£27.00

INTERNET WORLD™ GUIDE TO MAINTAINING AND UPDATING DYNAMIC WEB SITES

JEANNIE NOVAK
PETE MARKIEWICZ

INTERNET WORLD™ GUIDE TO MAINTAINING AND UPDATING DYNAMIC WEB SITES

JEANNIE NOVAK
PETE MARKIEWICZ

WILEY COMPUTER PUBLISHING

JOHN WILEY & SONS, INC.
New York • Chichester • Weinheim • Brisbane • Singapore • Toronto

Publisher: Robert Ipsen
Editor: Cary Sullivan
Assistant Editor: Kathryn A. Malm
Managing Editor: Marnie Shotsky
Text Design & Composition: Pronto Design and Production, Inc.

Designations used by companies to distinguish their products are often claimed as trademarks. In all instances where John Wiley & Sons, Inc., is aware of a claim, the product names appear in initial capital or all capital letters. Readers, however, should contact the appropriate companies for more complete information regarding trademarks and registration.

This book is printed on acid-free paper. ♾

Published by John Wiley & Sons, Inc.

Published simultaneously in Canada.

This publication is designed to provide accurate and authoritative information in regard to the subject matter covered. It is sold with the understanding that the publisher is not engaged in rendering professional services. If professional advice or other expert assistance is required, the services of a competent professional person should be sought.

Internet World, Web Week, Web Developer, Internet Shopper, and Mecklermedia are the exclusive trademarks of Mecklermedia Corporation and are used with permission.

Library of Congress Cataloging-in-Publication Data:

Novak, Jeannie, 1966-
     Internet world guide to maintaining and updating dynamic web sites / Jeannie Novak, Pete Markiewicz.
     p. cm.
     Includes index.
ISBN 0-471-24273-X (pbk. : alk. paper)
1. Web sites—Design. I. Markiewicz, Peter George, 1956-
II. Title.
TK5105.888.N693 1998
005.3'76--dc21
                                                              97-38093
                                                               CIP

Printed in the United States of America.

10 9 8 7 6 5 4 3 2 1

CONTENTS

INTRODUCTION

The static Web of 1994–1995 is gone; it has been replaced by sites that generate Web pages on-the-fly from databases, personalize information based on user profiles, provide daily and weekly access to news, and even allow an audience to tune into real-time audio and video Webcasts. The principles of dynamic Web design appear in the hottest, most trend-setting sites on the Internet. Cutting-edge online publications, virtual stores, real-time audio/video channels, online universities, cybercommunities, and competitive games and auctions have all been created through effective application of dynamic Web principles. Despite this growth, there is much confusion surrounding the most effective ways to make the transition from static to dynamic site development. This book is designed to help Web developers find their way out of the virtual fog surrounding all new technologies and develop a dynamic strategy that will work for them and their clients.

In writing this book, we soon realized that "dynamic" refers to much more than linking a Web page to a database; it covers the whole process of maintaining and updating content on the Web. We present a variety of strategies available to address all aspects of this issue. Dynamic content development is not for everyone (those who simply want to list their phone number on the Internet need not apply), but it is crucial to the success of groups that want to supply information, products/services, instruction, and entertainment to the Internet audience. Drawing from our own experience and that of others, we have attempted to provide a comprehensive introduction to dynamic sites that will benefit developers at all levels.

This book provides two complimentary forms of information that developers may use to assemble their own dynamic site strategies. Parts One and Two review the theory behind dynamic content, consider aspects of Web-site maintenance specific to dynamic elements, and discuss the tools and utilities available to create and manage dynamic updates. Reading through this area provides a feel for the capabilities and limitations of the current Web. In Part Three, theory turns to practice and we consider real-world dynamic sites developed for commerce, education, and other areas. This section focuses on a series of case studies—dynamic strategies developed and implemented by working sites on the Internet today. Each case study begins with the overall site goal, and lists the hardware and software infrastructure needed to support their plan. Case study analysis also includes strategies for organizing production and personnel, challenges faced by the site operators, and anticipated future developments. Short summaries at the end of each chapter compare the sites profiled in the case studies. The final chapter of the book (Part Four) moves from the present to the future and considers possible trends affecting the implementation of dynamic Web strategies—most notably media convergence and the increasing use of hybrid Web-disc technologies.

In the months we spent researching this book, we were constantly amazed at the rapid pace of development in dynamic Web technology. We expect our key concepts to be useful for quite some time to come, and we encourage you to continue checking on the current status of the industry by logging onto our supporting Web site at kspace.com/dynamic.

Good luck with your own efforts!

Jeannie Novak   Pete Markiewicz
jeannie@kspace.com   pete@kspace.com

PART ONE
THE DYNAMIC WEB

INTRODUCTION TO DYNAMIC SITES

In the beginning, the Web was a static medium. Designed as a system for exchanging research papers, its appearance bore many similarities to an electronic book. Web sites were built out of individual HTML files, which frequently were left unmodified for many months after their creation. The novelty of Web-based information coupled with a primitive development environment allowed content developers to follow production standards comparable to handwritten manuscripts. Errors in content and programming were frequent and expected.

But parallel to the explosive growth of the Web, there has been an increasing realization of its true potential. By its very nature, the Web transcends the static character of a book or billboard. Once the site is published on the Internet, the malleability of computer storage technology irresistibly suggests new possibilities for communication. Increasingly, the Web is moving beyond the electronic publishing model to a dynamic, two-way flow of information for which frequent change of appearance and content is the norm.

Avoiding the HTML Ghost Town

Nobody expects a CD-ROM-based game or word processing document to change each time it is used. But precisely the opposite is true on the Web—surfers increasingly expect new material every time they visit a site. Developing dynamic sites is rapidly becoming a necessity for everyone who expects to use the Internet effectively. Failure to do so leads surfers to conclude the site they have accessed is a ghost town—one that has joined the millions of Web pages left to virtually rot in forgotten corners of hard disks (see Figure 1.1). Such sites are not worth a return visit and cannot support a regular audience, promotion, or online sales. Some of the dynamic features the Internet audience increasingly expects are listed here:

- Time-sensitive rather than encyclopedic content
- Periodic interface "makeovers" that improve navigation and embody trends in style and design
- Compatibility with new generations of hardware, software, and standards for information delivery
- Support for communication with the site's visiting audience
- Effective management to handle ever-increasing quantities of available information

Static Web sites rapidly become a liability for their creators. In the June 7, 1997 issue of *Entertainment Weekly* (www.entertainmentweekly.com) magazine, several obsolete Web sites were lampooned for their breathless prose touting long-defunct events. Some of these sites were created by large entertainment companies, who presumably had the money and resources to keep them current. In a related observation, a recent study by Forrester Research (www.forrester.com) predicts that the average Fortune 1000 Web site will double in size in 1997, and triple in size in 1998! Clearly, the problems associated with maintaining dynamic Web content will only increase.

Figure 1.1 Example of a ghost town page on the Web.

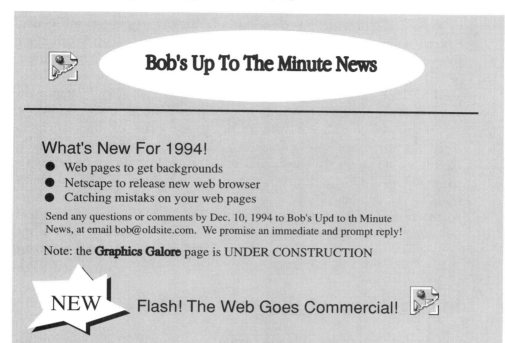

To avoid the ghost town syndrome, dynamic sites must provide the following features:

- New information available with each visit
- Interface and programming reflecting current trends in style and software
- Response to changes in visitor or server traffic, preventing users from experiencing frequent overloads or "lockouts"
- Nonexistence of typos, improperly designed graphics, and awkward interfaces
- Personal control and customization of content

Successful dynamic sites are at the forefront of the interactive revolution. Sites such as *USA Today Online* (www.usatoday.com) shown in Figure 1.2 provide up-to-the-minute access to news and events. Search engines such as Yahoo! (www.yahoo.com) and InfoSeek (www.infoseek.com) manage shifting databases with tens of millions of individual entries. Broadcast sites such as Liveconcerts.com (created by Timecast and House of Blues New Media; www.liveconcerts.com) and Audionet (www.audionet.com) provide access to real-time audio and video through the Web. A new class of sites such as NetGuide Live (www.netguide.com) has appeared simply to provide schedules of events elsewhere on the Internet. Dynamic catalogs with pages created on-the-fly from databases are characteristic of shopping sites such as CDNow (www.cdnow.com). Thousands of chatrooms linked with Web sites, summarized in listings such as Yack! (www.yack.com), allow the audience to communicate with each other as well as with experts, celebrities, and the site operators themselves.

Implications of Dynamic Content

The Web has converged books, radio, and television into a continuum. Put into electronic form, various media differ only in the extent to which they use dynamic information (see Figure 1.3). The fluid nature of digital information allows rapid, complete changes of content, and the Web can mimic anything from the broadcast system used in radio and television to a roadside billboard. But the Internet also allows two-way information exchange (Figure 1.4). This uniquely allows the Internet audience to contribute to content in a meaningful way, and adds a dimension that makes the dynamic Web site a unique entity in its own right. Through access statistics, email, online forms, response to advertising, and even direct content uploads, visitors make major contributions to dynamic Web sites. This creates an additional level for dynamic change that is controlled by the consumer as well as the content producer. Web sites

Figure 1.2 *USA Today Online* (www.usatoday.com) is an example of a dynamic Web site.

that post information contributed by their audience add a new communication channel running between the site visitors themselves.

To properly support dynamic Web content, it is necessary for the developer to make a clear break with software and CD-ROM distribution models. Developing these products traditionally involves a

Figure 1.3 Schematic of dynamic behavior in various media, plotted as update speed versus interactivity.

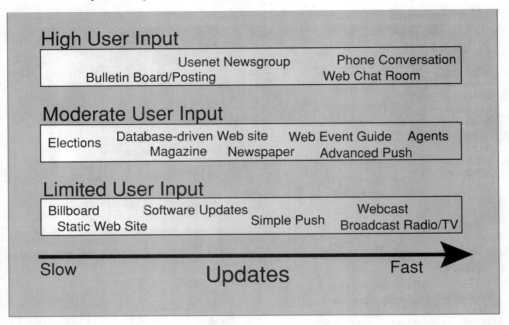

production schedule with a defined beginning, middle, and end. After completion, the end product may not change for months or years. In contrast, dynamic Web sites often change their content substantially in a matter of seconds or minutes. Due to this constant need for updates, the dynamic Web site is a moving target. Applying outmoded development concepts are of little use (e.g., putting a 2.0 version number for a Web site). On the other hand, the traditionally dynamic broadcast medium does not form an adequate model for the dynamic Web site. While broadcast radio and television have well-developed methods for dealing with continuous content flow, the media production model is one-way. The dynamic site's capacity to respond to visitor input blurs the boundary between producer and

Figure 1.4 Sharing of information (content provider-to-user and user-to-user).

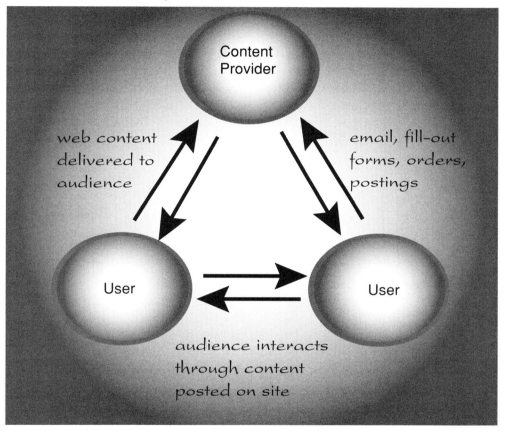

Content Provider

web content delivered to audience

email, fill-out forms, orders, postings

User

User

audience interacts through content posted on site

consumer, and makes its implementation fundamentally different from a traditional broadcast channel. As an example, consider the various *push* and *agent* technologies being developed to interface with the Web. With their increasing emphasis on controlling content delivery through user preference, they implicitly promote the consumer to the role of co-producer.

Figure 1.5 An example of a news site is Nielsen Ratings (www.ultimatetv.com/news/nielsen).

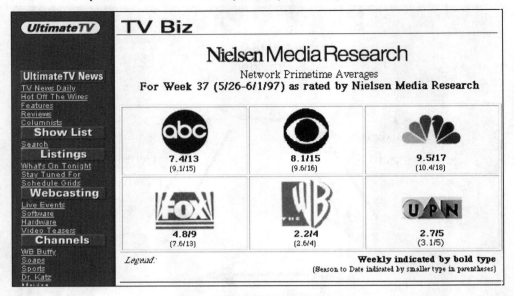

Here are examples of the many new forms of information enabled by the unique features of dynamic Web sites:

- Event reports (news, stock prices, weather) available 24 hours a day (Figure 1.5)

- Project management/workflow creating *Intranets* and *Extranets*

- Chatrooms, matchmaker environments, and virtual communities

- *Webcasting* (broadcast-style event reporting; see Figure 1.6 for an example)

- Search engines

- Serial entertainment (interactive Web "soaps")

Figure 1.6 Liveconcerts.com is an example of a broadcast site (www.liveconcerts.com).

- Product catalogs with changing inventories
- Travel guides/virtual travel
- Industry-specific databases
- Cutting-edge style and design shops

Maintenance and Updates for Dynamic Sites

The purpose of this book is to bring the scattered, rapidly evolving technology and principles needed for dynamic Web sites into a single place. Supporting dynamic sites requires new kinds of hardware and

Figure 1.7 Yack! (www.yack.com) is an example of an event-listings site.

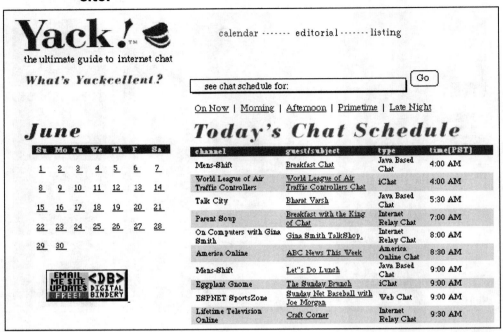

software, as it requires rethinking the way in which information is prepared and presented. When discussing dynamic sites, it is useful to divide tasks along the lines of maintenance and updates. While the distinction may at times seem artificial, it helps to simplify the development process and separates individual job descriptions along those already common in Web development.

Maintenance involves keeping the current Web site maximally functional with respect to errors, hardware/software changes, and the Web site's audience. Even if the content remains the same, the administrator must "run in place" to keep the site positioned.

Updates involve the introduction of new content, design/interface features, or adjustments to directory and file structure. Updates may be restricted to content, or may involve complete Web "makeovers," replacing an existing site's architecture with a new one.

Of course, the plans developed for maintenance and updates will mutually influence each other. For example, upgrading a site's presentation to include broadcast-style content will need substantial revisions in the maintenance plan for its hardware and software. For sites that record events such as sports or media (Figure 1.7), the associated network must be able to handle "spikes" of high visitor traffic. Expansion of the maintenance strategy to include detailed analysis of Web traffic may in turn suggest updates based on user preference or agent technology.

Distinguishing Dynamic from Interactive

CD-ROM and software developers frequently refer to "interactivity" as a key component of their products, and *dynamic HTML* providing CD-ROM-style interactivity is expected to make a major contribution to the Web experience. Many recent books and articles that promote dynamic site development provide tutorials in multimedia development rather than demonstrating how dynamic content can be managed. Since the dynamic and interactive approaches are frequently confused, their use in future discussions is explicitly defined in the next sections.

Interactive Systems

Interactive systems apply Newton's third law to computers by providing an equal reaction to each action taken by the user. For example, the onscreen buttons and controls found on many CD-ROMs often make a sound or change shape or color when they are selected by the user.

Development systems including Macromedia's (www.macromedia .com) Shockwave and Flash environments provide outstanding examples of interactive development. However, interactive systems are not necessarily dynamic. Unless a fresh supply of content is integrated into the existing system, multimedia content is interactive while remaining completely static. By themselves, interactive features do not create dynamic Web sites and simply provide a sophisticated interface to unchanging content.

Dynamic Systems

Dynamic systems add new content from the outside. A very simple example is a text-only Web page posting nightly weather reports with no hyperlinks. Even though the user cannot respond to or change the page in any way (making it noninteractive), it is highly dynamic. More sophisticated examples include linking music CD-ROMs to tour information posted on the Internet, live audio or video Webcasts, or displaying information on a Web page posted by visitors to the site.

The use of interactive software and systems will be considered in subsequent chapters, but will be told from the dynamic perspective. For example, the Flash program will be discussed with respect to its support for linking dynamic content on the Web and delivering streaming animation—rather than simply providing a tutorial on using its interactive features.

While "dynamic HTML" has been used by Netscape (www.netscape.com) and Microsoft (www.microsoft.com) to describe competing standards for advanced interactive Web interfaces, we feel that this is a misnomer that currently creates much confusion. "Interactive HTML" would be much better!

History of Web Maintenance and Updates

In the short history of the Web, dynamic systems have evolved rapidly. Following are some examples, along with their approximate time of appearance. The dates listed do not necessarily record the first use of the technology but indicate when they came into widespread use.

1994

During this period, the Web was almost completely static. The *CGI* (*Common Gateway Interface*) protocol for linking external programs was not widely used, and Web pages were exclusively created through manual editing of HTML files. Dynamic changes to sites were mediated exclusively through manual updates of individual pages. At the time, updates were not significant; the incredible growth of new sites provided a continual source of new information for the swelling ranks of surfers. What minimal dynamic content available was characterized by the following features:

Manual Web page creation. Originally, Web servers and browsers worked exclusively with HTML (HyperText Markup Language). Maintenance and updates were supplied, using a model similar to updating word processor documents.

Access log analysis. Programs allowing analysis of visitor traffic moving through a Web site appeared, allowing administrators to evaluate the success of their site and determine which areas needed improvement.

1995

In this period, the first dynamic sites appeared, characterized by CGI links to external programs. Most dynamism was confined to user input via fill-out forms. Database gateways were written, and a few pioneering sites provided links to dynamic information (Figure 1.8). Search engines using Web *spiders* collected and indexed the increasing number of static Web pages available online. The rising number of dynamic sites were supported by the following:

Pages generated by CGI scripts. CGI (hoohoo/ncsa.uiuc
.edu/cgi/) programs allowed the first customized extensions
to Web servers. By interfacing traditional programming languages (e.g., Perl, C) with HTML, they enabled automatic
response to fill-out forms, page customization based on the
user's software, and simple versions of online chat and discussion groups.

Interactive animation and multimedia plug-ins. Programs such as Macromedia's Shockwave (www.macromedia
.com) brought CD-ROM-style authoring into the Web,

**Figure 1.8 Shopping site CDNow (www.cdnow.com) with back-end
database.**

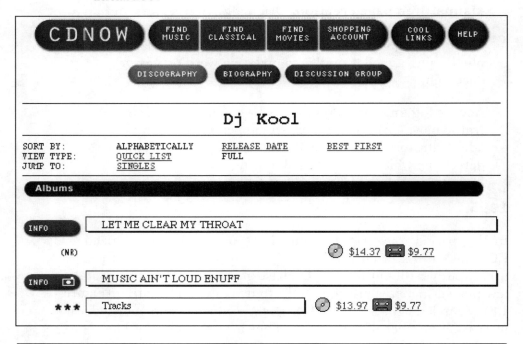

allowing designers to add interactive features to their Web sites without learning CGI programming.

1996

During this time, the Web acquired the features necessary to make it a serious publishing medium, and sites with dynamic content formed the cutting edge of development. As the Web became more popular, sites coped with repeat visitors by making frequent changes to their content. Database applications as diverse as movie archives, product catalogs, and email lists became more frequent. Instead of surfing new sites, Internet users increasingly demanded new information from their favorite hangouts. Increasing sophistication in dynamic content sprang from features including the following:

Database-generated Web pages. Initially, protocols and CGI programs were developed that created gateways between database languages like *SQL* (*Structured Query Language*) and the Web. Later, simplified scripting languages and programs such as Hughes Technologies' mSQL (hughes .com.au) and NetObjects' Fusion (www.netobjects.com) allowed designers to create database-driven pages without extensive database experience.

Streaming technology. Progressive Networks' introduction of RealAudio (www.real.com) brought real-time music and spoken word to the Web. By transmitting audio data in real time, RealAudio opened the door for broadcast-style dynamism. The concept was soon applied to video, videoconferencing, and multimedia delivery by companies including VDONet (www.vdo.net) and Xing Technology Corp. (www.xingtech.com).

Push technology. Early systems such as Pointcast (www .pointcast.com) delivered regular updates to end users through a proprietary interface. By setting up an automatic delivery channel, push systems let the user get information without having to conduct searches on the Web. More recent versions of push such as Marimba (www.marimba .com) and BackWeb (www.backweb.com) have incorporated Web-based content and added support for multimedia. More importantly, they have moved beyond broadcast-style content delivery by allowing users to precisely control the content actually pushed to their desktop.

1997

In this phase of Web expansion, commercial-level software supporting dynamic sites became available. Site operators no longer needed to program custom dynamic solutions, and the development process itself moved to a dynamic Web model with the introduction of Intranets. As the number of pages on the Web approached 100 million, users and developers increasingly turned to dynamic solutions that suggested or delivered content level based on preferences—determined actively through questionnaires and registration forms, and passively through tracking user movements and choices within sites. Currently, the growth of dynamic content is following these trends:

Commercial site management programs. As Web sites became more complex, the difficulty of keeping content current began to require custom programs similar to workflow and document management systems. These programs range from custom collections of CGI scripts developed in house to commercial programs such as Vignette's StoryServer (www.vignette.com).

Collaborative software. Programs such as Lotus' Domino (www.lotus.com), and Netscape's Collabora (www.netscape .com) software allow businesses to use the Web to manage dynamic information in workflow environments. Developed for Intranet and Extranet environments, they are likely to become common on the public Internet as well.

User-specific configuration and agents. Firefly (www.firefly.com) pioneered collaborative filtering of content contributed by its members to create dynamic music recommendations. Many other systems are being developed that use preferences supplied by audience members to narrow information searches to relevant domains.

Client-side interactivity. Netscape (www.netscape.com) and Microsoft (www.microsoft.com) have made competing proposals for a *Dynamic HyperText Markup Language* (*DHTML*). Sun's Java (www.javasoft.com) language and similar technologies support interactive controls, games, and development environments characteristic of CD-ROMs on the Web. By downloading applets or advanced HTML, they create local programs responsive to user actions without having to repeatedly access the Web server.

Server and network management tools. A variety of companies such as Mercury Interactive (www.merc-int.com) have introduced easy-to-use programs and technologies that enable pretesting Web sites for their response to high traffic, and allow Web-based monitoring of networks for overloads and bottlenecks.

Who Can Benefit from Running a Dynamic Site?

Any Web site, ranging from a personal homepage to a major media outlet, can increase its value by incorporating dynamic information. While some technologies require expensive outlays of technology and personnel, others demand little more than installation of a simple script available for free on the Internet. Small site operators may make their content dynamic simply by developing a regular calendar for making updates without any new hardware or software. As is frequently true on the Web, simple maintenance and update strategies often create results comparable to massive systems costing hundreds or thousands of times more. Here are examples of sites that may benefit from "going dynamic":

- Sites receiving rapid changes in visitor traffic, such as event sites
- Sites accepting and posting visitor content, such as bulletin boards and Web-based classified ads
- Sites that must stay at the cutting edge of technological advancement, such as Web development shops
- Sites that analyze visitor traffic and/or track visitor use for demographics or advertising purposes
- Sites maintained by large groups of individual content providers, such as online malls
- Sites with online catalogs and order processing
- Sites allowing visitors to interact in chatrooms, online gaming environments, or virtual communities

The challenge of dynamic sites is considerable, but the reward will be the evolution of the Web from a world away from the electronic library metaphor to a truly new form of media. Chapter 2 focuses on the first component of any dynamic site—the plan for its implementation.

DEVELOPING A DYNAMIC SITE PLAN

2

With a network of hyperlinks connecting virtually every page in cyberspace, it is easy to find what you're looking for through casual exploration. Unfortunately, the Web's ease of use sometimes invites developers to take an equally casual approach to managing their sites. Many locations on the Web are launched bearing excellent design and layout, but with time they become run down through inadequate, reactive, and haphazard attention. This is almost always due to insufficient preparation for the demands of managing and updating dynamic content.

In order to develop Web sites that retain their appeal, it is necessary to create a formal plan for production and management. This chapter considers the methods used to organize dynamic content in other media, and it builds on this to define a dynamic site plan specifically for the Web.

Features of Dynamic Content

All media may be described in terms of their *content* (raw information) and *presentation* (the interface that delivers the information to the audience). Content may exist in many forms, such as text, graphics, audio, video, animation, interactive multimedia, or even a broadcast signal. These content formats may comprise *media elements* and are contained within a presentation. An idealized dynamic media system is shown in Figure 2.1. The exact boundaries between individual media elements are arbitrary and are preassigned by the content developers. For example, articles (not just text) and images are media elements of traditional newspapers, and the overall layout, paper color, and font form the presentation. In television, the screen constitutes the presentation, and the linear broadcast stream may be divided into a variety of media elements (scenes within a

Figure 2.1 An idealized dynamic media system.

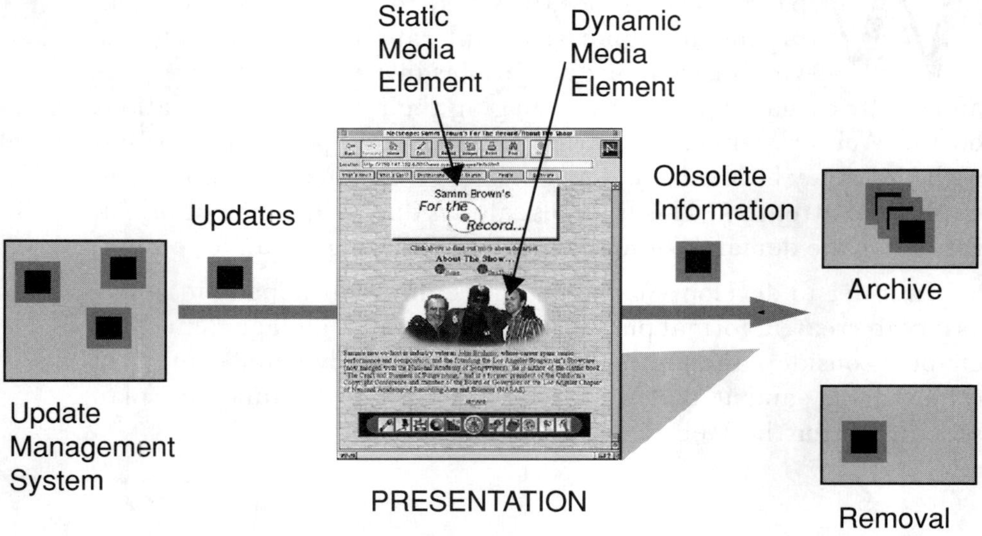

television show, title credits, end credits, commercials, station identification). On the Web, the computer screen forms the presentation, and the media elements may consist of a splash screen, chat transcript, navigation toolbar, MIDI file, Webcast, or animated GIF.

While there are almost infinite possibilities for dividing content into media elements, some assignments are more practical than others. For example, there is nothing stopping a Web developer from making each pixel on the computer screen a media element, but such a definition lacks utility. Elements will normally be defined by authorship (e.g., an article or photograph is often created by a single individual) or topic (e.g., a picture is a single element since it conveys a single idea). On the Web, common elements include scanned images, audio clips, and short animated sequences.

All media elements have the potential to carry *static* or *dynamic* content. Static content changes rarely, if ever, and creates a consistent look and feel for the presentation. The name of a newspaper or magazine is typically static and retains a specific size, color, and font from issue to issue. In contrast, dynamic elements change frequently. Underneath the edition's name, most newspapers print a picture related to their lead story. Since this picture changes with each publication, it is highly dynamic. A radio program may begin with a static prerecorded message or theme music, after which the body of the show consists of dynamic conversation. On a Web page, static layouts, background colors, and navigation toolbars are integrated with dynamic stock tickers, rotating banner ads, broadcast streams, and animation sequences.

Using this general model, dynamic media may be further characterized by the following features:

Number of distinct media elements. Each individual media element contains a complete piece of information and is created or modified as a unit. For example, a digitized image, audio clip, and any text from the same story constitute single media elements. An animated GIF file also forms a single media element, despite storing multiple images. Note that animation alone does not make it dynamic; it is static unless one or more of its images is modified on a regular basis. An HTML command that calls a date/time program also constitutes a single media element. Elements may also correspond to individual numbers in tables/spreadsheets, daily announcements, scores, polls, and survey statistics. In database-supported Web sites, elements often map directly to predefined database objects.

Update percentage. This variable measures the proportion of total media elements that are dynamic as opposed to static navigation or interface elements.

Update frequency. This variable measures the time interval between updates of individual media elements.

Synchronicity. This variable measures the degree of coordination between updates of individual media elements. Independent updates spaced randomly in time are asynchronous, while synchronous updates change all the media elements at once.

These basic features define a wide range of dynamic information. For example, a Web site such as the GVU Internet Survey conducted by Georgia Tech (see Figure 2.2), is updated every 6–12 months— a relatively low update frequency for the Web. Results appear on a completely new set of Web pages, making the percentage of the site updated relatively high. Since all the new survey information is posted at once, the updates are synchronous. On the other hand, the "ticker" page for the WebCrawler search engine (see Figure 2.3) consists entirely of static HTML, except for a single panel displaying a list of recently used search keywords. In this case, the update frequency is very high (approximately once every 3 seconds), but only a single media element is updated (preventing the synchronicity measurement from being applied).

Models for Dynamic Information

Dynamic content is far from new. Broadcast radio has managed dynamic information since 1920, and broadcast television is currently celebrating its fiftieth anniversary. Newspapers and magazines have existed for centuries. The rich experience of these other media provides a starting point for planning a dynamic Web site. Based on their unique characteristics, each of these media forms have developed their own models for presenting dynamic information. Three of the most widely used strategies (incremental, periodic, and streaming media, as shown in Figure 2.4) are discussed next.

Figure 2.2 GVU Internet Survey (www.cc.gatech.edu/gvu/ user_surveys/).

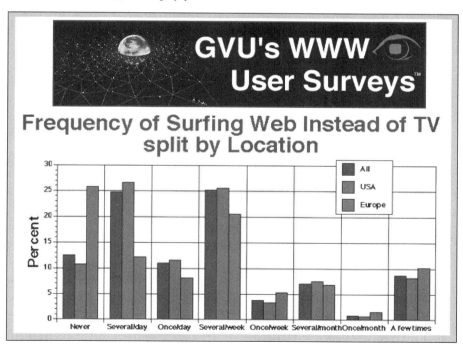

Figure 2.3 WebCrawler search engine (www.webcrawler.com).

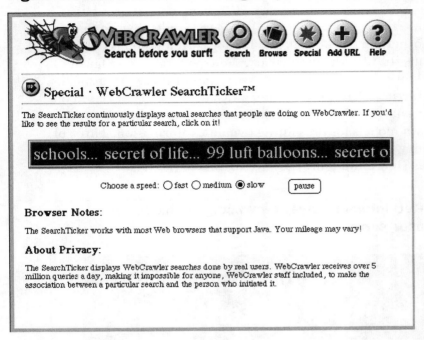

Incremental Updates (Bulletin Board Model)

This strategy is used when the desired information originates from multiple sources, submitted independently of each other. Examples include classified ads (see Figure 2.5) and the "personals" sections of weekly newspapers. The electronic *BBS* (*Bulletin Board System*)—in many ways a forerunner of the global Internet—takes its name directly from incrementally updated, real-world corkboards common at malls and meeting places. Incremental updates are ideally suited to content originating from a variety of sources, where each submission has intrinsic value independent of other submissions.

Electronic systems are particularly well suited for incremental updates. Unlike physical media, individual media elements on a Web site may be updated, added, or erased without affecting the rest of the content. In contrast, newspapers do not routinely issue single-page updates every time a new story is received!

Periodic Updates (Electronic Publishing Model)

Unlike incremental systems, periodic systems force synchronous content updates. Good examples are newspapers, monthly magazines, and regularly scheduled news shows in broadcast media. Periodic updates provide a good strategy for presenting information that is moderately time sensitive, but is able to retain its value for days or weeks. Examples include book reviews and editorials by featured columnists (see Figure 2.6). Periodic media do well at creating stable audiences, since users can reliably expect new information each time they tune in.

Figure 2.4 Diagram of incremental, periodic, and streaming media models.

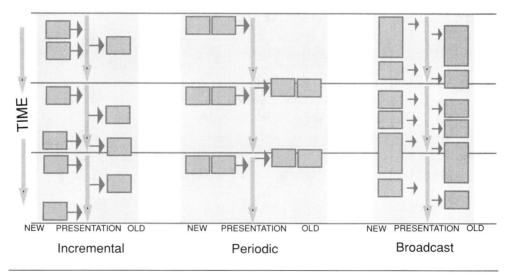

Figure 2.5 Example of highly incremental site (France Online Classifieds—www.france.com/classifieds).

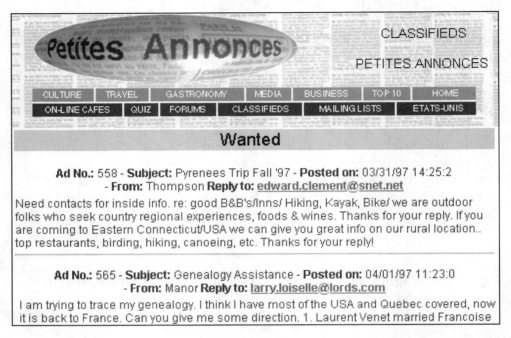

Since periodic media require large amounts of information to be updated at the same time, deadline pressure becomes an important part of development. On the other hand, the extended down periods between individual publications or shows make it easier to accommodate unexpected or missing content.

Media Streaming (Broadcast Model)

Streaming content updates occur at rates fast enough to create movement and sound. In radio and television, the broadcast stream usually consists of a single media element—while streaming multimedia technologies allow delivery of multiple elements. Examples of streaming

Figure 2.6 Example of periodic update site (Slate—www.slate.com).

media (see Figure 2.7) include live television broadcasts, stock tickers, Internet push channels, and music playlists on the radio. By requiring nonstop updates of information, the broadcast model puts the greatest demands on the developer, who must continually guard against static dead time. Supporting broadcast information frequently requires creating a script or storyboard specifying exactly when each piece of information will be presented to the audience.

Staging (Development Model)

To varying degrees, all dynamic media have adopted the concept of *staging*, sometimes referred to as *pipelining*. In staging (see Figure 2.8), an informational assembly line converts raw content to a form suitable for the presentation. Raw data entering the staging process

Figure 2.7 Example of a broadcast site (GRIT—www.grit.com).

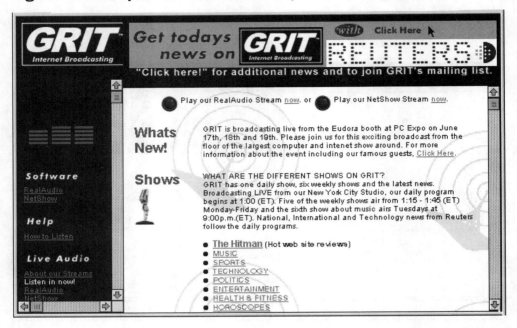

is converted to a media element or element update after digitization and preliminary formatting. Each new element is edited and checked for mistakes, integrated with interface/style elements, and finally uploaded into the presentation. As in an actual assembly line, a high level of efficiency results from admitting new information to the beginning of the staging process before finishing the old.

Each staging process contains its own internal set of uniform guidelines, or *templates*, that impose a common operation on introduced data. These templates may be font/style manuals (text) or sampling rates/formats (audio). *Cascading style sheets* (www.w3.org/pub/WWW/REC-CSSI), for example, are often used to control the layout for a group of files, for example, individual pages in a product catalog.

Figure 2.8 Staging diagram.

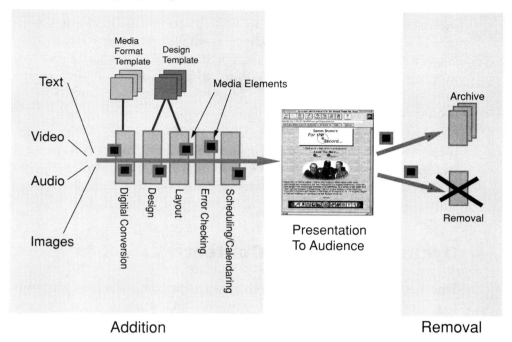

Web-based media development frequently employs *staging servers,* which are copies of all or part of the public Web site containing content at different levels of development. Most developers maintain local copies of Web sites on their workstations and check them in this environment before uploading to the main site. More sophisticated systems like Interwoven's Teamsite (www.interwoven.com) provide commercial software for automating the staging process. This $40,000 product (20 users) runs multiple Web servers for the authoring, editing, and administrator-level approval prior to final publication. Media elements advance through each level during the staging process, and the administrator can roll back all or part of the site to earlier file versions.

Like other media, Web sites frequently support multiple staging streams. For example, a Web classified directory might support hundreds of streams for each ad, with each stream operating independently of the others. In periodic content, the staging streams may start independently, but they are synchronized to deliver media elements to the presentation at publication. Broadcast media streams may be assembled from a series of individual media elements delivered one after the other to a presentation.

Staging can apply to maintenance as well as updates. For example, a Web Administrator might create a staging system to process raw user-access data. Steps in the staging process might include conversion to database format, statistical analysis, and final delivery as charts and diagrams.

Dynamic Web Site Content

Due to the flexibility of the Web's underlying architecture, dynamic models from other media may be mixed and matched with a freedom unavailable elsewhere. A single Web page could display a running list of user-contributed commentary (incremental), a regular column written by a featured writer (periodic), and a real-time audio channel (broadcast). Dynamic mixtures rare or impossible for other media are easily developed. For example, Web pages such as GhostWatcher (see Figure 2.9) broadcast images from a haunted house on a scale of hours to days. A site supporting real-time auctions such as Internet Shopping Network's FirstAuction (www.firstauction.com) might update its display every few seconds, using incremental content from a variety of sources.

In the past, new media have initially emulated older forms containing similar attributes. For example, early feature film duplicated the experience of live theater before developing its own style in the 1920s. It is likely that dynamic Web site development will follow a similar trend. Evidence of a unique style is already apparent in the tendency to write Web articles as short paragraphs connected by graphics and hyperlinks, instead of longer continuous narratives fond in other media. While Web sites emulating existing media may be easier to sell to potential backers, the most exciting projects transcend existing media to create a unique and useful environment.

Figure 2.9 GhostWatcher Web site (www.flyvision.org/sitelite /Houston/GhostWatcher/index.html).

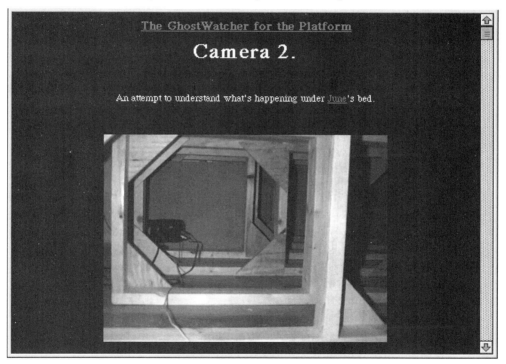

Developing a Dynamic Site Plan

Once a decision is made to support dynamic content, the next task for the developer is to develop a plan. Creating a formal plan will introduce a sense of reality by converting hazy goals into specific production directives, dates, and schedules. For larger groups, a dynamic site plan serves to coordinate the individuals contributing to its content. Writing an explicit plan helps to expose flaws in the general concept itself, and it also helps establish effective communication between everyone involved. Dynamic site plans should be written out explicitly, even if the site is maintained by a single individual.

Depending upon the proposed content, the style of writing used in the dynamic plan may vary. For example, a plan describing an online news service or virtual university might simply list the features it will make available to its audience. Sites following broadcast-style models (such as regular shows on push channels) may benefit from a written treatment similar to those developed for film and television projects. One possible organization for a site plan is given next.

Part 1—Description of the Site

The first section of the plan should lay out general goals for the project and demonstrate the site's unique contribution to the Web. The plan should also indicate if the proposed goals are conservative or ambitious, and possibly indicate fallback alternatives if they are too hard to develop.

Dynamic Content Features

Using the basic features of dynamic content (including synchronicity, update percentages, and interval between updates), the developer should characterize the proposed site. This should be done for the Web site as a whole, as well as for individual dynamic media elements. The site should be characterized as incremental, periodic, broadcast, or a mixture of these models.

Anticipated Market/Audience

The introduction should also describe who will be interested in the content and how much new content must be supplied to maintain audience interest. If the site carries advertising or supports financial transactions, the demonstrated market should be large enough to make the site profitable. If the site is already online and being upgraded, it is extremely useful to analyze current access statistics as thoroughly as possible.

Expected Benefits from a Dynamic Approach

The benefits of going dynamic are pivotal points of the plan. Since dynamic Web sites often require substantial financial outlays for their implementation, the true benefits need to be determined. Is the goal higher traffic, greater sales volume, or retaining existing traffic through repeat visits? Benefits need to be laid out clearly and, in the case of Web sites that generate revenue, financial projections should back them up.

As an example of relative benefits, consider the difference between an online catalog whose individual products attract cyber-shoppers, and an entertainment site whose brand name alone is the primary draw. At present, most shoppers find products on the Internet by accident, discovering them by typing keywords in search engines. For sites of this nature, it is less important to conduct repeated graphical facelifts than to make sure that prices are correct and order processing is prompt and efficient. On the other hand, repeat visitors to strongly branded sites tend to enter through the same page each time. It is essential to present them with something new each time they log on—possibly a rotating "selection of the day" or frequently updated graphics and animation.

Figure 2.10 Dynamic content on the Comedy Central site (www.comedycentral.com).

For operators producing content for broadcast media (radio and television networks), dynamism is a double-edged sword. For example, the Comedy Central cable channel (see Figure 2.10) was an early user of Webcast technology. In 1996, it featured a dynamic image uploaded directly from its broadcast stream, which updated every few seconds. This created a positive perception in its audience (e.g., "they're really serious about the Web"). Unlike some other broadcast sites, Comedy Central did not place its Webcast on the site's homepage. Since it is impossible to transmit the immediacy of live performance through the small, jerky video supported on most of the Internet, the operators realized that the Webcast would be of secondary interest to their audience. Instead, the homepage features other forms of dynamic content including scrolling jokes, contest announcements, and updated broadcast schedules.

Part 2—Implementation of Dynamic Content

Here we cover specific details of the production system used to support staging and presentation of dynamic content.

Design Plan

This section describes the interface that will contain dynamic content. In most cases, the preliminary design should consist of rough sketches or storyboards showing the site's appearance before and after updates. Individual media elements should be clearly defined in a list. The overall look and feel of the site—as well as toolbars, headers, buttons, and other navigational tools—should be described. It is also helpful to include a site flowchart showing the main pages in the presentation, important media elements, and the connections between them.

Staging

The requirements for individual components of the staging process— along with the underlying hardware, software, and personnel needed for their operation—should be listed. If complex or multiple media types are to be used, staging could form a major portion of the entire plan.

Hardware and Software

This section should list the various components of technology needed to construct the Web server, including computer platforms, operating system, Web programs and utilities, document management software, and workflow software for organizing updates.

Maintenance Plan

The requirements for keeping the virtual assembly line running—as well as strategies for detecting broken links and other errors on the site—should be detailed in this section. Maintenance concepts should also include plans for archiving old information, system-wide backups, and management of servers and networks.

Figure 2.11 Personnel flowchart.

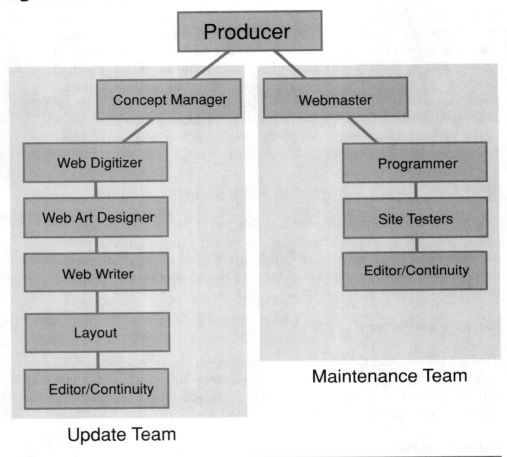

Part 3—Personnel Description

For static Web sites, only two jobs are typically defined: the developer (or Web designer) and the individual responsible for ongoing maintenance (or Web Administrator/Webmaster). Dynamic sites require a greater diversity of job descriptions for effective operation.

The dynamic plan should show an organizational flowchart (see Figure 2.11) for the production team that summarizes individual jobs and superior/subordinate relations. It is necessary to define specific responsibilities for each person involved, as well as a method for communication and arbitration of disputes. Individuals can benefit from writing out distinct descriptions, even if they personally attend to each of the tasks listed.

Existing models for production have differing advantages and disadvantages when applied to the Web environment. Newspaper production bears many similarities to Web development; however, most newspapers and magazines have production staffs several times the size of the typical Web team. Editors used to handing off material to subordinates may find themselves called upon to do HTML layout, uploading, and fact checking. CD-ROM production teams work in the same electronic environment as the Web, but they normally spend months readying a static product. Web development may be more similar to current broadcast teams. In recent years, the size of broadcast productions has dropped, and reporters are often responsible for writing and even editing the story. A possible organizational scheme is described in greater detail next.

Producer

This individual carries and sustains the overall vision for the site through changes and updates in its content. The Producer's main role is to coordinate the site team so that the members function effectively together. The Producer takes responsibility for the overall long-term vision for the site and makes sure that everyone understands their individual roles in developing it. The maintenance team under the Producer is headed by the Web Administrator, and the update team is headed by the Content Manager. In small groups, all three positions may be combined into a single individual's job description.

Content Manager

This individual organizes information destined for the Web site and works with the Web Administrator to optimize its presentation. Often combined with the Web Administrator (or Webmaster) position, Content Managers have the primary responsibility for all work by the update team. Under the Content Manager, possible job assignments include:

Web Digitizer. Conversion of raw content to Web-compatible media, and management of standard staging templates for media formatting. Different individuals may be assigned to handle conversion of text, graphics, audio, video, and Web-based multimedia.

WebWriters. Provide stories, commentary, and other original text for the site.

Web Art Designer. Creates a graphical look and feel for the site, develops a navigation architecture, and is responsible for creating staging templates used for layout of dynamic content.

Layout. Takes dynamic content and templates staged by the Digitizer and Art Director, and integrates it into each final Web page.

Copy Editors/Continuity. Read and examine material critically, looking for awkward, ungrammatical, and just plain boring writing. By fact-checking, they protect the site from inaccuracy, unconscious bias, and copyright violation. For sites following incremental and periodic updates, the Copy Editors' role is quite similar to comparable positions in newspapers and magazine publishers. For broadcast sites, the Copy Editors' role resembles Continuity Editors, who ensure that facts or other information aren't presented out of sequence.

Figure 2.12 The Cave (www.new-kewl.com/web-noir/index.html).

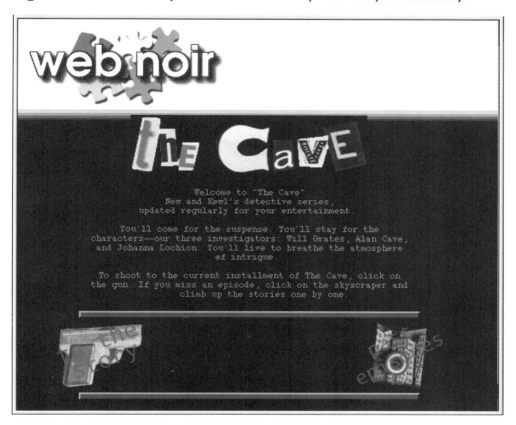

Certain jobs are absent from this description. The most significant gap is the position of Director, a critical member of teams for film and television production. The Director's traditional role is to take material assembled in preproduction and create a finished product. On the Web, interactivity, agents, and user preferences combine to let the audience direct their own experience directly from the preproduced materials. The clearest example of this is found in Web-based soaps such as The Cave (see Figure 2.12)—modeled on dramatic presentations in other media. Instead of watching a completed shoot, the user's exploration of the site reveals a detective drama in prepared diaries, letters, and announcements.

Web Administrator/Webmaster

The Web Administrator/Webmaster oversees the maintenance team and is responsible for the day-to-day operation of the Web site. This individual also administers server hardware/software, manages network connections, is responsible for data backups, and may forward visitor access statistics to the appropriate group. While not responsible for content presentation, the Web Administrator acts as the gatekeeper, managing updates and corrections made to the site. Under the Webmaster, possible job assignments include:

Web Programmer. Selects and develops the actual software used on the Web site, such as HTML, Java, or CGI scripts.

Hardware/Software/Network Testers. Evaluate the site under real-world conditions, and "push until it breaks." Testers confirm the logic of the site's navigational structure, ensure its cross-platform capabilities, and measure the average download time for individual Web pages. Professional beta testers may be used in this position, but it is a good idea to include individuals with little or no professional background to duplicate the experience of the audience.

Site Integrity Checker. For some very large sites, a specific individual may be assigned to handle fixing broken links and removing obsolete files.

Part 4—Communication between Team Members

Depending upon the size and location of the production team, communication may be organized in several ways.

YellNet/SneakerNet

Suitable for small groups well acquainted with each other, YellNet usually features a single person who gives verbal instructions for maintenance and updates to a group within shouting distance of each other. Informal scribbled notes past between individuals forms the parallel SneakerNet. Since the dynamic site plan exists largely in the Producer's mind, it stands or falls on memory and attention to detail. Most sites pass through a YellNet phase during their startup, but they need to move quickly to more formal methods.

PaperNet

Another tongue-in-cheek name describes the more formal organization possible via a mixture of printouts, calendar entries, faxes, bulletins, and copied documents. Since many groups already use dead trees for organization, PaperNet has the advantage of familiarity and a low learning curve. Organizing dynamic content in this way is also necessary if material passes through the hands of individuals who do not use the Internet. The chief disadvantage of PaperNet is that dynamic content may have to be processed several times. Thus, a marketing representative may type a press release on a word processor, print it, and pass it along to the Web site digitizers who then retype it into their HTML editors!

EmailNet

Surprisingly effective communication is possible using basic email accounts. In order to implement EmailNet (see Figure 2.13), members of the production team create email addresses corresponding to various "in" and "out" boxes for dynamic content, such as "database," "updates," "redo," "errors," and "obsolete." Instead of verbal or phone communications, the developers send messages to these boxes, which are in turn assigned to be read by individuals in the group. Converting to email allows an extremely powerful integration

Figure 2.13 Diagram of EmailNet.

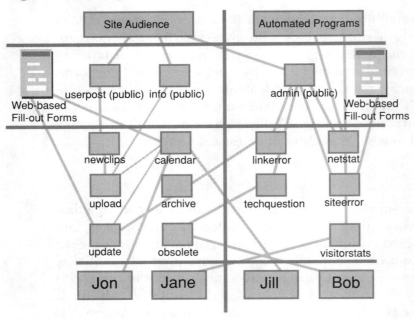

with the Web site. User queries can be routed to appropriate email boxes, and automatic programs on the site can be configured to send reports through email. To standardize message content sent between boxes (e.g., work orders), simple Web-based fill-out forms using the "mailto" command can be created. It is even possible to systematize staging by exchanging media elements as mail attachments. Since commercial workflow software is frequently expensive, EmailNet provides a good way for smaller independent sites to build their own Intranet-style management system.

Workflow

Custom workflow programs and Web-specific site management software are useful for managing large sites and production groups whose members are geographically dispersed. Workflow programs usually start with a version of EmailNet and add calendars and scheduling systems. Advanced workflow programs often include the ability to arrange virtual meetings and collaborations.

Part 5—Financial

The last section of the plan should include an estimate of the ongoing cost of providing dynamic information. Careful analysis of the outlays necessary may help small operators avoid a virtual albatross—a large Web site receiving sporadic and inconsistent updates because of limited resources. A few well-maintained pages with regularly refreshed content are far preferable to a shoddily operated giant! The financial analysis should include startup costs for equipment, Internet access, software, and personnel necessary to implement a dynamic strategy, as well as ongoing costs of maintaining the network and content staging.

Additional Questions to Consider in Developing a Dynamic Site Plan

As the dynamic site plan is being developed, it is often helpful for the developers to brainstorm starting from a series of questions. Here are some examples.

Maintenance Questions

The maintenance team needs to concentrate on the steady-state operation of the hardware and software, and with variations introduced by activities of the update team and users visiting the site. Questions should concern what equipment to purchase and what will be necessary to install and maintain it. In addition to normal operation, the maintenance team will also have to plan for the unexpected, whether it is equipment failure or too much success in attracting visitors to the site. Here are some sample questions:

How will the site respond to surges in visitor traffic? Sites that cover occasional events of widespread interest (e.g., holidays) have drastically different hardware and network requirements than those providing the same service day after day.

How will individual pages on the site be created? Options include manual layout using HTML editors, or Web page assembly on-the-fly using scripts and databases. If manual editing is used, it will be necessary to hire enough developers to manage updates. If automated systems are used, top-level programmers will have to install and fine-tune expensive software. Database-driven sites also require faster server hardware.

How will the site respond to requests and suggestions from the audience? Even if the site doesn't post user submissions in its content, there will be a steady stream of email queries, form-based product orders, suggestions, and proposals via email—and possibly via phone and fax. For large sites with multiple mailboxes, the problem of unsolicited spam email may be a significant factor.

How will the site respond to the sudden loss of personnel, Internet connection, Web server, or hard disk? If hardware or software is lost, or if a member of the team is absent, alternate workarounds should be developed. The production team may also have to plan a response to "stop the presses" news that necessitates interrupting the staging process.

Will obsolete content be archived or destroyed? This is of primary importance from a maintenance standpoint, since archive data can quickly occupy more disk space than the site itself. If changes are necessary to archived content (e.g., someone listed in old documents changes his or her legal name), how will this information be added?

Update Questions

The update team will need to consider its own internal organization, hardware and software necessary to support dynamic data, and interaction with the maintenance team. Since the update team will operate at every level between raw data and finished product on site, the questions will need to cover a greater breadth than those considered by the maintenance team. Another critical area that needs to be considered is how the team will coordinate update efforts, and whether custom software will be necessary for this. Some sample questions appear next:

What proportion really needs to be dynamic? While it may be tempting to plan for massive updates of content, much smaller changes are frequently more appropriate. For example, a site listing the address of a small business may have largely static content, but it will also need to reassure potential clients that it hasn't been abandoned. In this case, dynamic content could consist of date and time counters, as well as short "quotes of the day" from the operators. Larger sites will want to prioritize the hotspots that require the fastest updates. It is also important to subdivide dynamic content between purely automatic updates and those which require intervention by a human operator.

Is content or interface most important? Web design shops may make few changes in their services and pricing, but they will need to make frequent adjustments to their interface to ensure clients they are at the cutting edge.

Will users contribute content? Allowing significant audience input to the site's pages implies developing automated programs for collecting user postings, and a human editor to analyze them for appropriateness.

Will user preference control content delivery? For sites whose typical audience is interested in only a small portion of its total content (e.g., world news), screening, message forwarding, push channels, and agent software should be considered. Since these are new technologies, provisions need to be made for additional research and programming.

How will the team communicate? If several individuals cooperate to develop dynamic content, it will be necessary to define how information, development, and responsibility will be set up within the group. Smaller groups will be able to use a version of EmailNet, while larger groups will need to consider specialized *groupware/workflow* software, discussed more fully in Chapter 5.

This completes the basic discussion of dynamic site plans. In the following chapters, the hardware, software, and techniques needed to implement maintenance and updates are explored in greater detail.

PART TWO
DYNAMIC SITE MAINTENANCE

BASIC DYNAMIC
SITE MAINTENANCE

T he Web Administrator and additional members of the maintenance team are responsible for keeping the dynamic site in a steady state. This "running in place" mode of operation includes keeping standard programs and services online, responding to problems that affect the site's performance and delivery, and ensuring that information resulting from the site's operation is routed to the Producer and update team. Specific jobs that fall under maintenance (see Figure 3.1) include:

- Purchasing, evaluating, and integrating hardware and software

- Enforcing hardware, software, HTML, and program compatibility standards

- Confirming that the Internet connection remains active, and responding to sudden surges in traffic and bottlenecks in server performance

- Installing, configuring, and maintaining server software

Figure 3.1 Jobs of the maintenance team.

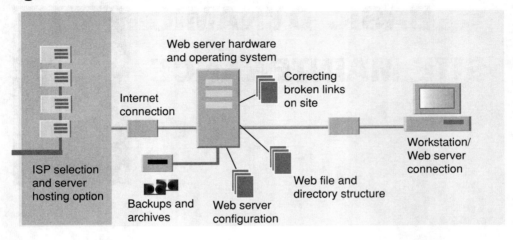

- Policing the site for incompatible or obsolete content, and identifying and fixing broken links

- Ensuring that access statistics to the Web site and elements including banner ads reach the Producer and update team, as well as email and user input from programs and fill-out forms

- Managing major upgrades of the site's hardware and software, such as moving content to a new server or operating system

- Managing security on the Web site, and developing an access policy for members of the update team

Styles of Maintenance

Maintenance of most Web sites falls under one or two general strategies—one occurring by default, the other by design. Reactive strategies are inefficient and dangerous, but are nevertheless the mode that most site operators fall into. Reactive maintenance results in problems being addressed only when they occur. The most common cause of reactive maintenance is poor planning, in which the basic tools of maintenance—hardware, software, and an overall plan—are lacking.

A more effective strategy for supporting dynamic sites involves preventive maintenance. This strategy goes beyond simply responding to problems and encourages an active pattern of looking for trouble in the system. Regular schedules for routine tasks help to catch small problems before they become larger.

Maintenance Models Based on Server Type

As discussed in the previous chapter, a dynamic site team usually has at least one public Web server, coupled with one or more private staging servers which will normally reside on one or more of the per-

Figure 3.2 National access providers and hosting services.

BBN Planet	http://www.bbn.com
Netcom	http://www.netcom.com
PSINet	http://www.psi.net
UUNet	http://www.uu.net
IBM Global Web Solutions	http://www.ibm.com/websolutions
MindSpring	http://www.mindspring.com
Earthlink Network	http://www.earthlink.net

sonal workstations used by members of the site team. The public Web site will be connected to the Internet though an *Internet Service Provider* (*ISP*), examples of which are shown in Figure 3.2. The current economics of Web site hosting fall naturally into three models distinguished by the type of Web server hardware, method of connection used to connect the private and public servers, and the size of the monthly maintenance budget. These options (shared server, bandwidth rental/dedicated server, and inhouse network—illustrated in Figure 3.3) are compared next.

Figure 3.3 Shared, dedicated, and inhouse servers.

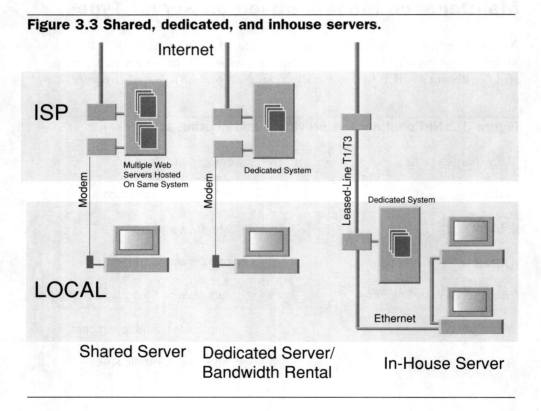

Shared Server

The cheapest option (approximately $20–$500/month) for development puts the site on a shared virtual server, often on the same account that provides consumer-level dialup access. A single computer hosts multiple Web sites which optionally have their own unique domain names. The ISP generally has full responsibility for hardware/software maintenance, and the production team accesses the public server through modem or ISDN accounts. This option offers extremely low costs (right down to the $19.95 monthly rates charged for basic Internet access), but ISPs usually limit installation of the databases and CGI scripts necessary for dynamic sites. Sophisticated site management and groupware (beyond the basic EmailNet described in the previous chapter) are difficult to implement, though recent moves by Lotus (www.lotus.com) to put Domino-based groupware/workflow accounts on national ISP networks may change this situation.

Virtually all ISPs offer some form of shared server rental. Quality of service varies tremendously and unpredictably, since several Web sites compete for access to the shared server's processing power. Some small ISPs even host sites on systems already burdened with dialup modem traffic. Finding a useful shared service requires investigation. The Web Administrator should contact other clients of the same ISP and ask about the service they have received, and personally visit these sites to check for slowdown caused by overloaded servers.

Bandwidth Rental/Dedicated Server

Groups with larger sites demanding more power and control will need to purchase their own server or rent a dedicated system from the ISP which contains only the group's content. In either case, the computer would be housed at the ISP's location (approximately $200–$1,500/month). Like shared server options, the development team connects to the server through dialup accounts. With exclusive use of the server, the developers and programmers have full control over the operating system, programs, and storage space. The ISP usually provides basic maintenance and may offer additional bandwidth management, backups, and security services. Unlike the shared option, maintenance of dedicated systems requires the full-time attention of at least one Web Administrator. Fully dynamic sites can be supported through this option, though reliance on low-speed Internet connections between the development team and server may make updates difficult.

Dedicated servers present particular challenges for the maintenance team. Since the server will operate remotely, the maintenance team needs to have full control over the system. Dedicated servers are usually installed to handle high traffic and to support complex sites requiring advanced programming. Despite this, the connection between server and administrator often remains at the modem level. This makes it difficult to upload large audio or video files. The maintenance team will also be restricted to hourly or daily checks on the server, which makes it harder to catch developing problems before they get out of hand. To maintain consistent access, the maintenance team should have at least two distinct accounts with different ISPs. This way, if one ISP goes down or overloads, there is an alternative available for handling maintenance problems.

In-House Network

Groups with large sites may elect to keep their Web servers in house and connect their local network to an ISP through a high-speed Internet connection (>$1,500/month). Updates are fast and easy, since the production team accesses both staging and public servers directly through the local network. If the company runs an internal Intranet, the public server can be connected seamlessly to its information. In-house networks give the Web Administrator physical access to the Web server(s), making system backups and other operations easier to manage. In addition to being responsible for the server, the maintenance team must ensure that the Internet connection remains functioning at all times. Placing the Web server on a company network can also cause potential security problems. Due to this, the resources of an internal *Information Services* (*IS*) group are needed to maintain the server in house.

The Internet Connection

Dynamic Web sites demand more reliable Internet connections than static sites. This is because dynamic information encourages visitors to return to the site again and again. Surfers will judge the site by its ease of access, and slow or broken connections will reflect directly on the site's content. The update team also requires reliable access to the Web server and often will be connected 24 hours a day. There are several factors influencing the reliability of connections, some of which are discussed next.

Connection Speed

Common access speeds include T1 (1.54Mbps), T3 (45Mbps), and OC-3 (fiber-optic T3) bandwidth connections. Many Internet providers also advertise "fractional" services allowing access to a portion of the total T1 or T3 bandwidth. (The "10-megabit" connection offered by some ISPs is an example of the latter.) The maintenance team will need to get enough bandwidth to handle the anticipated routine traffic, as well as occasional or planned spikes of much higher traffic. While a detailed discussion of bandwidth management is reserved for the next chapter, a simple rule-of-thumb estimate for site requirements can be derived by the following:

number of users in a given time/average connection time per user) = average number of connected users

Thus, if a site has 30,000 unique visitors per day, and their average connection time (e.g., the time in which data is actually being downloaded) is 1/1000 of a day (14.4 minutes), then the average number of users is 30,000 /1000 = 30 at any one time. Note that this calculation does not correct for fluctuations in access. Assuming the majority of users log on using 33.6 (~33 kilobits/second) modems, the minimum bandwidth necessary for the site is 33,600 * 30 users = 990,000 bits/second, or about one megabit per second. Since T1-level bandwidth is about 1.5 megabits/second, a line of this speed in principle is adequate for normal traffic on the site. In practice, content type and variations in traffic must also be considered. The simple calculation just shown assumes users download up to two megabits of information per visit, a value characteristic of a site rich in graphics, audio, or video. Sites providing access to text and numerical information (e.g., database results) will be able to tolerate a greater number of users without choking, while those providing streaming audio and video will overload.

Leased-Line Connections

Inhouse servers get their access to the Internet through T1/T3 leased lines maintained by the local phone company. ISPs usually will take care of ordering this line, but the maintenance team should also request contacts at the phone company so that they can reach them directly in emergencies. While not common, phone companies occasionally switch off leased lines or scramble one line with another. When setting up the service, the ISP should make sure the leased line doesn't cross the territories of rival regional phone companies. While signals will pass between their networks without degradation, fixing any problems will require cooperation from two business rivals—never an inviting option!

Redundant Connections

Traffic from ISPs flows into several large Internet backbones, traditionally routing their traffic through *Network Access Points* (*NAPs*). By connecting to multiple NAPs, ISPs ensure that if a portion of the Internet goes down, traffic can be rerouted through an alternate path. For even greater redundancy, large ISPs may also establish nearest-neighbor agreements with other ISPs to exchange traffic independently of the NAPs.

If you expect a high volume of traffic on your site, or plan to offer audio or video Webcasts, redundant connections through a national ISP are absolutely necessary. Local hosting services can sometimes also provide redundancy. In contrast, smaller local ISPs usually resell bandwidth provided by a larger ISP. With only one connection to the Internet, they cannot compensate for network problems. If redundancy and low costs are required for the dynamic site, it may be preferable to outsource the Web server to a national ISP or hosting service, rather than paying a smaller amount for an inhouse connection from a regional ISP.

Guaranteed Bandwidth

Some T1/T3 services actually provide shared access. Shared access occurs when data from several incoming T1 or T3 lines are combined on the ISP's internal *Local Area Network* (*LAN*), or when a group of Web servers share a common LAN on a Web hosting service. Depending on the bandwidth demands of the other clients, the minute-to-minute quality of access can vary widely from the advertised ideal. While this may not pose a problem for Web servers delivering basic HTML, sites downloading large multimedia files or streaming audio and video will require guaranteed bandwidth. Guaranteed options ensure that a given bandwidth is always available independent of traffic produced by other clients using the service. These options are usually at least twice as expensive as shared bandwidth. Guaranteed options are ISP specific, and the maintenance team should examine the specifics of their implementation to ensure they are adequate.

It is worth noting that many ISPs that do not provide guaranteed bandwidth nevertheless charge by the amount of data transferred from their clients' sites. Some seemingly inexpensive services begin charging exorbitant rates if data transfer exceeds a few hundred megabytes daily. Popular sites with a few thousand daily users can easily exceed this value.

In the future, Internet-wide bandwidth reservation through *RSVP* (*Resource Reservation Protocol*; www.ietf.org/html.charters/rsvp-charter.html) will augment the current system. RSVP will allow ISPs to guarantee a level of access for traffic throughout the Internet, but several years are likely to pass before it is implemented.

Traffic Spikes

If your dynamic site hosts transient events causing surges in visitor traffic (e.g., the annual awards ceremony on the Association of Motion Picture Arts and Sciences site; www.oscar.com), you may want to negotiate temporary increases in bandwidth use for specific times. Some ISPs will allow short-term purchase of additional guaranteed bandwidth. Shared access accounts generally do not allow additional bandwidth to be added in this way.

Security

Developers who put their sites on shared servers are vulnerable to vandalism from other clients, ISP employees, or random hacking of the ISP's network. The maintenance team should ask for a copy of the guidelines the ISP uses to increase security, and emergency contact information if hacking or site vandalism occurs.

Tech Support

Contact with the technical support staff of the ISP is an absolute necessity for dynamic sites, and it should be the deciding factor in choosing an ISP. The ISP should provide a support number specifically for its high-speed connection or Web hosting clients, and should be reachable by email and fax. If the development team doesn't have a programmer, check to see if the ISP has support for CGI scripts and a library of default programs. Also inquire whether the ISP can supply basic tech support through an automatic notification service. For example, some ISPs are implementing Clear Communications

Figure 3.4 Example of a statistics report (Earthlink—www.earthlink .net).

Current System Status	
This page was last updated on : Wed Jun 18 13:09:25 PDT 1997	
Peak Usage is currently: 6:00pm - 12:00mid PST.	
News:	• Online and Operational.
Mail:	• Online and operational. • These mail tips may help to improve email performance. • Important announcement regarding our email service.
DNS:	• Online and operational
California Dialup:	Please check with your local phone company to ensure that your access number is a local toll free call. All numbers require you to prefix your username with **ELN/** • Online and operational
Nationwide Dialup:	Please check with your local phone company to ensure that your access number is a local toll free call. All numbers require you to prefix your username with **ELN/** • Online and Operational.
Registration:	**EarthLink Registration Server:** • Online and operational. **Microsoft Referral Server:** • Online and operational. **Netscape Referral Server:** • Online and operational.

Corp. (www.clear.com) push channels running through Pointcast (www.pointcast.com) to send statistics and performance information directly to their clients, often saving a call to the support staff. Other ISPs make similar information available on their public Web server. An example of an ISP's statistics report is shown in Figure 3.4.

Alternative Connectivity Options

The ISP market promises to become even more complex with the entry of new players.

Cable operators. Time-Warner's RoadRunner (www.rdrun.com), @Home's @Business Network (www.work.home.net), MediaOne (www.mediaone.com), and Comcast (www.comcast.com; recently purchased by Microsoft) are developing cable-based ISP networks. At present, cable ISPs number their customers in the thousands, and the design of existing cable networks may pose security problems for business. Most offer basic Web hosting services on shared servers and plan to expand to dedicated servers as well. A good resource for capabilities and limitations of cable modems can be found at Motorola's Multimedia Group (www.mot.com/MIMS/Multimedia/).

Power, water, and gas companies. These utilities are using their rights-of-way to construct ISP services. With extensive experience in the business of providing service to the general public, they may provide significant competition for the phone companies.

Broadcasters. Some satellite operators have announced Internet access, but in most cases their service runs one way, and is therefore unsuitable for Web hosting.

ADSL-based ISPs. A few ISPs have begun to offer *Asymmetrical Digital Subscriber Line (ADSL)* technologies, which can use ordinary phone wire for T1-level access. ADSL uses advanced signal technologies to push T1 or higher speeds over ordinary phone lines.

For a good heads-up page for cable, ADSL, and other alternatives, check out the High Speed Access Page (www.specialty.com/hiband/). An excellent discussion of ISP and hosting issues is available at sites like WilsonWeb's How To Choose A Web Hosting Service (www.wilsonweb.com/articles/webhost.htm).

Server Operating Systems

The choice of Web server hardware is governed by requirements for speed and capacity—and the proficiency of the maintenance team with the hardware and operating systems. At present, there are three basic platforms widely used to host Web servers: Unix, Windows NT, and Macintosh.

Unix

This command-line operating system is currently the best choice for dynamic Web sites. Unix servers show superior performance at high-traffic volumes and under heavy computing loads—a fact of life for dynamic sites. Multiprocessor Unix systems also show greater scaleability than competing platforms. Due to scaleability, multiprocessor RISC/Unix systems show nearly linear increases in performance, whereas comparable multiprocessor Windows NT/Intel platforms show less improvement. Unix is less appropriate for staging servers, since the learning curve for effective use is steep and individual team members are likely to prefer Mac or Windows systems.

Unix systems provide several additional advantages. Since they were designed for multiple users and Internet access from the start, server implementation tends to be very efficient. Once online, they can take advantage of a vast bulk of free Web-related software.

High-performance Web servers such as Sun Microsystems' (www.sun.com/products-n-solutions/hw/servers/index.html) Ultrasparc, or Silicon Graphics' (see Figure 3.5) WebFORCE offer the best developed solutions. Berkeley Software Design, Inc. (www.bsdi.com) makes a commercial hacker-resistant version of Unix for Intel platforms that is extremely popular with ISPs and Web hosting services. Sites trying to keep expenses low can go with Linux (www.linuxhq.com) or FreeBSD (www.freebsd.org) software and build credible servers for under $2,500. For more information, check resources including Jeff's Resources Vault (www.nda.com/~jblaine/vault/) or Mark's List of Unix Resources (www2.quickweb.com/~mark/unix.html).

Windows NT

Many administrators in corporate IS departments will be drawn to Microsoft's Windows NT platform (www.microsoft.com/NTServer/) because of its compatibility with their existing networks. NT is steadily acquiring essential Internet functions, including mail and proxy servers, firewalls, and Web servers. For Web servers hosted in house and receiving less than 100,000 hits/day, NT provides a good option. The current implementation of NT is less useful for remote Web hosting. Since some NT functions still require direct, console-level access, servers cannot be maintained over modem connections. In this case, it will be necessary to pay the ISP for administration or get walk-in access to the server.

NT's major advantage appears on the back end of maintenance. Much of the new commercial software for expanding Web servers and linking databases is specifically developed for NT. For this reason, NT systems are excellent staging servers. Comparable Unix software is generally more expensive, or exists as unsupported freeware. Resources for using Windows NT on the Internet can be found at sites such as the Microsoft Windows NT Sites list (www.indirect.com/www/ceridgac/ntsite.html) and Windows NT Web Server Tools (www.primenet.com/~buyensj/ntwebsrv.html).

Figure 3.5 Silicon Graphics' WebFORCE site (www.sgi.com/Products/ WebFORCE/).

Macintosh

A surprising number of Web servers run on Apple Computer's Macintosh (www.apple.com) platform, despite uncertainty about the company's long-term prospects. Macs offer the easiest environments for development by nontechnical personnel and provide a complete set of tools for supporting standard Internet services. It is estimated that up to 70 percent of professional developers use Macs for their work. Macintosh servers are also harder to hack than Unix or NT systems; Internet access was added so recently to the Apple OS that low-level security holes are nearly nonexistent. Middleware providing Web access to common Mac databases such as FileMaker (see Everyware's Tango; www.everyware.com) provide tools for constructing dynamic sites and staging servers.

Despite their ease of use, Macintosh servers have some serious limitations. The fastest Macs (about 300MHz) still perform more slowly than NT or Unix servers. In addition, the lack of true multitasking on the Macintosh operating system leads to frequent and unpredictable crashes, making it a poor choice for public servers hosted on a remote ISP.

In 1997, Apple began to merge its existing operating system (www.macos.apple.com) with the NeXT computer platform, indicating that the promised Rhapsody OS will include robust multitasking similar to NT and Unix platforms. Internet-related resources are available at Apple's main site, and at Jon Weiderspan's Macintosh Internet Resources Directory (www.go-nexus-go.com/macresources/).

Web Server Software

There are hundreds of Web servers available for Internet and Intranet applications. Lists and reviews are maintained at Web Compare (webcompare.internet.com), W3 (www.w3.org/pub/WWW/Servers.html), and Serverwatch.com (www.serverwatch.iworld.com/about.html). Despite this diversity, most dynamic sites use one of the software packages listed next.

Apache

This public, free package for Unix (see Figure 3.6) is the most popular and widely supported server on the Internet. The availability of the complete source code, combined with the ease of compiling external modules (www.zyzzyva.com/server/module_registry/) into the main server, have contributed to Apache's success. Modules supporting *Secure Sockets Layer* (*SSL*) transactions are available, and the commercial Stronghold (www.c2.net/products/stronghold/) version also implements SSL security. Apache implemented the more efficient HTTP 1.1 (ftp://ds.internic.net/rfc/rfc2068.txt) standard well ahead of commercial servers and should continue to provide cutting-edge performance for the foreseeable future. News and technical support are available at Apache Week (www.apacheweek.com). Apache is an excellent choice for sites running local or remote dedicated servers willing to develop and customize their own dynamic applications.

Figure 3.6 Apache site (www.apache.org).

Netscape SuiteSpot

Netscape provides an industrial-strength collection of servers enabling Web access, messaging, and collaboration. The SuiteSpot server family (www.netscape.com/focus3/comprod/server_central) combines cutting-edge performance coupled with tight integration with a comprehensive suite of Intranet and collaborative software. The Netscape Enterprise server features LiveWire, which enables JavaScript-based connectivity to databases and Web Publisher content management tools. Able to handle the demands of large organizations, SuiteSpot is most appropriate for a mix of public and Intranet servers within larger corporations. Netscape's unmatched experience in this area makes it a superior enterprise partner.

Microsoft Internet Information Server (IIS)

Another free server (www.microsoft.com/InfoServ/), this provides a comfortable way to add Web connectivity to Windows-based systems. IIS helps create staging servers on local workstations and hosts moderate-traffic sites on NT platforms. Strengths of the product include its status as free software, relatively simple setup/maintenance, and tight integration with other Microsoft BackOffice products (particularly databases). Limitations include lack of cross-platform support for Unix and Macintosh environments. Microsoft is steadily developing enterprise solutions comparable to Netscape's and will form a competitive alternative in the future.

America Online Server

Not widely appreciated, the AOL server and publisher packages (www.aolserver.com/index.html) provide a remarkable mix of performance and dynamic database integration for Unix and NT platforms. Performance is robust and suited to high traffic loads. Until May 1997, AOL distributed a free version of Informix's Illustra (www.illustra.com) object/relational database with the server, and continues to maintain tight integration with the product. Object/relational databases are widely considered to be the best solution for multimedia-based dynamic Web sites. The server also includes its own internal search engine, and simple integration with AOL's Web authoring tools. Despite these advantages, the AOL server is used on only a small fraction of public Web sites. Due to its small marketshare, many groups worry that AOL will ultimately terminate its support for the software.

Starnine

Starnine's WebStar server (www.starnine.com) is the system of choice for Macintosh platforms. While not compensating for the limitations of the Mac OS, it does provide simple setup, efficiency, and integration with Mac databases and software. Server setup and customization is simpler than other Web servers, and support is available for CGI and database gateways. On the other hand, the server is not suitable for high-traffic public sites. The fastest (300MHz) Macs still fall short of NT or Unix performance, and the Mac OS remains uniquely vulnerable to system crashes. In practice, Starnine servers are restricted to sites maintained by groups that can afford inhouse networks. With simple operation, the server may provide a useful platform for staging content before uploading content to a Unix or NT Web server. Starnine servers may also be useful in a university environment with a large installed base of Macintosh computers.

Web Server 4D

Web Server 4D (www.mdg.com; $245; Macintosh, Windows NT) is an unusual system that consists of a Web server fused with the 4th Dimension database and a large, built-in feature set of dynamic modules. Built-in server routines provide site performance monitoring, log analysis, cookie tracking, and lists of recently modified pages. Management tools include access control from users, groups,

and realms—with complete tracking histories for each. W4D directly supports up to 100,000 domains on a single IP address. The server
can listen on multiple IPs and deliver true multiple-domain virtual
servers. Email support for domains is also implemented, making
establishment of a complete domain far easier than it is for Unix systems. At its price, the system is hard to beat for a one-step system
leading to dynamic sites on Macintosh and Windows systems.

Web Server Configuration

Running a Web server supporting dynamic data requires frequent
changes in configuration. When installing the server, the maintenance team should consider the following issues:

- How hard will it be to upgrade the system if the size of the
  Web site grows by tenfold?

- What can be done to simplify moving the server to different
  hardware and software platforms?

- How will access to areas of the Web site be controlled? Will
  individual members of the maintenance and update team
  be restricted to specific files and directories?

- On large sites, access logs may add hundreds or even thousands of megabytes to the disk. How can this information be
  stored and transferred to the appropriate access programs?

With these questions in mind, consider the basic configuration
issues common to most dynamic servers.

Document Access

Web servers are usually set to access documents and programs under
specific directories. Files outside these directories are invisible to the
Web server. It is extremely important to set document/program
roots such that Internet users cannot see critical operating system or

program files. Within the directory tree, most servers allow access to be password protected for individual files and directories, often employing an .htaccess name/password system. A good discussion of access on Unix systems is provided at The Htaccess Authentication Tutorial (faq.clever.net/htaccess.htm).

If a goal of the site is to manage large numbers of authorized users, DBM authentication should be used instead of the ".htaccess" file. A discussion of DBM is provided in an ApacheWeek article at www.apacheweek.com/features/dbmauth. DBM is specific to Unix and requires the presence of custom libraries such as GDBM (www.mit.edu:8001/afs/athena.mit.edu/project/gnu/doc/html/gdbm _toc.html).

File Permissions

Since multiple developers may be adding and deleting files on the Web site, it is important that file permissions are set properly. Files can be set for read-only, read-write, or read-write-execute. Under Unix, the "chmod" command should be used to set file permissions. Executable CGI programs should be set to 755 (i.e., everyone can read and execute the program, but only the owner can write to it), and HTML files should be set to 744 (i.e., no execution possible). Read-write privileges can be assigned to a single user, a defined group of users, or any user using the "chown" command under Unix. Windows NT offers a comparable utility called CACLS.EXE for setting permissions. Setting permissions is discussed at NYC Unix Help (www.tac.nyc.ny.us/manuals/UNIXhelp) and at many other Web sites. Several site management software packages provide document check-in/check-out privileges that function independently of system-level permissions.

Administrative Servers

For security reasons, a public Web server frequently runs as a highly restricted user called "www" or "nobody." Programs launched from

Figure 3.7 Suggested breakdown of files and directories facilitating expansion.

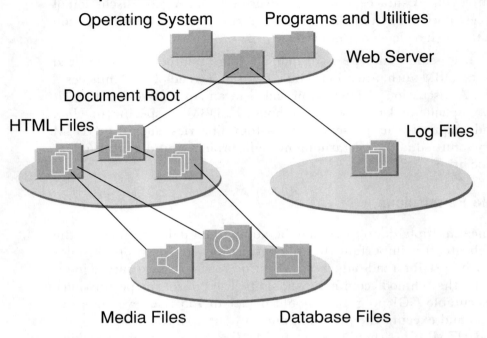

the Web server (such as CGI programs) inherit the user's privileges and thus will have the wrong permissions to modify files. This is a problem if the developers want to use a Web-based interface to manage their sites. In order to circumvent this problem without compromising security, many sites run a second Web server under a user with more privileges. These administrative servers should only be available to the site team, and access to them should be password protected. Many commercial packages include a special administrative server by default. If you are using a freeware system such as Apache, it is possible to launch a second server by having it run at a different port assignment (e.g., yoursite.com:2093).

Media Configuration

Multipurpose Internet Mail Extension (*MIME*) types originally were designed to provide an exchange standard for email attachments, but they are now widely used for identifying Web-based media. MIME entries map a media type (e.g., QuickTime) to a file extension (e.g., .mov). Most Web servers that encounter a filename extension not listed in their MIME configuration file will instruct the user's Web browser to treat the information as text or HTML. Misspelled filename extensions (e.g., file.htmlx) can result in multimedia being downloaded as text characters on screen. If new media types are installed on the site, a MIME entry may need to be added. It is also important to test the download to make sure that the MIME type is being read correctly.

Directory Structures

Dynamic Web sites often grow rapidly in size and may require frequent changes in their directory or file structures. By selecting the proper organization of files and directories, updates requiring installation of new hard disks can be made much easier. A suggested breakdown of files and directories facilitating expansion is shown in Figure 3.7.

With increasingly cheap disk storage, sites running their own servers may want to set the Web server's document root to a second disk containing all the HTML files. If this is not done, adding more storage space may require reinstallation of the operating system. Moving the documents to a separate disk also allows better access control; the entire disk can be set to Web-specific permissions.

The main directories holding HTML files should be divided as nearly as possible along departmental lines. Since individual members of the update team usually produce content for specific departments, such an arrangement also simplifies access control. Within departmental directories, most sites subdivide files based on media type. Individual HTML, graphic, audio, and video files should be named whenever possible to reflect some aspect of their content. This will make it easier for the update team to manually locate and replace files from a directory list. It also makes it easier to segregate media requiring extensive disk space (e.g., movie files) from text files occupying little volume. For example, a directory containing large (10-megabyte) video files could be moved to its own disk, and an *alias* directory could be added to the main site pointing to it.

Log files can add hundreds of megabytes a day for sites with high traffic (e.g., 100,000 hits/day). Since log analysis programs typically put a heavy load on the server, it is a good idea to transfer log data to either a second hard disk, an analysis computer on the local network, or a remote log analysis service over the Internet (see Chapter 4).

Link Validation

After server and site installation, checking dynamic Web sites for broken links is one of the most important responsibilities of the maintenance team. Broken links appear regularly on dynamic sites; errors in writing or removal of a file frequently create a swarm of broken links scattered throughout the site. There are a variety of ways links can break, many of which are listed here:

HTML. Broken HTML links are caused by either misspelling the link to an existing file or removing a file without removing the links pointing to it. Extra or missing quotes or brackets in an <A HREF....> tag can also break a link, as well as confuse the browser's presentation of the remainder of the Web page.

Imagemaps. Older versions of HTML do not provide direct support for linking the XY coordinate selected on a graphic with a hyperlink. To get around this, many sites implement *client-side* imagemaps using the <MAP> tag, or a *server-side* imagemap program (usually in CGI). Frequently, site developers update their HTML files but forget about the imagemaps. Since imagemaps are frequently used to construct graphic navigation tools, this can be a major problem.

External programs. Hyperlinks to CGI, databases, Java, Shockwave, or other non-HTML programs can fail through misspelling, movement of the program file, or an incorrectly configured program returning a system error.

Orphan files. When a site is updated, links to older files are often changed without removing old files they pointed to. For example, a site visitor could stumble upon an obsolete page that describes a contest that ended years earlier, or one that links only to pages that no longer exist! These orphan files can confuse users who find the page through a search engine and find themselves trapped in an obsolete environment. In this case, it's better to have a 404 error generated. However, instead of showing the user the error file, the server should present a page that lists valid links to the site.

External links. Links to other Web sites provide a valuable method for traffic exchange and promotion. Unfortunately, the "favorite links" page will rapidly become obsolete as sites move or disappear.

Back links. Even if you keep track of everyone who has contacted you for link exchange, popular sites and search engines will accumulate back links without your knowledge. These links will break when local errors are corrected or site content is updated.

Domain names. Many Web sites start out as single pages maintained by an individual. When they expand, the operators usually will get a new, often custom domain name. Large corporations with well-known names frequently put up temporary Web sites while negotiating for their brand name on the Internet. When the new domain names become operative, bookmarked URLs and links on other Web sites will fail unless steps are taken to automatically redirect the obsolete link to the new domain.

Programs for Link Analysis

A wide variety of free and commercial programs exist for checking links. Freeware provides basic functions and access to source code, but it may be difficult to install and maintain. Commercial programs provide more comprehensive link checking in environments suited to nonprogrammers, usually coupled with other site management tools.

Web-Based Validation

Several Web sites run back-end scripts that can be used to validate individual Web pages and entire sites. The virtual shingles of Dr. HTML (www2.imagiware.com/RxHTML/) and Dr. Watson (www.addy .com/watson/) lead to linkchecking, HTML language validation, and even spellchecking for text. The latter feature is very useful to anyone who has tried to use a word processor to spellcheck HTML. A newer service, Net.Mechanic (www.netmechanic.com), allows linkchecking of large sites as a background process and sends the results as email. WebCrawler (www.webcrawler.com) has an unusual option that allows users to find all the Web sites that point back to a given URL. While not comprehensive (Webcrawler only checks sites listed in its internal database), it does provide a free service capable of discovering broken backlinks on remote Web sites. InfoSeek (www.infoseek.com) recently added a "remove dead URL" button to its "add URL" page. If other search engines follow suit, it should simplify updating remote backlinks.

Freeware/Shareware

Siteman (www.morning.asn.au/siteman/; $50.00) provides linkchecking for individual files, directories, or whole sites. Interesting features of this Windows 3.x/NT package include a utility that changes the name of a file on the site, then goes through the entire site updating the appropriate links. Other options check external links and list all links pointing to a particular file. Additional NT link validators are available at the CSE 3310 Link Validator Site (htmlvalidator.com) and BiggByte Software (www.biggbyte.com). Other free or low-cost programs for Unix include Missinglink (www.rsol.com/ml/), Linklint (www.goldwarp.com/bowlin/linklint/), and Lvrfy (www.cs.dartmouth.edu/~crow/lvrfy.html).

Commercial Software

Getting a commercial program may greatly simplify the management of broken links. With friendly interfaces, some of the responsibility for dead links can be moved to the update team, with the maintenance team providing a second-pass monitoring. A large number of programs are currently available.

Microsoft FrontPage (www.microsoft.com/frontpage/; $395) and Adobe PageMill (www.adobe.com/prodindex/pagemill/main.html; $195) provide an analysis of broken links within individual Web pages, as do most high-end site management packages. For smaller Web sites and for sites that need to check backlinks and external URLs, one of the following programs will provide a reasonable option:

Coast Web Administrator (www.coast.com; $495), a commercial Windows NT/95 application, combines broken-link detection, identification of orphan pages, and drag-and-drop site management. Designed to integrate with HTML editors, it can repair broken links on remote servers via a built-in FTP function. An interesting feature called ActiveScan allows the program to test imagemaps, fill-out forms, and database links with default data. This makes it much easier to test non-HTML links. During the first site check, the Web Administrator provides dummy form entries, which are remembered and used by ActiveScan on subsequent runs. The program also supports password management, allowing the administrators to restrict access to some areas of the site.

InContext WebAnalyzer (www.incontext.com/products/analyze.html; $249.95; Windows NT) combines linkchecking with graphical maps of the site. Maps can display the site as directory trees, tables of contents, and a unique circular ("Wavefront") map showing directory relationships. Individual files are analyzed for URL name, MIME type, size, depth in the directory tree, last modification date, title, and all "in" and "out" links. WebAnalyzer also features report generation and automatic scheduling for linkchecks.

Site Technologies SiteSweeper (www.sitetech.com; $249.95; Windows NT/95) combines comprehensive broken-link detection with estimates of download time for individual Web pages. SiteSweeper provides access to page properties, dividing links to and from pages, external links, and image sizes.

Adobe SiteMill (w1000.mv.us.adobe.com/prodindex/sitemill/overview.html; $195; Macintosh), one of the very first management programs, has recently received a much-needed upgrade. The 2.0 version generates site maps and finds and fixes broken links. It also adds the option of working with remote Web sites via an integrated FTP upload utility.

Additional Methods for Management of Broken Links

Besides linkcheckers, there are additional steps the maintenance team can take to reduce broken links:

404 errors. Most Web servers allow specifying an HTML file in place of the default 404 error. Simply adding a custom HTML page can greatly increase a visitor's confidence that the site has not been abandoned. For more sophisticated behavior, a CGI script can be used. The script can report the problem via EmailNet and even suggest an alternate page to the visitor. For example, on the authors' Kaleidospace site (kspace.com) visitors sometimes look for artists that are no longer online. On receiving a URL for a vanished artist, a custom CGI suggests artists with similar work.

Server redirects. If the Web site is moved to a new Internet domain, a "redirect" command can be installed at the old server URL to route visitors automatically. Most Web servers support redirecting access for individual files, programs, and directories. CGI scripts are also available for routing visitors to the new URL. The latter method allows the programmer to create a custom "we've moved" sign for their audience. CGI-based redirection scripts can be found at CGI/Perl Tips, Tricks and Hints (www.halcyon.com/sanford/cgi/cgi-tips.html#redirect).

Backlink monitoring. The open communication characteristic of the Internet has fostered an informal approach to links between Web sites. If the maintenance team searches for invalid or unwanted links to their site on other servers, they should use appropriate "netiquette" in requesting changes. Most Webmasters will respond to a formal email message informing them of changes in a site's structure or movement to a new domain name. To reciprocate, the maintenance team should make sure their links to other sites are periodically checked. If a broken link points to a valued partner, associate, or sponsor, the Web Administrator should send email informing them of the problem and requesting new information. In a few cases, the site may insist that links pointing to it be removed. As an example, a site containing adult content might link directly to one carrying financial information. In this case, the maintenance group will need to consult to determine if legal action is necessary.

Site Code Compatibility

In addition to major programming errors, the maintenance team needs to be aware of more subtle problems which may not bring the site down, but cause errors in the page display. The maintenance team should take responsibility for flagging Web pages with subtle errors in HTML coding, such as unmatched quotes or extra brackets. Such mistakes may not be immediately apparent in the Web page display, but could result in content being rendered invisible. The effect of minor HTML errors is often browser dependent. Development groups that program exclusively with the help of HTML editors won't experience this problem, but groups upgrading from manual coding to HTML editors usually need to "clean" their files with a validation program. Web sites such as A Kinder, Gentler Validator (ugweb.cs.ualberta.ca/~gerald/validate) can be used to create reports of inconsistent HTML coding and list standard and nonstandard HTML tags on the site. As more sites use JavaScript and other client-side languages (see Chapter 5) with variables and if/then branching, the possibility for errors will increase.

Storage and Archiving

Only 20 percent of all businesses using computers do regular backups! This means that the remaining 80 percent are destined to experience the pain of lost data. Backups are an absolute necessity for public Web sites handling dynamic information. Even if local copies of the site remain on developers' systems and staging servers, the public server invariably contains unique configuration files and data which will be lost during a disk crash. In addition to safety backups, dynamic sites frequently need to archive earlier versions of the site. The following provides pointers for managing storage and archives:

Backups by ISPs. Reputable ISPs always back up data on shared servers. The ISP should provide the maintenance team with their backup schedule. Dedicated servers may back up over the ISP's network, or may use a local drive connected to the server.

Inhouse servers. Many administrators install tape drives on their server and set the system to run automatic backups.

Backup servers. For sites with critical information, the Web Administrator can set up a second "shadow" server that mirrors content on the primary server, or an additional hard disk on the main server.

Remote backup services. Web Administrators wanting additional security may elect to store copies of their sites with an Internet-based backup service. Several companies including SafeGuard Interactive (www.sgii.com), Connected (www.connected.com), and XactLabs (www.xactlabs.com) provide backups directly over the Internet using the *Secure Sockets Layer* (*SSL*) protocol. Remote backups add a significant cost to the maintenance budget, and the Web Administrator needs to make sure that the company can supply their archives on demand.

Archiving. In some cases, it may be desirable to copy a snapshot of the Web site for later access. Such a solution can provide an instant replacement for a crashed site without the reinstallation of software necessary with tape backups. Programs offering the ability to create shapshots include Ingot Software's (see Figure 3.8) Disk Imager, and Hicomp's (www.hicomp.com) Hiback software available for Unix and NT platforms. To use the programs, an additional disk is designated for automatic or manual backups. Since

Figure 3.8 Ingot Software (www.ingot.com).

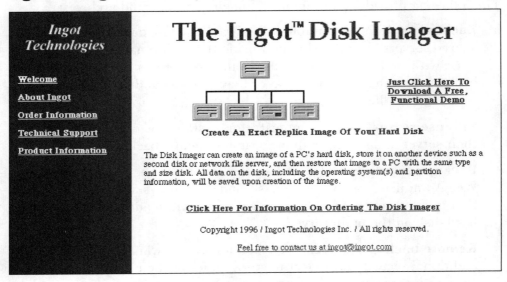

Ingot Technologies

Welcome
About Ingot
Order Information
Technical Support
Product Information

The Ingot™ Disk Imager

Just Click Here To Download A Free, Functional Demo

Create An Exact Replica Image Of Your Hard Disk

The Disk Imager can create an image of a PC's hard disk, store it on another device such as a second disk or network file server, and then restore that image to a PC with the same type and size disk. All data on the disk, including the operating system(s) and partition information, will be saved upon creation of the image.

Click Here For Information On Ordering The Disk Imager

Copyright 1996 / Ingot Technologies Inc. / All rights reserved.

Feel free to contact us at ingot@ingot.com

the exact structure of the disk data is preserved, there are no changes required if the snapshot must be swapped for a crashed disk.

Web-to-CD publishing tools provide an alternative means of archiving complete, working copies of an entire Web site. Out of various hybrid CD solutions, Marketscape's WebCD (www.marketscape.com) has been used primarily to distribute copies of Web sites on CD, but has the potential to save backup snapshots of a Web site. The 650MB limit of CD-ROMs may pose limitations for some large sites, but the advent of read/write DVD (4GB) drives in the near future will make it an attractive option for some sites. Using a functional medium allows rolling back all or part of a Web site, since consecutive backups record the site's update history.

Backup Management Strategies

As part of the overall maintenance plan, the Web Administrator should keep records of the backup times and media swaps.

Backup Frequency

Since ISPs are responsible for virtual hosting, the maintenance team should ask them for their backup schedule. Typical backup schedules followed by most ISPs involve incremental storage every night, alternated with full weekly backups. If updates to the site are very frequent, the development team should consider incremental saves to a backup company.

Backup Media Rotation

If the hosting service does not provide this service automatically, the team needs to get the ISP to do regular media swaps, or get permission to do the swaps themselves. Tapes should be swapped every few weeks, and a "golden" backup should be kept separately for several months. The maintenance team must keep in mind that the read heads in tape drives can easily become dirty or misaligned, and fail to successfully back up. Unless administrators periodically check administrative messages generated by the server, failed backups may not be noticed for some time. More than one site operator has responded to a hard disk crash only to discover that their tape drive had been malfunctioning for months! A good discussion of backup scheduling tradeoffs can be found on the Web for Legato Software's (www.sresearch.com/search/113002.htm) NetWorker package, which apply to other backups systems as well.

Correlating Backups with Site Updates

The Web Administrator needs to coordinate with the Content Manager and Producer to provide for special backups outside the standard calendar. If a well-developed backup schedule is already in place, the update team may consider modifying its schedule so that major additions to the Web site occur right after major backups.

Putting It All Together: A Preventive Maintenance Calendar

To implement a preventive maintenance strategy, a detailed manual should be created describing all aspects of maintenance. In the first part, information necessary for maintenance should be summarized in a manual-like format. Areas to cover include:

- Internet connection and network information, and contacts for the Internet Service Provider, or ISP.

- Specifics of the hardware and software used to maintain the Web site. Check a site like Web AdministratorResources (www.cio.com/resources) to get a feel for the most recent tools available.

- Personnel and organization of the maintenance and update teams, including email and phone numbers.

- A scheduling calendar assigning maintenance tasks designed to catch problems before they become too severe.

- Product information such as software version numbers, license numbers, tech support, and key configuration file-names.

- Estimates for financial outlays necessary for effective ongoing maintenance.

In the second part of the manual, dates and times should be established for routine checks on the integrity of the Web site. A possible maintenance calendar could use the following breakdown:

Monthly. Messages to external sites when URLs have changed on the site; rotation and backup of the entire Web site; and backup of access logs and rotation of backup media. Operating-system-level tests of hard disk integrity. Research online to discover if security patches and/or software upgrades have become available.

Weekly. Tests for broken links covering the entire Web site; checks for unexpected and/or unknown files added to the system; and analysis of recent access to password-protected areas. Also, system-wide checks for spelling and HTML code compatibility. Incremental backups of portions of the Web site that have changed. Communication with the update team about new site policies, problems on the site, and planning for spikes in visitor traffic. Archive Web site using a CD or DVD-based system if necessary.

Daily. Checks on network access, connection speeds, and server traffic. Make sure daily incremental backups are occurring normally.

With essential hardware, software, and a preliminary plan in place, the maintenance team can proceed to implement features and policies designed to make the dynamic Web site run at peak performance. These advanced features are discussed more fully in the next chapter.

ADVANCED MAINTENANCE

4

Dynamic sites with high visitor traffic require more sophisticated management techniques than those discussed in the previous chapter. These sites put greater demands on infrastructure and need continuous monitoring for optimum performance. Figure 4.1 illustrates a possible breakdown of advanced maintenance jobs common to dynamic sites. This chapter considers the analysis of site performance in greater detail from the perspective of network and visitor traffic.

Site Performance Issues

The complexity characteristic of large dynamic sites creates many potential performance bottlenecks (see Figure 4.2), some of which are:

> **End user's hardware.** Cutting-edge enhancements to Web sites (such as real-time audio) require that visitors have relatively new and fast hardware. For example, the newest

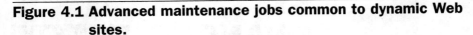

Figure 4.1 Advanced maintenance jobs common to dynamic Web sites.

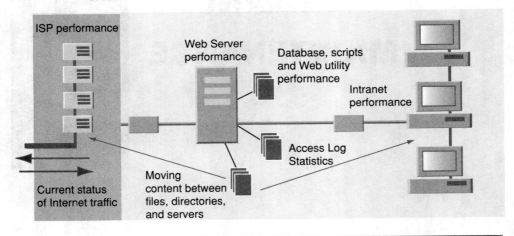

Web browsers from Netscape and Microsoft need several megabytes to run—while a significant fraction of the audience still has under 4 megs of RAM in their systems. Older Mac Quadras and 486 PCs may process information more slowly than can be sent over the network, greatly increasing connect times.

Internet-wide traffic slowdowns. During the rapid growth of the Internet, bandwidth has largely kept up with the rise in traffic, but just barely. During 1996, there were several regional network blackouts affecting ISPs and online services. This problem is particularly acute for U.S. sites that attract a large international audience.

ISP traffic slowdowns. ISPs vary widely in efficiency of data transmission. Most ISPs are growing rapidly, which means they repeatedly pass through a cycle of increasing pressure on their network, followed by the installation of

Figure 4.2 Potential Internet performance bottlenecks.

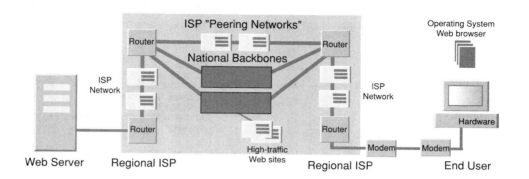

new equipment to alleviate the problem. America Online (www.aol.com)—an online service that contributes the largest single source of Web traffic—experienced this situation in a major way in early 1997 after they announced their conversion to a flat-rate Internet access service. After slowdowns caused by millions of new users, AOL solved the problem by making a massive investment in network infrastructure. ISPs may also experience slowdowns by losing one of their connections to either the Internet's national backbones or private ISP-ISP *peering networks*.

Traffic spikes on event sites. Popular events can slow access to unrelated sites. Events the size of the Academy Awards (www.oscar.com), NASA's Mars Pathfinder Site (mpfwww.jpl.nasa.gov), and IBM's 1997 rematch of Deep Blue versus Kasparov (chess.ibm.com) created traffic levels affecting the Internet as a whole.

Streaming media/Webcasts. In the absence of effective bandwidth reservation systems, streaming live audio and

Figure 4.3 Daily and weekly traffic cycles for a sample Web site using Marketwave (www.marketwave.com) software.

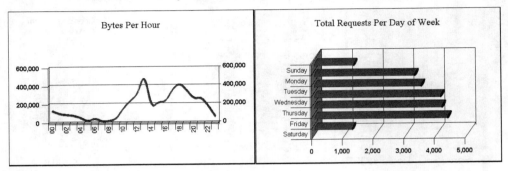

video are particularly sensitive to the ISP's traffic and the current state of the Internet.

Daily and weekly traffic cycles. Since about half of all Internet traffic originates in the United States, most sites can expect to experience day/night and weekday/weekend shifts in traffic following U.S. time zones. Figure 4.3 shows these daily and weekly traffic cycles for a sample Web site using Marketwave software.

Server overloads. When Web requests hit a server faster than it can process them, individual requests queue up and the system slows to a halt—its memory filled with unprocessed HTTP requests. This "snowball" effect can strike suddenly and convert a normally operating site into one that is completely inaccessible.

CGI bottlenecks. Even on fast sites with moderate traffic, relatively inefficient CGI scripts may tie up much of the server's processing power in requests from a few users. Other internal operations (such as rebuilding a database index file) may cause major slowdowns. Figure 4.4 shows

Figure 4.4 Hourly delay in processing time for CGI scripts, broken down by time of day using Accrue Software (www.gauge.com).

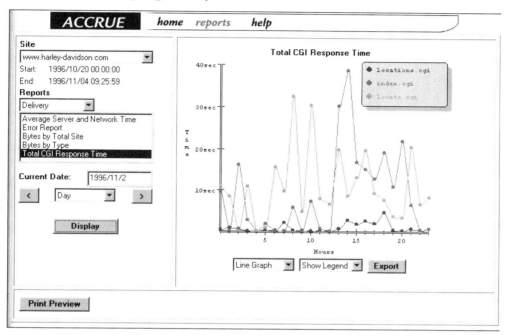

the hourly delay in processing time for CGI scripts, broken down by time of day using Accrue Software.

Email blackouts. A high traffic of email involving graphic, audio, and video attachments can put considerable strain on the mail server. Since most mail servers automatically accept traffic from other domains, an email-oriented event (e.g., auction bidding) on one site can tie up others. Mail servers may experience slowdowns when processing third-party *spam* mail.

In order to effectively manage these problems, the maintenance team should develop a general plan for assessing and managing site performance. The plan should detail how performance information will be collected and distributed, and how the team will respond to bottlenecks and overloads when they occur. Based on the information just given, the following areas should be considered:

- The current state of the Internet
- The ISP hosting the Web site and/or the high-speed connection between the ISP and the inhouse network
- The local area network (LAN) or Intranet connecting individual workstations in the development group
- Access statistics recorded for visitors to the Web site
- Performance bottlenecks in Web site hardware and software

It is the job of the maintenance team to do the following:

- Acquire information for each of these points
- Assess each of the potential problems
- Monitor ongoing effects of these problems on the site
- Take action when these problems impede the normal access and update process

The following sections consider these aspects of site performance in more detail and illustrate strategies for keeping performance at its optimum.

Internet and ISP Traffic Monitoring

Internet-wide traffic monitoring is traditionally done by ISPs, but that doesn't mean that the maintenance team can't get and use the information to its advantage. If the maintenance team is aware of the current state of Internet traffic, it has the ability to quickly distinguish problems with the Internet or ISP from those arising within the network. There are a variety of free and commercial services that may be used to monitor the Internet and individual ISPs, such as outage notification and ISP report cards.

Outage notification. Most local and national ISPs provide reports detailing the state of Internet traffic across their networks. If major increases in traffic are expected for new content or special events, the maintenance team should check with its ISP or hosting service and request access to network status reports. Web-based reports are publicly available on the Web from large ISPs such as Uunet (www.noc.uu.net), and AGIS (www.agis.net/outages.htm). Metropolitan Fiber Systems (MFS) provides near real-time traffic reports (ext2.mfsdatanet.com/MAE/) for the major NAP (Network Access Points).

ISP report cards. The status of the site's immediate ISP (or the ISP that a site customer is using for access) may be determined through the Internet Weather Report (www.internetweather.com) or Netstat.net (www.netstat .net). These free services check how fast information is being transmitted by the ISP to the test site and the percentage of errors that occur during transmissions. A similar service with graphical maps and animation is available at the MIDS Internet Weather Report (see Figure 4.5). Since only a single site is monitoring the ISPs, the report's usefulness is limited to particular geographical areas. Notification of the loss of access to a particular URL is provided by Red Alert (www.redalert.com) starting at $19.95 a month.

Other commercial services provide for more detailed monitoring and notification. Freshwater Software's (www.freshwater.com) SiteSeer service can show access times to Web pages scattered across the United States, determine that fill-out forms and databases are working, and verify that individual Web pages were updated based on

Figure 4.5 MIDS Internet Weather Report (www3.mids.org/weather/) for a day in June 1997 throughout the San Francisco Bay area, with large circles indicating congested traffic.

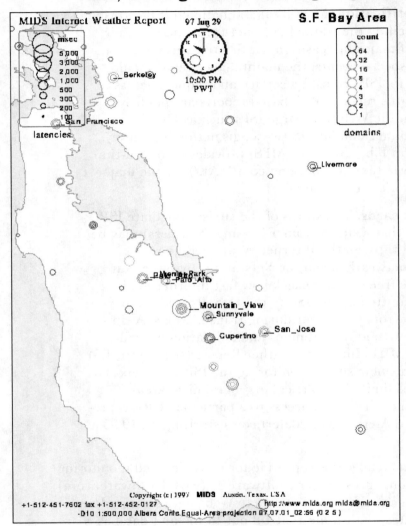

their text. The last feature is useful in distinguishing update lems on the development team's server from *caching* of old Web on an ISP's network or user's computer. The net.Sweep servi net.Genesis (www.netgen.com) is more comprehensive. Ranging i.. price from $100 to $7,000 a month, the various versions of net.Sweep analyze a site's performance using a nationwide mix of modem and high-speed connections. The net.Sweep service reports the frequency of transfer times, stalled downloads, and lost connections. Inverse Network Technology (www.inverse.net) provides more sophisticated performance profiles for ISPs for about $5,000 per month. At the top end, the Benchmark Report Works ($100,000–$250,000) places 125,000 calls to 670 ISPs per month, and provides detailed reports on call failure during day, download times, and connect failure rates. While few sites have traffic justifying such expensive reports, the companies also provide public information on their Web sites.

Intranet Network Monitoring

In many cases, the maintenance and update teams share a high-speed network with workstations and staging servers. In order to keep internal traffic running smoothly during development, the administrator or IS manager can install Intranet network management software. Apparent slow connections within a corporate Intranet are often due to repairable defects (e.g., incorrect information loaded into network routers) rather than an intrinsic lack of bandwidth.

VitalSigns Software's NetMedic (www.vitalsigns.com; $49.95) is an end-user tool that can determine the speed of Web connections broken down by the individual "hops" taken by the information over the Internet. It also provides the ability to monitor slow processing by the end user's computer—a valuable tool for customer support. The software can also track the percentage of successful connections through dialups from ISP accounts, providing a low-cost alternative to ISP report services. The program can function in interactive mode, or send email or beeper alerts to the maintenance team.

Ipswitch's WhatsUp (www.ipswitch.com; Regular $195; Gold $495) is especially useful for network administrators, providing a graphical map enabling management of local client computers, servers, routers, hubs, and printers. When functioning in notification mode, the software may be set up to automatically deliver alerts through digital beepers, pagers, email, and alarm tones through a workstation speaker.

Freshwater Software's SiteScope (www.freshtech.com; $500) on Unix and NT workstations allows administrators to control several Web servers through a standard browser interface. The manager can initiate real-time updates and change configuration of individual servers. The software can detect URL availability, correct functioning of CGI scripts, mail server operation, disk space usage, efficiency of the ISP connection, router operation, and traffic spikes. SiteScope can fix some problems itself by triggering automatic programs or send email alerts if manual intervention is necessary. Programmers may easily add their own recovery scripts to the set provided in the package. SiteScope also produces reports that summarize errors over time; these may help the maintenance team spot long-term usage problems.

Web Site Performance

As sites grow in complexity and begin to incorporate a variety of media, it is no longer possible to predict the overall site's behavior based on homepage access. The problem is even more significant for dynamic sites that continually update their content. To answer this problem, principles and tools developed for traditional software testing are migrating to the Web. Using these tools, the administrators can conduct automated "dry runs" to predict performance under heavy traffic. Programs are not cheap and typically require a dedicated computer to generate the test traffic.

Segue Software's Silk (www.segue.com; $3,995 and up) set of tools provides a comprehensive test suite originating from a client-server *Quality Assurance* (*QA*) testing background. SilkTest can analyze a Web site's performance for delivery of HTML, Java, ActiveX, database, and large tables. A companion program, Surf!, automatically tests for broken links.

Mercury Interactive's Astra SiteTest (www.merc-int.com; $9,500; Windows NT/95), a high-end program, is the Cadillac of performance software. The program will simulate as many as 4.3 million daily hits on the Web server. SiteTest is one of the most highly visual of the current crop of performance tools, and it provides multiple graphical views of data with zoom and other features. The program can run tests on HTML access, cookies, proxy server efficiency, reliability of user authentication, performance of CGI scripts, and fill-out forms. Customized tests can be generated by the site administrator by "walking" the program through probable access scenarios including text entry and database calls. SiteTest combines individual scenarios to create multiple virtual users during test runs. The product is designed to integrate with Mercury's $495 SiteManager product. A security plug-in for testing sites running secure (SSL) transactions is available for $995.

RadView Software (see Figure 4.6; $1,000–$50,000 depending on size of installation) also sells a test suite that can analyze Web server performance under extremely heavy traffic loads. The WebLoad program generates virtual users. With Pentium Pro and faster hardware, the site can be tested with the equivalent of several million daily users. Testing can include standard HTML, Java applets, cookies, and secure transactions. The program can be installed on several workstations and send multiple requests, thereby providing a more realistic simulation of actual operation. The program also includes the Agenda tool, which allows recording manual tests and

Figure 4.6 Measuring server performance using RadView's (www .radview.com) WebLoad software.

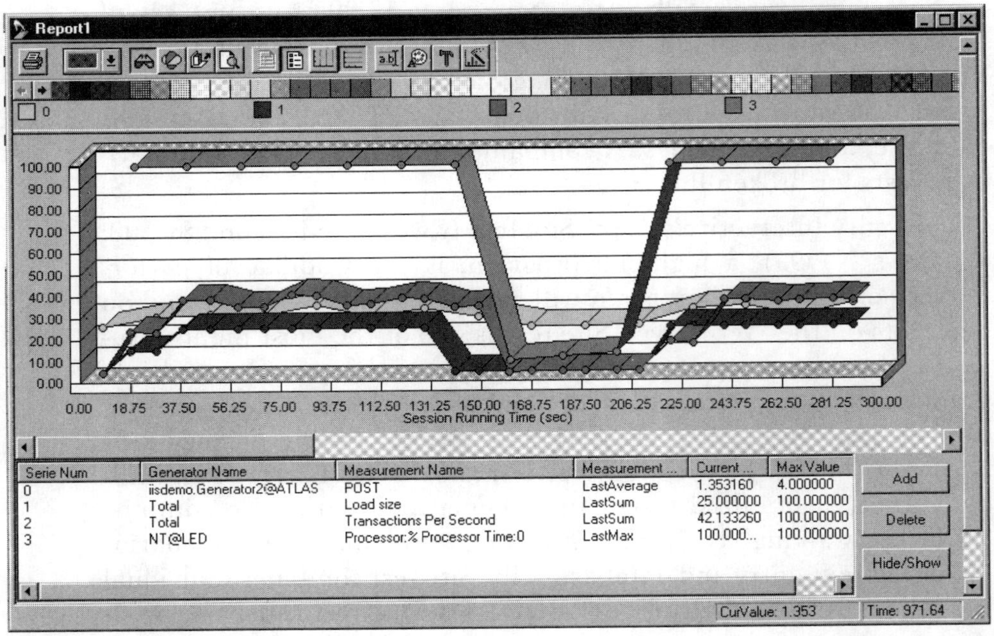
Report1
0
1
2
3
100.00
90.00
80.00
70.00
60.00
50.00
40.00
30.00
20.00
10.00
0.00
0.00 18.75 37.50 56.25 75.00 93.75 112.50 131.25 150.00 168.75 187.50 206.25 225.00 243.75 262.50 281.25 300.00
Session Running Time (sec)
Serie Num | Generator Name | Measurement Name | Measurement ... | Current ... | Max Value
0 | iisdemo.Generator2@ATLAS | POST | LastAverage | 1.353160 | 4.000000
1 | Total | Load size | LastSum | 25.000000 | 100.000000
2 | Total | Transactions Per Second | LastSum | 42.133260 | 100.000000
3 | NT@LED | Processor:% Processor Time:0 | LastMax | 100.000... | 100.000000
Add
Delete
Hide/Show
CurValue: 1.353
Time: 971.64

saving them for later automatic execution. Like many other performance managers, it includes a broken-link tester called WebExam.

Management of High-Traffic and Traffic Spikes

Despite the best laid plans of the developers, a dynamic site will occasionally experience a surge in traffic that was greater than anticipated. Such behavior is particularly common on dynamic sites, where new information provided by the update may drastically increase the audience interest in the site or portions thereof. When traffic rises and there isn't time or funds to change the hardware, there are several methods the maintenance team can apply to provide relief. Typically, a few pages on the site will receive a vastly disproportionate numbers of hits. These may be the site homepage, site directory listing, help pages, or popular content. The maintenance team should check the access logs and identify bottleneck pages for reduction of download size by one of these methods:

Keep common pages as HTML. Dynamic construction of pages takes significantly more processing power than file transfer. If the pages receiving the most hits are converted to HTML files, access time will drop. If the site displays a frontispiece, slideshow, or splash screen prior to the main page, it can be removed to reduce server load.

Reduce graphics and multimedia. Modern Web pages frequently load hundreds of thousands of bytes on a single page. With typical modem access restricted to about 3,000 bytes/second, this can prolong average connection times—increasing server load. Depending on page content, small "thumbnails" can replace full-sized graphics and animated GIFs. Background audio linked to a Web page should also be removed, since this slows down processing by both the Web server and visitor's computer. Multimedia and animation programs such as Macromedia's Shockwave (www.macromedia.com) should be removed from all high-traffic pages, and should not be used on homepages or navigation pages as well.

Turn off streaming audio and video. Real-time audio and video put much greater demands on the server than access to download-and-play audio/video clips or static HTML pages. If a high-traffic site is also running special servers for real-time audio or video, the management team should consider moving them to a different computer or, in extreme cases, temporarily shutting them off.

Increase server memory. Web servers may begin to use the hard disk for virtual memory when they run out of RAM; this can drastically slow down their operation. Since memory is cheap and easily installed, the maintenance team should consider increasing it on the Web server to the largest practical size. Increasing memory will benefit most servers with less than 64 megs, and upgrading to 128 megs or even 256 megs is not unreasonable for high-traffic servers.

Frequent reboots and process "kills." If traffic snowballs despite all efforts, there may be no choice but to repeatedly reset the system. In some cases, stopping and restarting the Web server every few minutes can keep the site "up" with only occasional glitches. If server access does not improve after restarts, the system should be rebooted.

Server Clustering and Load Balancing

Clustering and load balancing programs and hardware dynamically allocate traffic between a group of computers that was initially sent to a single Internet domain. By distributing traffic across several processors, it is possible to greatly increase efficiency. In addition, advanced clustering software can find the least-loaded server in the group and preferentially send new requests to it. During the early history of the Web, many large dynamic sites wrote their own balancing software. Now as more sites receive high traffic, specially designed solutions have become available.

BIND (ftp://ww.net/networking/ip/dns/), useful when the maintenance team runs its own nameserver, allows the team to configure the nameserver to send requests in a "round-robin" fashion. Standard *Domain Name Service* (*DNS*) lookups use the BIND program to map the domain request to a unique IP address for a single computer. In a round-robin strategy, BIND consults a list of IP addresses for a given domain name. Each new request sent to the domain is mapped to the next IP address on the list, equally and consecutively distributing requests among a set of computers. This simple solution may be adequate for many sites. Round-robin strategies do not route traffic dynamically because they distribute traffic independently of server load. Thus, the round-robin system will send a request to the next IP on the list, even if the server at that IP is currently bogged down with a lengthy request. More information on round-robin strategies can be found at The DNS Resources Directory (www.dns.net/dnsrd/servers.html) or Ask Dr. DNS (www.acmebw.com/askmr.htm).

HydraWEB Technologies (www.hydraweb.com; $7,000–30,000) provides network hardware systems specifically designed to route HTTP traffic between several Web servers. HydraWEB hardware operates at up to 80MB/second total throughput, and handles up to 2.8 million hits per hour on 100MB ethernet. The system uses intelligent load balancing, dynamically expanding requests to more servers as traffic increases. Traffic for a subset of the Web site's content can be routed to particular servers. This allows the administrators to replicate a few high-traffic pages instead of creating complete mirror sites on each server in the cluster. The system is Unix and NT aware, and can load-balance in mixed clusters of Unix and NT servers. Persistent sessions for HTTP and FTP are supported so that servers can maintain state information about individual site visitors.

Cisco Systems (www.cisco.com; $17,000–$37,000, depending on Cisco router model) offers a load-balancing system called Distributed Director for installation on its popular network routers. The system works in two modes. In the nameserver mode, it adds intelligence to standard DNS operation, dynamically building a table of potential IP addresses to which it can send an HTTP (or other) request, and choosing the destination based on server loading. In the HTTP redirect mode, it dynamically routes HTTP requests based on traffic and sends appropriate commands back to the user's Web browser to enable a transparent "jump" to the least-loaded server. Cisco plans to introduce a dedicated hardware product similar to HydraWEB in the future.

Inktomi's (www.inktomi.com/Tech.html) Network Of Workstations (NOW) cluster technology is designed to handle the most demanding traffic and specifically provides support for dynamic Web sites using databases distributed over several servers. Its flagship product powers the HotBot search engine (www.hotbot.com), among others. While this technology is currently restricted to search engines, Inktomi's new Virtual Network Cache software can reduce redundant traffic requests. An advanced feature system produces a "virtual network cache" shared by multiple servers, which helps to reduce redundant request processing. This service is primarily useful for large ISPs, though extremely high-traffic Web sites may find it valuable in the future.

Microsoft's (www.microsoft.com) Wolfpack is an NT-specific solution for clustering and load balancing that received a gradual rollout beginning in 1997. The first incarnation of the technology links two NT servers, primarily for the purpose of providing redundancy and fault tolerance. Later versions scheduled to ship in 1998 will increase the cluster size to 16 servers and will add dynamic load balancing.

Log Analysis Software

Once the server is processing HTTP requests, the next job of the Webmaster is to ensure that the traffic is monitored and recorded. Virtually all Web servers record delivery of pages, graphics, and multimedia objects to their visitors. Primary analysis of visitor access logs has traditionally been the responsibility of the Web site Administrator and maintenance team, though new generations of analysis tools are making it useful to the production team as well.

Log analysis typically falls into two levels. In the first, the software simply sorts individual values written to the access log. Examples include pages receiving the most hits, or number of requests coming from particular countries. Basic statistics of this type can:

- Show which pages receive the most visits
- Break down access by domain and nationality
- Demonstrate traffic patterns that contribute to server loading
- Be reformatted and loaded into databases, spreadsheets, and workflow software
- Provide input for personalization systems that dynamically adjust site content based on the visitor's actions
- Reveal demographic and preference information that can be used to control updates

Web servers typically record the visitor's date and time of access, domain name or computer IP address, requested URL, and amount of data transferred. A separate error log records broken links and failed access, and the *agent log* provides information about the Web browser and operating system on the visitor's computer. If an automatic program (like the Web "spider" on a search engine) is visiting the pages, this is also recorded in the agent log. If *referer log* information is recorded, each hit also lists the last URL the visitor accessed. This kind of information can be used to reconstruct individual meanderings through the site, or show which remote Web sites send traffic to the site.

More sophisticated log statistics examine correlation between URL requests. This level of analysis requires loading the logs into a database and applying algorithms that can reveal patterns in the information. Correlation converts a collection of hits into visits, and turns averaged traffic values into features of individual behavior. Among the specific kinds of results correlation can provide are:

Entry point. Since many Web surfers discover sites using search engines, they do not necessarily enter through the assigned homepage of the site. Knowing entry points can lead to redesign of the site so that visitors are not trapped in a local dead end. Entry points are also prime targets for promotion, ordering information, and banner advertising.

Number of pages visited. Careful analysis of the extent of each visitor's exploration will show if the site's content is generally useful, or whether a few pages contain all the information the audience wants. The information may be used to adjust dynamic sites to shorten the path to the audience's usual goal, or divert their attention to other content they might otherwise miss.

CGI/database processing times. By analyzing the delay between user requests and subsequent server output, the analysis program can determine how long it takes a CGI script to execute. This information can help pinpoint troublesome scripts that are incorrectly configured or take too much processing time.

Time spent on page. This statistic will show the developers if individual pages are doing their jobs. Examples include site directories and help pages (visits should be short), or interactive games (visits should be long). Figure 4.7 shows an example report with this information.

Clickstream. Advanced software can recover the unique path each user has taken through the Web site. Using this information, the developers may determine whether individual visitors browse through a variety of information or rapidly "drill down" to specific content. It may also demonstrate correlations between content. For example, clickstream analysis might show that visitors reading a news page tend to search for editorial information found on a sec-

Figure 4.7 Report from net.analysis program by net.Genesis (www.netgen.com) showing the average time spent viewing individual Web pages.

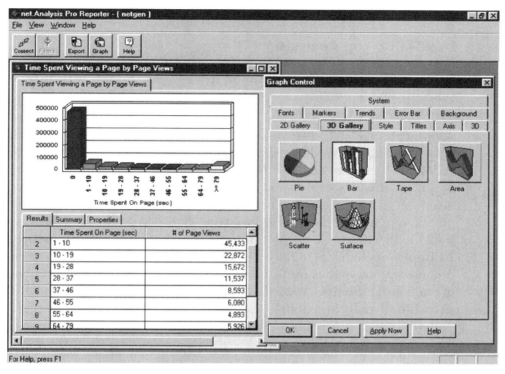

ond page. This information may be applied by adding a link to editorials directly on the news page.

Return visits. Knowing whether visitors return to the site is the single best test of effectiveness. If visitors come back repeatedly, it indicates that they most likely find the site's dynamism useful. Return visits can thus guide the positioning of dynamic versus static content on the site. They are also important for online advertising, since an ad viewed several times by a small number of visitors has a different effect than the same ad viewed once by a larger audience.

Auditing. Specialized programs such as those provided by BPA International (www.bpai.com) can provide authenticated "page views" and *click-throughs* of banner ads. This information can be used for audited sale of advertising on Web sites.

Low-Traffic Log Analysis

Sites with less than a few thousand visitors per day may take a relaxed approach to log analysis and typically analyze traffic at weekly or even monthly intervals.

Matt Kruse's Mkstats (www.mkstats.com; free if noncommercial; $50–$300; Unix/Windows supporting Perl 5) outputs its results in HTML, which can be directly read through the Web browser. The program provides tables and charts of information in the log, but does not cross-correlate information in a database. Due to its simplicity, one of the most appropriate uses for Mkstats is to provide individualized statistics for multiple clients sharing a Web server. Examples include ISPs delivering basic access information to their members, and virtual malls or similar sites hosting a large number of individual clients. Mkstats has no features specific to dynamic sites, but its daily and hourly statistics can show daily traffic flow and pinpoint pages receiving the highest access.

NetTracker by Sane Solutions LLC (www.sane.com; $295; Unix/Windows NT) outputs results to a Web browser using Java. Due to this design, it is a good solution for providing access reports to nontechnical personnel and for sites using connections too slow to download log files to a local computer. It includes common reports for access analysis and may generate clickstream profiles for individual visitors. Output may be exported to Microsoft Access and Excel for sophisticated analysis. Like Mkstats, NetTracker is a good solution for distributing access reports to large numbers of visitors. For these customers, Sane Solutions sells site licenses that require paying a monthly per-recipient fee.

net.Genesis (see Figure 4.7; $295; Windows 95/NT) produces the Net.Analysis Desktop program, which uses a special non-Web client to analyze and display access information for moderate-traffic sites. The program is restricted to local analysis, but it does provide built-in FTP for transferring log files from the Web server to the developer's workstation. The program provides a variety of analysis reports that are more sophisticated than Mkstats but reveal essentially the same information.

Bazaar Analyzer Pro from Aquas, Inc. (www.aquas.com; $599; Macintosh/Unix/Windows NT) is written entirely in Java, so its operation is platform independent. The Java client is a Web browser reading standard HTML, which allows anyone with a password to examine and analyze access logs. The Bazaar Analyzer EasyView enables user-configured Web analysis—even for Web sites hosted on virtual servers by Internet Service Providers. The combination of platform independence and sophisticated reporting makes Bazaar Analyzer the method of choice for smaller dynamic Web sites.

High-Traffic Log Analysis

Sites that have high hits ($>$10,000 unique visitors/day) generate volumes of data that can choke the fastest Web server's operation. Consider a site receiving 50,000 unique visitors a day. Since the average Web user looks at about 20 pages (check current statistics at www.cyberatlas.com) during each online session, the daily log will list 1 million individual hits. Since each entry uses 200–500 bytes of information, the log will experience a daily increase of 200–500 megabytes! Such enormous files strain the capacity of servers, disk storage, backup systems, and software. As a rule of thumb, when a site receives more than 10,000 visitors daily the maintenance plan should enumerate a strategy for moving and processing large amounts of data. Examples of possible strategies are illustrated in Figure 4.8.

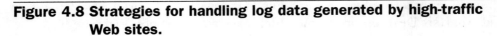

Figure 4.8 Strategies for handling log data generated by high-traffic Web sites.

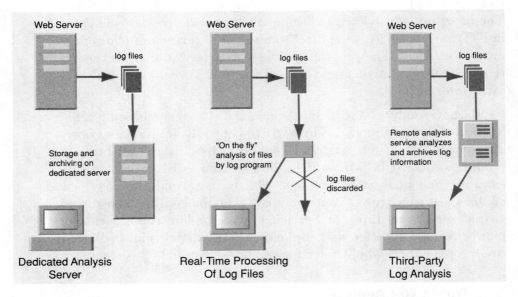

Analysis server. To reduce the load on the Web server, the log may be written directly to another "analysis" computer, or it can be periodically retrieved by the log analysis program. This system may then devote its computing time to analyzing the log information, generating reports, and archiving. Allowances will need to be made for the daily transfer of up to 1 gigabyte of information to the analysis server, and this solution is impractical unless both computers are located in house or on the ISP's network.

Real-time processing of log files. On sites that don't run a separate analysis server, the log program can be set to run continuously in the background and process information as fast as it comes in. This approach can save disk space and prevent periodic slowdowns caused by batch analysis of stored log files.

Backup/archive strategies. If the site administrator decides to archive access logs, the maintenance team will need to dedicate resources to house hundreds of backup tapes per year, or purchase a specialized system designed specifically for high-volume backups.

Software

Software useful for high-traffic sites shares several common features. In most cases, it moves access information directly to a database file and increments it as necessary. Programs are written in compiled languages such as C, instead of running as lower Perl scripts. To reduce downloads, the program may be installed directly on the Web server or (for the highest-traffic sites) require a dedicated analysis computer.

WebTrends (www.webtrends.com; Windows NT), recognized as the leader for high-traffic sites, is the best solution for groups running an inhouse Web server on a high-traffic NT platform. Unlike most other packages, it is largely self-configuring during installation. Once installed, it operates in the background, continually converting access information into analysis reports. The program can provide results at the console or email them on a regular basis. Among its many features is direct support for advertising analysis of page impressions and click-throughs. While the program can be used with remote non-NT servers, most of its speed advantages are lost. Output format includes HTML, Microsoft Word, and Excel. A wide variety of standard reports are available, and custom reports can be created using the template wizard.

net.Analysis PRO by net.Genesis (www.netgen.com; $495/individual client; $200/user site license; Sun-Solaris/Unix/Windows NT) provides outstanding visitor path analysis, studies of entry and exit points, and other sophisticated correlation of access data. Reports include technical information useful to the maintenance team and marketing information useful to the rest of the development group. Many reports are interactive and let the user modify parameters to reveal specific features of the data. Information is aggregated into one or more existing databases, so comparing new data to old doesn't require reanalysis of the entire log file.

O'Reilly & Associates' Stratisphere (www.stratisphere.ora.com; $399; Windows 95/NT) can create real-time graphs tracking current and past usage on a minute-by-minute basis. The program is useful for high-traffic sites because it immediately transfers log information to an internal database. Due to this, the program doesn't have to store or reanalyze old log data to combine it with new information. The program is also good for analyzing multiple Web sites, and it can process up to 16 log files at one time.

Accrue's Insight (www.gauge.com; $15,000 and up; Sun-Solaris) software provides good performance with high-traffic sites receiving several million hits per day. The program can correlate log information to track access by visitors on different days and in different areas of the site. Data is available as averaged statistics or as individual user sessions. It also contains features useful in precisely understanding the experience of site visitors, including estimates of average page download times, capability and performance of the visitor's hardware and software, round-trip times for HTML requests sorted by ISP, and execution times for CGI scripts.

IBM's Surf-Aid (www.ibm.com) program applies "data-mining" principles to log analysis, drawing on the company's experience with the Intelligent Miner toolkit for large databases. Data-mining strategies apply complex programs to detect subtle patterns in large amounts of information. The Decision Support Query and Reporting system moves beyond reporting access statistics and allows the site operators to construct and test hypotheses against the database. For example, the program might highlight differences in page viewing between visitors that chose to buy a particular product versus those that didn't, and correlate this against other demographic features supplied from a third database. Combined with IBM's Predictor software, the mined information could be used to present information to the visitor based on previous choices.

MarketWave's HitList (see Figure 4.9; free Standard version; $995 Pro version; Enterprise version released late 1997; Windows 95/NT) provides direct support for Lotus Domino and Microsoft's IIS Web server. The program generates a large variety of impressive reports and has 175 predefined report elements for designing custom output. With an ability to extract and separately report information sent to multiple domains on a virtual server, the program is particularly useful for sites with multiple content providers. HitList

Figure 4.9 Breakdown of browser types for a hypothetical Web site generated with Marketwave Software's HitList (www. marketwave.com) program.

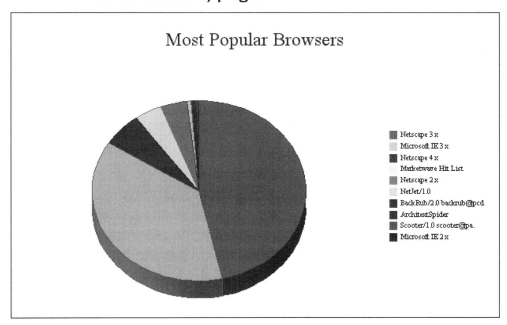

can display results on the Web or send a Microsoft Word file to the administrator as an email attachment. The high-traffic Pro version is 100 times faster than the Standard. It specifically focuses on tracking advertising, and it can generate impression/click-through reports for banner ads. It can also record the search terms used by visitors coming in from major search engines and monitor banner ad click-throughs on remote servers.

Third-Party Log Analysis

Another option for companies with high traffic is to transfer log files over the Internet to an analysis service. Outsourcing log analysis may make sense for large, well-funded sites that need third-party auditing for advertising sales or other reasons, or who don't have a large inhouse staff capable of supporting internal analysis. Price-Waterhouse (www.pw.com) and I/PRO (see Figure 4.10) have combined to provide the best-known service, Netline. Companies using Netline send their access logs to I/PRO, which returns reports to the site operators. Additional services include data management, archiving of log data, training, and technical support. The service costs $1,000 and up per month, depending on the number of servers or amount of data being analyzed. I/PRO also offers a sophisticated audited service, I/COUNT, for use in advertising sales.

Advertising Logs and Statistics

Sites that base their economic model on banner advertising may not need the power of a comprehensive log analysis program. Instead, advertising performance statistics may be the only information used in making site modifications. Advertising software acts as a combination miniserver and log analysis program, posting banners on Web pages, tracking views, keeping audit logs, and even dynamically adjusting which ads are shown to given visitors. There are several ways the maintenance team may collect advertising information for use in operating dynamic sites. CGI scripts set to run as *server-side includes* will "fire" each

Figure 4.10 I/PRO (www.ipro.com), which provides Netline service.

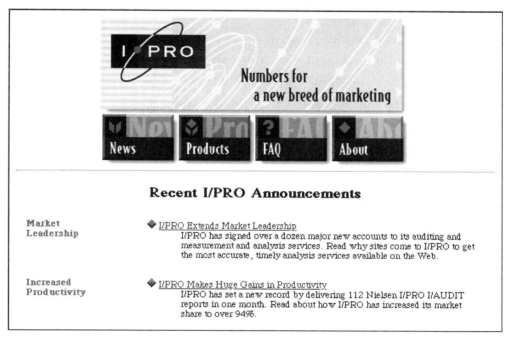

time a page is loaded. Since the Web server provides the program with the same environment variables it uses, the ad software can write its own access log. By using this information, the script can keep a sub-log that exclusively records only ad views, whether or not the visitor clicked through to the advertiser's site. Free and low-cost CGI banner ad scripts for Windows are available from Meysoft (www.meysoft.com/scripts/scripts.html), Selena Sol's Public Domain CGI Script Archive (www.eff.org/~erict/Scripts/classified.html), and Black Cat Communications (www.blackcat.net/redir/). Commercial software packages such as ClickWise from ClickOver Software (www.clickover) and Central Ad Software (www.centralad.com) provide an additional log interface the advertisers using the service can check independently of the site administrators.

Site Performance Strategies

After determining the hardware and software needed to assess and maintain the site's performance, the maintenance team should prepare a maintenance plan that describes specifically the information that will be collected and used to plan dynamic site maintenance.

Access and log stats. Information from network analysis programs and log analysis should be reviewed regularly by the maintenance team and compiled into an overall picture of the site's current dynamic state. Long-term trends (such as deterioration of the ISP's service) should be easy to identify in the report. If the log analysis software provides reports useful to maintenance (e.g., the length of time it takes a CGI script to execute), these should be added to the plan.

Hardware/software capabilities of the average visitor. Using the agent log or its equivalent, the administrators may develop a model of the hardware and software limitations of the site's typical visitors. For example, if the site attracts large amounts of university traffic, provisions may need to be made for users restricted to text-only access. If the site caters to the Web developer/multimedia market, features that cannot be seen by Macintosh Web browsers should be avoided. The maintenance group should provide this information to the update team, along with tips for making updates compatible with the audience's equipment.

Communicating with the ISP. The plan should describe how to get traffic reports from the site's ISP. It should also list contact email and phone numbers in the event of emergencies.

Communicating with the update team. The maintenance team should be aware of the kind of content used to update the site. If content will have a major impact on visitor traffic, the maintenance team needs to know about it. Conversely, maintenance that affects site updates, such as temporary maintenance shutdowns, should be relayed to the site development group by the maintenance team.

Emergency measures. The maintenance team should have the necessary information available to quickly reconfigure a server to handle increased traffic. For example, an alternate low-graphics homepage might be designated for heavy traffic, or a mirror server might be held ready in case of failure of the primary system.

Check for improvements in hardware and software. The maintenance team should visit hardware/software vendor Web sites on a periodic basis, since useful upgrades may appear at any time. For example, Web servers supporting the HTTP 1.1 protocol are significantly faster at downloading Web pages, and most vendors have posted upgrades taking advantage of the new protocol.

Web-Specific Security Problems Associated with Updates

Dynamic sites require analysis of security in their maintenance plan on two levels: (1) standard security used for public Internet servers applies equally to dynamic sites, and (2) security must be maintained within the site group, particularly with respect to the update team's ability to modify the Web site. The maintenance groups should set up clear standards to follow for access:

Access levels. The software or operating systems should be set to allow individual members of the update team access only to those areas that they need to modify. A second authorization level should be set for changing configuration files on the Web server and programs, and the highest level should be reserved for modifications of the programs themselves.

Keeping mailing lists private. It is an unfortunate fact of life that mailing lists and personal email are routinely scooped into the maw of spam email programs. To reduce problems with unsolicited email in internal boxes, the maintenance team should investigate using features in their mailer restricting messages to the allowed senders in the site team. One option is Sendmail 8 as described at the Sendmail Modification Site (www.informatik.uni-kiel.de/~ca/email/check.html) to keep lists of allowed and disallowed users. The maintenance team should consider modifying the mail program so it cannot act as a remailer for spam email. Since some ISPs report that as much as 20 percent of their traffic comes from junk email, this is a problem not to be taken lightly.

Break-ins and unauthorized access. While the scope of damage possible through HTTP is generally less than other protocols such as Telnet, the maintenance team needs to take account of these issues. Potential security problems occur in the operating system, the use of server-side includes for adding dynamic information to a Web page, improperly designed CGI programs, and document access. The administrators should read a comprehensive HTTP security document such as the WWW Security FAQ (www.genome.wi.mit.edu/WWW/faqs/www-security-faq.html) to better understand features relevant to their particular installation. Information and comic relief for current security problems like those shown at Digicrime (www.digicrime.com) may provide a useful reality check to security discussions.

Confidential information. Dynamic sites frequently provide information whose effect depends on being presented only after a specific time. Examples include contest or product announcements, ratings, and exclusive stories or interviews. Often, the maintenance team will be aware of this information before it is posted, and can diminish its value by "slips" in email or other communication. In addition to Web security, the site should implement a general policy making everyone responsible for keeping confidential information confidential.

Year 2000 Problems

The Internet is largely immune to the problems expected in older systems that will not generate accurate information after 1999. Despite this, a study by the Gartner Group (www.gartner.com) indicates that older routers and switches may have unexpected errors at the millennium, as will operating systems including Windows NT. Interestingly, Macintosh systems are believed to be completely free of millennium bugs. Though major problems are not expected, the maintenance team should occasionally check sites such as The Year 2000 Information Center (www.year2000.com) 'til the party's over.

Moving Content between Files, Directories, and Servers

On dynamic sites, it is often necessary to alter the location of individual files and directories in the Web server's document tree. This usually requires changing numerous hyperlinks on the site, and almost ensures that visitors who bookmarked the old page will run into the "file not found" 404 error. While linkchecking programs may repair the problem after it occurs, the maintenance team should establish rules that facilitate upgrades and movement of content through the Web site.

Establishing File Naming Conventions

Whenever possible, files and directories should have consistent names. For example, the default file in any directory (e.g., index.html) should be the same across the entire site. This allows the Programmer to make major simplifying assumptions. Metasites containing content from many sources should use a parallel naming structure. If templates are used to create HTML files, the templates should themselves be named in a consistent and easily understood fashion. The update team should also be made aware of one of the most common mistakes site developers make—overwriting files with the same names in the wrong directories. Figure 4.11 shows representative strategies for managing file and directory names that are used by many Web sites.

Naming conventions can have a major impact on site updates. For example, some sites deliberately name individual files to reflect the directory they are located in. Thus, for a directory called "project1," a navigation icon might be called "project1icon.gif." Use of this convention will prevent accidental overwrites such as those discussed previously. However, if the directory name is changed to "project2," the administrator will need to change the filename to "project2icon.gif" in order to preserve the convention. Since most linkchecking programs don't change filenames, the administrator will have to rename the file manually.

Consistent Link Naming

HTML hyperlinks may be absolute (listing the entire directory path from the document root of the Web server) or relative (referring only to files and directories within the current working directory). On sites updated with manual HTML, it is easy to be inconsistent in writing hyperlink paths, which will lead to problems if files or directories are later moved. By keeping all paths local, portability of content between directories is enhanced, but other simplifying conven-

Figure 4.11 Aliases and parallel naming structures that make updates easier and increase site portability.

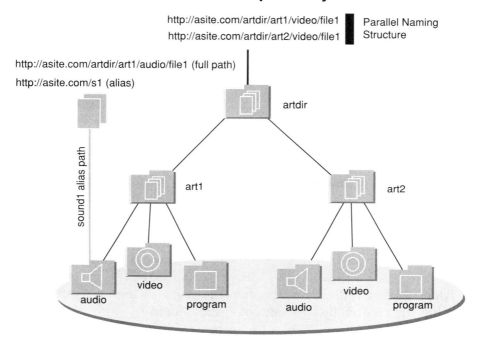

tions will not work. The Web Administrator should consult with the update team and establish standard path conventions.

Using Aliases for Major Pages

An alternate way to avoid long pathnames is to use *aliases*. For example, consider a site with an announcements page located at:

http://yoursite.com/usr/www/files/html/bob/files/announce.html

By creating an alias to the file (the ln -s in standard Unix), the path can be shortened to:

http://yoursite.com/announce

If this alias is used during site development, moving files on the Web server will only require changing the alias rather than modifying individual hyperlinks. The only requirement is that all links in HTML code be *absolute* (starting at the document root) rather than *relative* (applying only to the directory at which the server is currently accessing). Note that if the .html or .htm suffix is left off, the alias will not work, unless the default MIME type is set to "html" instead of "text."

In many Web servers such as Apache, an alternate way of creating aliases is defined in the server's configuration files. This method can be used when the creation of aliases at the operating system level is undesirable. However, administrators should note that search engines using automated spider programs may reject this form of aliasing and post an error 202 message.

While aliases allow filenames to be moved and renamed within the Web site with relative ease, they may make it difficult to move the files to a radically different operating system. For example, the alias file created by a Macintosh is incompatible with those supported by Unix. Aliases may have to be created independently on the staging and public Web servers. Aliases also cannot be detected or modified by the current generation of site management programs. Improper use of aliases could also link the Web site to sensitive areas of the computer's operating system.

Moving the Site to a New Server

Successful dynamic sites often move to new servers, often to migrate to a new operating system or to change from a shared Web server (maintained by an ISP) to a dedicated or inhouse server developed specifically for the site. With virtually every aspect of the site's configuration subject to alteration, a server move is one of the hardest projects the maintenance team may undertake.

Server configuration. The location of the *server root* may have to be changed if the directory structure of the new server differs from the old one. The MIME type file may also cause problems, since the default MIME file provided in new server software may not list custom MIME types currently being used by the site.

HTML files. Provided that the files were placed under the same *document root*, there should be little problem with the transfer. Difficulties arise if certain documents and directories are actually aliases to locations that do not exist on the new server. Problems may also occur if hyperlinks include the specific name of the server (e.g. firstserv.company .com/home), while the new server has a different name (e.g., secondserv.company.com/home).

CGI scripts. Unlike HTML, scripts will almost invariably need modification if there are changes in the operating system. Script programmers usually hard-code directories and filenames that may not exist on the new server. For example, Macintosh and Windows NT do not normally include Perl—the common code of most CGI scripts. Many CGI programs may also encode a specific Internet domain name or IP address that will also have to be changed. Finally, scripts may assume the presence of particular programs or function libraries that may not exist in all operating systems.

Server-side *imagemaps*. Many sites use a CGI script to process mouse clicks on graphics with the <IMAGEMAP> tag. Common imagemap programs store the URL for selections in a separate file. Unless this is updated at the same time the site is moved, navigation toolbars and other clickable graphics will cease to work. Imagemaps constructed for client-side processing using the <MAP> tag do not have this problem.

Copies of information running under secure servers.
Many sites run one standard Web server for most pages and
a second secure server for order forms and other sensitive
information. In order to maintain a secure transaction, the
secure server cannot access any HTML files, graphics, or
directories under the insecure server and require copies of
this information under their document root. Moving the site
to a new system is almost certain to disrupt these interactions, unless care is taken to reconfigure the document
trees for both servers.

Compiled programs. Programs written in C, C++, or other
languages will experience all the problems of scripts, along
with additional difficulties with system-specific directories
and function libraries necessary for recompiling. Most public-
domain programs can be recompiled without major reworking
between common Unix platforms. Migration between Unix
and NT systems presents a greater challenge. Since source
code is not available for most of the NT operating system,
programmers may have difficulty adapting their programs.
For large sites, migration utilities such as the Datafocus
(www.datafocus.com) Nutcracker suite may help the transfer.
Such systems may also be useful if custom programs are being
written to function on a variety of Web servers.

Once the principles of maintaining dynamic sites have been
established, the next step is to investigate the update process itself.
The next two chapters cover basic and advanced update strategies,
detailing tools and resources valuable to the update team.

PART THREE

DYNAMIC SITE
UPDATE TECHNIQUES

BASIC DYNAMIC SITE UPDATE TECHNIQUES

W hile the maintenance team's concern is to "run in place" and maintain stability, the update team's job is to disrupt it! In operating a dynamic site, the update team will be changing all or part of the site, or facilitating changes made by site visitors or automatic programs. While developing the site plan, the following areas will need to be considered:

- Source of content
- Conversion of content
- Integration of new content into the Web site
- Detection and removal of obsolete content
- Content personalization

This chapter discusses content sources, formats, and integration into the Web site. Advanced topics including removal of obsolete content and content personalization are considered more fully in Chapter 6.

Sources and Formats of Dynamic Content

With its deserved status as a "convergent" medium, the Web accepts content from a large variety of sources, many of which are unique to the medium. While developing their update plan, the site team should list all potential sources of dynamic content relevant to the goals of the site. Final implementation will depend on the reliability of the content, the expected audience, and formatting and editing requirements. The following sections, along with Figure 5.1, provide an overview of major content types available on the Web, along with brief descriptions of standard formats and conversion.

Printed Documents

Printed documents may be rekeyed in a word processor or HTML editor. *Optical Character Recognition (OCR)* software is used in some cases, though program errors almost always require additional manual editing. Most groups that use printed documents as content for their sites will also need to edit them for spelling, grammar, clarity, and consistency with the existing style of the Web site. The Copy Editor position—essential to most update teams—is almost always necessary for processing printed content. It is advantageous to avoid using this nondigitized content to avoid having to go through the added processing. If the update team is receiving this content from an outside source, it's best to make sure the source understands that digitized format would be easier to process. Many individuals unfamiliar with electronic technology assume that OCR is a simple and flawless conversion of printed documents, and even more do not realize that formatting digitized documents is far easier than retyping them! It is also necessary to define how far to go in reproducing the printed document's layout on the Web. In many cases, printed material uses font sizes and styles that do not reproduce well on screen. If large numbers of documents are routinely processed, the update team may need to develop a conversion guide specifically for printed

Figure 5.1 Areas of the dynamic site used by the update team.

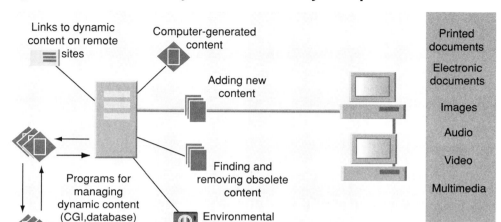

material. Update teams may outsource document rekeying to services such as WebTyping.com (www.webtyping.com).

Electronic Documents

When material destined for the Web site already exists in another electronic media format (e.g., word processors or desktop publishing programs), special conversion utilities are required. In the past it was impossible to replicate most documents accurately on the Web; however, recent additions to HTML have allowed a freedom comparable to other media. Useful conversion programs include:

> **Solutionsoft WordToWeb.** (www.solutionsoft.com; Windows NT/95; $279) This program functions with Microsoft Word 7. Document conversion is managed through Windows software Wizards, which allow users to set background colors, place images, and create tables of con-

tents. The program batch converts a set of documents and automatically breaks large documents into a series of hyperlinked pages.

Infoaccess HTML Transit. (www.infoaccess.com; $149) This program supports the conversion of a broad set of standard word processing and database formats. HTML Transit also converts images and Microsoft *Object Linking and Embedding* (*OLE*) objects, which become static graphics as well. When the original document is too long for comfortable onscreen reading, the program automatically breaks it into several smaller pages linked by navigation buttons.

Hexmax HexWeb XT. (http://www.hexmac.com; Mac/Windows 95; $149/$399) This program converts QuarkXPress files to HTML. To facilitate the conversion, HexWeb XT includes linkchecking, automatic tables of contents, and support for frames and layered documents.

Images

Graphics destined for the Web are input using flatbed scanners, slide/transparency scanners, or digital cameras. The most common image type on the Web is the *GIF* (*Graphics Interchange Format*). This standard allows up to 256 colors, with one color optionally being specified as transparent to the underlying background. The GIF standard also supports simple animation that most Web browsers interpret without plug-ins. The *JPEG* (*Joint Photographic Experts Group*) format is also common on the Web, particularly for larger "blow-up" versions of GIF images or those requiring thousands of colors for proper rendering. Some Web sites use the newer *PNG* (*Portable Network Graphics*; www.boutell.com/boutell/png/), a GIF replacement that includes alpha channels (variable transparency), gamma correction (cross-platform control of image brightness), and two-dimensional interlacing (a method of progressive display)—but it does not support animation. PNG also supports zooms and pans, searchable metatags with picture information, and digital water-marks embedded in the image itself.

Web browsers generally use a specific 216-color palette original-ly developed by Netscape (www.netscape.com) to display images on computers with 256 or fewer colors. In order to ensure compatibility with all potential site visitors, graphics should be saved using these palettes. Failure to do so might result in unreadable screens. For example, if a set of subtle grays are used in a background graphic, the browser might dither them into ragged lines, or render them with a single color that makes the overlying text unreadable. Programs like DeBabelizer (www.equil.com; $399/$599; Macin-tosh/Windows) choose the best mix of colors for several images dis-played on the same Web page.

Audio

Sound is recorded live, or it is sampled directly from cassettes, CDs, or DATs using standard music processing software. Many Web pro-grams (including background <SND> HTML and JavaScript) use the Sun audio (AU) format. The low quality of AU audio is directly comparable to telephone audio, which uses a similar coding algo-rithm. Web sites might also contain high-quality *AIFF* (*Audio Interchange File Format*) formats common in music editing software, and the somewhat lower-quality WAVE form native to Windows sys-tems. Since most Internet users are restricted to 28.8/56k modem speeds, AIFF/WAVE audio is usually provided in 8-bit, mono format with sampling rates of 11k or 22k. This sound quality is adequate for recorded music but is still well below the 16-bit, 44k stereo quality found on audio CDs.

Real-time audio is currently dominated by Progressive Network's (www.real.com) RealAudio format. Over a 28.8k modem, RealAudio quality is comparable to a mono FM radio, and ISDN format files provide near CD-quality stereo. New real-time audio formats include Microsoft's Netshow (www.microsoft.com/netshow), Beatnik from Thomas Dolby's company, Headspace (www.headspace.com /beatnik), and Liquid Audio's (www.liquidaudio.com) authoring system. Beatnik is unusual in supporting both MIDI and digital audio files over the Web, and in providing prepackaged sounds for interactive controls. More information about Internet audio is available at sites like Soundorama (www.soundorama.com/formats.html).

Video

The majority of download-and-play video uses Apple's QuickTime (quicktime.apple.com), though AVI (Video for Windows) and *MPEG* (*Motion Picture Expert's Group*) formats are also found. Due to bandwidth limitations, most video is recorded in 160×120 pixel windows, with limited color and slow (>10/second) frame rates. Under these conditions, it still takes about 5–10 minutes to download 30 seconds of video over a modem.

Real-time video is also available on the Web—but just barely. Among a large number of companies, VivoActive (www.vivoactive .com), VDO (www.vdo.net), and XingTech (www.xingtech.com) have established followings for their proprietary streaming formats. While all formats support Windows, Macintosh and Unix support is spotty to nonexistent. In 1997, Progressive Networks (www.real.com) introduced the RealVideo format, which could become the streaming video standard on the Internet. RealVideo runs on multiple platforms and offers a variety of compression options, from a slideshow presentation suitable for 28.8 modems to real-time video delivery on corporate Intranets.

Links to Dynamic Content on Remote Sites

Virtually any site may include dynamic components through banner ad swapping or membership in a banner exchange network. Free banner networks like the Internet Link Exchange (www.linkexchange.com) and the Commonwealth Network (commonwealth.riddler.com) provide sites with dynamic elements. Groups with larger sites may sell banner space through commercial ad companies like Doubleclick (www.doubleclick.net) and NetGravity (www.netgravity.com).

Content Aggregation

Developers may also add useful dynamic elements simply by linking to content on related sites. For example, a site dealing with Canadian content might provide links to the online version of regional newspapers, or audio/video feeds from Canadian Web sites. While most sites welcome the additional publicity, occasional problems may occur. In the recent Ticketmaster (www.ticketmaster.com) versus Microsoft (www.microsoft.com) lawsuit, the Microsoft Seattle Sidewalk (www.seattle.sidewalk.com) site linked directly to pages deep within the Ticketmaster site, allegedly depriving visitors of the chance to view Ticketmaster's advertising banners. Regardless of the validity of this case, the update team should always clear links to dynamic content with the site operators.

Environmental Information

This small but significant class of dynamic content includes information supplied from the environment by nonintelligent means. Examples include date and time information, Web access statistics, "spy" cameras, temperature/pressure sensors, and audio feeds. More information about hooking environmental sensors to the Web is found at Anthony's List of Internet Accessible Machines (www.mitchell.net/ant/machines.htm) or bsy's List of Internet Accessible Machines (www-cse.ucsd.edu/users/bsy/iam.html).

Computer Generated

As hardware and software become more powerful, computer programs that spontaneously generate dynamic content are being developed. *Artificial Intelligence* (*AI*) programs have found applications in *chatterbots*, which are programs designed to prime conversations in chatrooms. An extensive list of chatterbots is maintained on the Simon Laven Page (www.student.toplinks.com/hp/sjlaven/). Other examples include fractal image generators such as those listed at the Fractory (tqd.advanced.org/3288/), and *Artificial Life* (*AL*) simulations on the Live Alife Page (www.fusebox.com/cb/alife.html), shown in Figure 5.2. Not currently in widespread use, these systems might become major dynamic content sources in the future.

Integrating Dynamic Content

Once the sources of dynamic content are established, the next job for the update team is to create a staging process that places content into media elements on the site. There are two main approaches to doing this. In the *direct* approach, the update team makes modifications directly to HTML pages that are subsequently uploaded to the site. These techniques (e.g., manual HTML editing, search/replace, and cascading style sheets) require greater personal effort by update team members, but they have the advantage of allowing arbitrary changes to be made on short notice. Since a human editor is involved, any combination of HTML, JavaScript, or other markup/programming languages may be added in a single session, and changes in content do not require modifying the update strategy. In the *indirect* approach, content is loaded into an automatic system that generates the final Web page. For example, instead of editing HTML, the update team may enter database information that, in turn, automatically appears in Web pages delivered from the server. Such systems (e.g., database-generated pages and media elements generated by CGI scripts) are easier to manage, but they usually restrict the type of content that is used in updates. If content changes format or media type, adjustments may need to be made in the programs processing it. The update team should examine both methods and develop a strategy that optimizes automation and flexibility.

Figure 5.2 Example of computer-generated dynamic content—an artificial ecosystem at the Live Alife Page (www.fusebox.com/cb/alife.html).

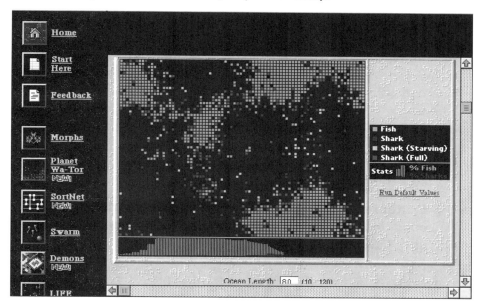

Manual Updates

A basic update strategy follows the "word processor model," allowing individual documents to be edited in a word processor style environment. Most commercial HTML editors provide direct manual editing in this mode. Manual editing also includes operations applied to groups of HTML files, including format changes and search/replace functions. In cases where these options are unavailable in the editor, the update team installs a custom search/replace CGI script such as HTGrep (iamwww.unibe.ch/~scg/Src/Doc/htgrep.html) or ht/dig (htdig.sdsu.edu). A custom search/replace script used on the authors' Kaleidospace (kspace.com) site is shown in Figure 5.3.

Cascading Style Sheets

The *Cascading Style Sheet* (*CSS*) specification adopted by the W3 consortium (www.w3.org/pub/WWW/style/) in December 1996 provides an alternate method of global control for document features. By creating a single file, the update team instantly changes features such as font type, point size, leading, drop caps, and first-line effects across the entire site. To make global changes across the site, the update team simply edits the CSS file with commands similar to the following:

```
<STYLE TYPE="text/css"> H2 { color : red }</STYLE>
```

Figure 5.3 Custom search/replace program showing options for conditional searches and restriction to particular files or directories.

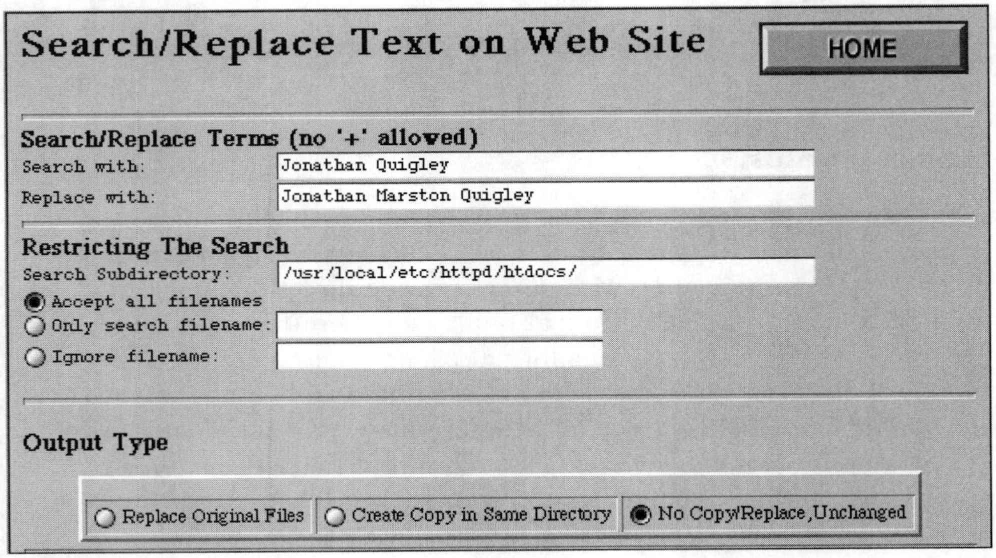

Search/Replace Text on Web Site   HOME

Search/Replace Terms (no '+' allowed)

Search with: Jonathan Quigley

Replace with: Jonathan Marston Quigley

Restricting The Search

Search Subdirectory: /usr/local/etc/httpd/htdocs/

● Accept all filenames
○ Only search filename:
○ Ignore filename:

Output Type

○ Replace Original Files   ○ Create Copy in Same Directory   ● No Copy/Replace,Unchanged

This command, or rule, will cause all HTML files that contain the following tag to color <H1>...</H1> titles red:

```
<LINK REL=STYLESHEET HREF="file.css" TYPE="text/css">
```

On sites with standardized formats for content (e.g., online catalogs), CSS greatly simplifies document management and eliminates the need for formatting search/replace operations. On the downside, older Web browsers will often display style sheets as text. Microsoft provides support for the standard in its Explorer Web browser, but support by Netscape and other platforms (such as TV/Web hybrids) is far from complete. Backward compatibility is assured by putting the style command inside an HTML comment, for example:

```
<STYLE TYPE="text/css" <!-H2 { color : red }-></STYLE>
```

Unless the site is assured of an audience with cutting-edge software, the CSS system should not be implemented.

Dynamic Links to External Programs

The second most common method for enabling dynamic content is to link to external programs from HTML pages (see Figure 5.4). Most links to external programs use the *Common Gateway Interface* (*CGI*) (hoohoo.ncsa.uiuc.edu/cgi/interface.html). CGI programs are usually implemented as scripts in the Perl language (www.perl.com), although Microsoft's Visual Basic and compiled languages such as C or C++ are common alternatives. Once the program is written, a standard HTML tag creates the dynamic media element:

```
<a href="/cgi-bin/programs/dynamic.pl">Link to dynamic
content</a>
<img src="/cgi-bin/programs/dynimage.pl" ALT="Dynamic
image">
```

This simple strategy separates program code from the HTML pages, and keeps the HTML page clean and readable by all Web browsers. Since program execution occurs on the Web server, high

Figure 5.4 Dynamic links to external programs.

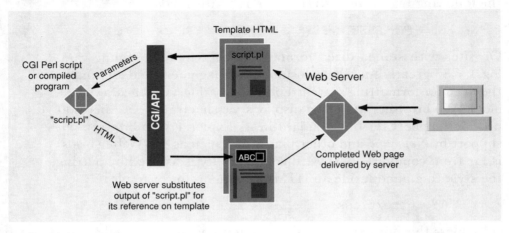

traffic might lead to reduced site performance. General information for developing programs with a CGI interface is found at W3c (www.w3.org/pub/WWW/CGI/) and NCSA (hoohoo.ncsa.uiuc.edu/docs/cgi/overview.html). Windows NT-specific CGI information is available at (website.ora.com/wsdocs/32demo/windows-cgi.html). Mac and Windows NT systems will need the Perl programming language installed to run CGI scripts. CGI programmers should also pick up Thomas Boutell's CGI (www.boutell.com/cgic/) library for serious work. If searches on these sites don't turn up the required information, the update team should try searching Verity Web Publisher's Virtual Library (www.verity.com/vlibsearch.html) or The CGI Resource Index (www.cgi-resources.com), shown in Figure 5.5.

Since CGI execution is slow and involves considerable processing overhead, many Web and database servers implement a custom *Application Programming Interface* (*API*). APIs sacrifice portability to increase execution speed and reduce memory requirements. High-traffic Web sites will frequently need to convert generic CGI applications to platform-specific APIs.

Figure 5.5 The CGI Resource Index (www.cgi-resources.com).

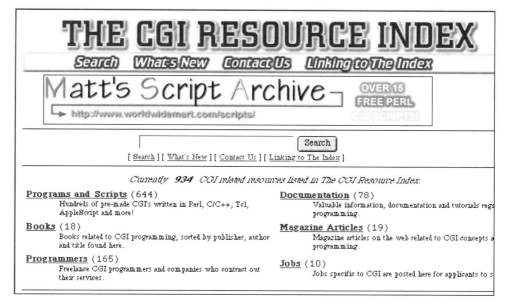

Web/Database Gateways

Due to their power and flexibility, Web/database gateways form a special class of dynamic links. By providing access to information in organized arrays, Web/database links greatly expand the power of dynamic sites. Despite this potential, simple methods for linking standard database formats to the Web have taken some time to appear. Major vendors including Oracle (www.oracle.com), Sybase (www.sybase.com), Informix (www.informix), and Microsoft (www.microsoft.com) provide free or low-cost gateway software for their platforms. Most database gateways consist of an *Open DataBase Connectivity* (*ODBC*) module providing a standard interface for database queries, and graphical tools that simplify the design of individual database-driven applications. Currently, Web/database gateways

Figure 5.6 Web/database gateway design.

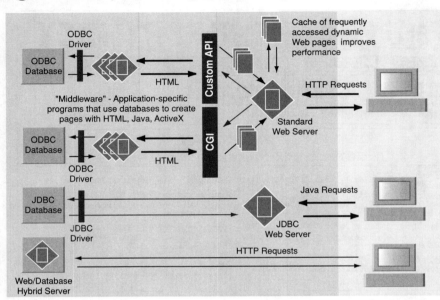

are divided into the following classes described next and shown in Figure 5.6.

CGI gateways. In these implementations, a standard CGI script or program translates commands sent from the Web server into standard ODBC format and sends them to the database. Intermediate programs (middleware) perform additional logic with database information to dynamically construct Web pages. To support non-ODBC databases (e.g., dBase), custom gateways are required.

API gateways. To speed up the slow process of running CGI programs, some Web servers implement custom APIs that allow direct communication with the database. Common formats supported by many vendors include Netscape's (NSAPI) and Microsoft's (ISAPI) API formats.

JDBC gateways. Since the Java programming language has become more popular, many developers have needed to provide direct database access to downloaded applets. In order to meet this need, a database gateway (JDBC) comparable to ODBC gateways has been developed. Some Web servers process Java requests and send them to standard databases using a JDBC-compliant gateway.

Web/database hybrids. Some databases such as Oracle's Universal Server respond directly to HTTP and/or Java requests over the Internet, eliminating the need for gateways or a separate Web server. This approach provides the fastest method for constructing dynamic Web pages; however, it may be difficult to serve static HTML and link to CGI programs.

For general gateway information, the update team should check sites such as Accessing a Database Server via the World Wide Web (cscsun1.larc.nasa.gov/~beowulf/db/web_access.html) or the sites of their current database vendors. Database and gateway development is proceeding very rapidly in the industry, and development of database-enabled sites will become simpler in the near future.

Web Programming Languages

More sophisticated external links define mini-programming languages within the HTML file itself. As shown in Figure 5.7, upon encountering a non-HTML program, the server is configured to pass it to a CGI or API interpreter for execution. Web programming languages typically implement the basic features of standard procedural languages, including variable assignment, if-then conditionals, functions, and program loops. This approach has substantial advantages compared to simple CGI programming. Placing scripts directly into HTML, it eliminates the need for a large number of separate CGI scripts—and the CGI/API interpreter is usually much faster than standard Perl. By including support for various databases, Web

Figure 5.7 Web-specific programming languages used to generate dynamic content.

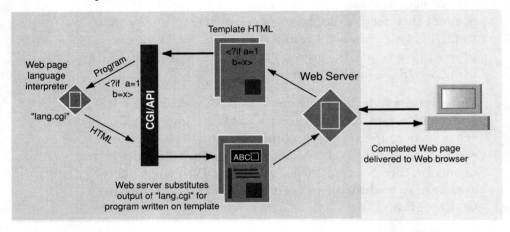

programming languages make it much easier to develop database-enabled Web pages. Example of languages are given next.

Freeware/Shareware

Nearly all Web servers support a simple *server-side includes* language that adds programming commands to HTML pages with an .shtml extension. Server-side includes appear in comment tags. Common commands include:

```
<-!- #command variablex="value" -> assigns a value to a
variable name
<-!- #echo var="LAST_MODIFIED"-> displays last time doc-
ument was changed
<-!- #include files="file.html"> puts contents of file
at place where include command appears in document
```

For sites requiring a full Web-based language, PHP (mcsv.com/php-1.95/doc/php.html; Unix) is a good choice. This Unix-specific language combines a C-style programming syntax with access control and direct support for *SQL (Structured Query Language)* databases. PHP interprets commands placed within a <?> construct, and PHP-active files are referenced with a .phtml extension. The language supports variables, arrays, function calls, and conditional branching.

Commercial

Compared to free languages, commercial offerings have better support and more sophisticated programming interfaces. Commercial systems currently in use include the following:

MetaHTML. (www.metahtml.com; Unix; $2500) Recently migrated to commercial status, this advanced Web page language is used on many large sites. Commands appear within < > constructs and support a full-featured programming language with a Lisp-style syntax. Current versions include support for commercial databases and provide site management through the PowerStrip function. A free version lacking the database and PowerStrip modules is available for download.

Alliare Cold Fusion. (www.allaire.com; Windows NT/Solaris; $995) Currently the leading general-purpose tool for database linking and dynamic site management, Cold Fusion defines a custom HTML-like tag language (CFML) for database/Web integration and a server-side engine that generates HTML on the fly. This program supports Java, JavaScript, ActiveX, and VB Script, but it requires knowledge of database programming languages for effective use. The program works with ODBC-compliant databases including Microsoft Access, Oracle, and Unix SQL servers; and it is compatible with Netscape, Microsoft, and O'Reilly Web servers. Cold Fusion also provides management tools enabling file uploads and site administration.

ExperIntelligence's Webberactive. (www.webbase.com; Windows NT; $149) Similar to Cold Fusion, this package uses a custom "tag" markup language to simplify page design. Options include quick access to all available tags, attributes of all tags, and possible values of all attributes. New tag definitions are downloaded directly from the Web. A built-in preview using Microsoft Internet Explorer technology ensures accurate and feature-rich previewing that includes ActiveX controls, email generation, and support for Microsoft's dynamic HTML (DHTML) and *Channel Definition Format* (*CDF*).

IDS Software. (www.idssoftware.com; Windows NT/95; $495) The IDS server provides a gateway to standard relational databases through HTML and Java environments. The Java version employs the efficient JDBC Type 3 database driver (splash.javasoft.com/jdbc/jdbc.drivers.html) and supports secure SSL transactions. The HTML version supports ODBC databases and provides a custom page language with variables, conditionals, and program branching.

Virtuflex Software. (www.virtuflex.com; $2495/$495; Unix/Windows NT) This modular system is designed to integrate Web pages with databases, faxes, and pagers. The core program provides links to add-on gateways for ODBC databases, email, Internet faxing, chat, bulletin boards, form letters, threaded discussions, surveys, and online quizzes.

Maxum Development. (www.maxum.com; $395; Macintosh) NetCloak and NetForms allow Macintosh developers to create forms, banners, counters, targeted search and retrieval abilities, "crawling spiders," archive and mirroring systems, reporting, and site management. An excellent way for Mac-based developers to add dynamic functions to their site without platform migration.

Net Dynamics. (www.netdynamics.com; $5,000; Unix/ Windows NT) This system consists of a Java-based server coupled with a visual development environment that integrates Java, HTML, SQL, and legacy business applications. The program links Web pages to PeopleSoft, SAP, Informix, Oracle, SQL Server, Sybase, DB2, and ODBC data sources.

Client-Side Programs

Client-side programs are executed after a page is downloaded by the Web browser. As shown in Figure 5.8, these programs run on an end user's computer and no special programs need to be installed on the Web server. The Web browser provides direct support for interpreting the programs, or requires downloading an additional plug-in for execution. Next we'll discuss the client-side programs currently in widespread use on the Web.

Java

The most common client-side language on the Web is Sun Microsystems' Java (java.sun.com; free—built into Netscape, Explorer, and other Web browsers). This extremely powerful, object-oriented programming language is supported by all major Web browsers. Often used to write client-side applets, Java is increasingly being used to write Web servers and databases. Due to its complexity, Java requires professional training for effective application development. Information on Java programming is found at the Sun Microsystems' site, and an exhaustive library of free and shareware programs is maintained at Gamelan (www.gamelan.com), shown in Figure 5.9.

JavaScript

To open up Java-style programming to a larger audience, Netscape developed JavaScript (home.netscape.com/eng/mozilla/Gold/

Figure 5.8 Dynamic content through client-side programs.

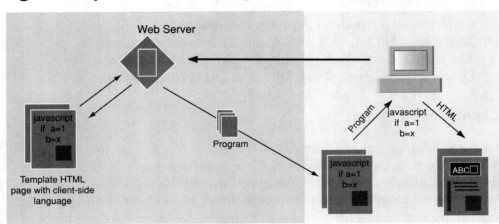

handbook/javascript/index.html; free—built into Netscape and Explorer). This client-side language implements a subset of Java commands but is simpler to program and implement. JavaScript capability is built directly into most Web browsers. Information and tutorials are available through Netscape and at JavaScript World (www.mydesktop.com/internet/javascript/).

Weblet Programming

Eolas Software's Spynergy Weblet Developer (www.eolas.com; Windows NT/Unix; $49.95) is a Java competitor that implements an alternate applet technology through "weblets" running the Tcl/Tk programming language. Available on most Unix systems, Tcl/Tk is popular for cross-platform graphical development. Weblet programming features a much shorter learning curve than Java, but end users must download a plug-in for use.

Figure 5.9 Gamelan Java/JavaScript site (www.gamelan.com).

Shockwave

Macromedia's Shockwave (www.macromedia.com; $495; Macintosh/Windows) implements a subset of the CD-ROM authoring environment of Director. Requiring a plug-in for execution, Shockwave movies access and dynamically display data stored on Web pages, execute CGI scripts, and pass objects between movies. Shockwave's programming language, Lingo, is specialized for the development of animated graphical and multimedia objects that are responsive to visitor input. Full-featured Shockwave programs have long download times and often execute slowly. To reduce this problem, Macromedia recently released Flash, a small and fast development environment/plug-in suited to most Web-based multimedia developments. Macromedia also recently put the ShockWave player into a Java wrapper, allowing individuals without plug-ins to download and play the media.

DHTML

Dynamic HTML (DHTML) is not dynamic in the sense defined in this book, but it refers to client-side programs that support the download of multiple *layers* or objects for a single Web page. After download, only some of these elements are visible, and user interaction might expose or conceal different areas of the content. Two competing standards for DHTML exist. Netscape has developed a DHTML system based on its <LAYER> tag. Microsoft has developed a competing standard using the new eXtensible Markup Language (XML), a standard proposed by W3C (www.w3.org/pub/WWW/TR/WDxml .html) that allows content providers to create their own commands without losing compatibility. The end result of either approach is a page that provides a more CD-ROM-style interface to the Web, through scripted interactions between page elements. In effect, DHTML turns individual pages into mini client-side programs. Unlike Java/JavaScript-based languages, DHTML only works with content that has already been downloaded, and it cannot request new content. As such, its use is primarily in creating a more responsive interface than in providing new content, or in exploring a large amount of static content a little at a time. As an example of the latter, consider a floor plan for a building. Using DHTML, constraints in furniture placement are coded into the page, and the user could progressively discover these by moving icons around on the screen.

For dynamic sites, the use of DHTML will depend entirely on content. If the site provides simple online games, models of physical objects, or responsive interfaces suitable for children, a DHTML script is sufficient to deliver the content. Since DHTML pages have no ability to call updates, new versions will need to be developed for each change in content.

Remote Hosting of Dynamic Programs

Many ISPs do not allow program installation on shared Web servers. To overcome this problem, the use of dynamic media elements and databases is rented from remote program hosting services. When developing the site plan, the update team should check to see if the ISP supplies remote program hosting. If the required programs are not available locally, additional resources can be explored through the CGI Resources Index (www.cgiresources.com/Programs_and_Scripts/Remotely_Hosted/). An example of a company providing this service is i-depth (www.i-depth.com; $10/month; all platforms), a service that provides a variety of remote dynamic banner ads, forums, guestbooks, hit counters, classified ads, chat, and calculating order forms. As the complexity of Web software continues to grow, this strategy is likely to become increasingly common. Some major software developers such as Lotus (www.lotus.com) have already announced that Web-based versions of their groupware packages are available over the Internet for a monthly fee.

Integrated Database Development Packages

Some systems provide a database tightly integrated with development tools in one package that promises true on-the-fly site generation. Many of these software packages actually include the database bundled with the product, making the package a particularly good choice for development groups that haven't already purchased a database. Other program suites implement radically new database models suitable for multimedia environments. Following are some examples of integrated database development packages.

Flat-File Databases

These databases contain lists of information that is stored in simple lists of text and numbers. Many small sites use a proprietary database available in Selena Sol's Public Domain CGI Script Library (www.eff.org/~erict/Scripts/). WODA Web-Oriented Database System (www.fagg.uni-lj.si/~zturk/works/wb/) is a comparable flat-file database written in Perl. Features include built-in support for output from Web fill-out forms, and a "new to me" function that lists all changes since the command was last run. This feature is useful in managing updates or versioning. WODA also imports and exports data from Microsoft Excel or Access.

Relational Databases

Relational database packages provide greater power and flexibility than flat-file systems. Unlike flat-file systems, the contents of one database entry are implicitly related so that changes to one affect the other. Using relational databases allows the complex coding necessary for most dynamic sites.

Hughes Technologies MiniSQL. (hughes.com.au; Unix; $250) This is a Unix SQL database that costs much less than other similar commercial packages. It implements the subset of SQL most commonly used in database operations, and it is distinguished by its fast response in common operations. The package also provides W3-SQL, an interface package for creating SQL databases and accessing them from dynamic Web links through its custom page description language. W3-SQL also provides access control and authentication for administration of the database. While containing the features of a full database, it falls short of providing a complete Web development environment. Its primary use is in providing Web access to information, rather than constructing complete pages on the fly. The program is free for nonprofit, educational, and research groups.

Microsoft Visual InterDev. (www.microsoft.com/vinterdev/; $499; Windows NT/95) This package provides a graphical authoring environment for *Active Server Pages* (*ASP*), which support a variety of languages for database integration including Java/JavaScript, Visual Basic Script (VBScript), C++, and Perl. The program also defines a custom Web programming language and recognizes files with an .asp extension. Database calls are made directly through SQL/HTML commands. For non-Microsoft servers, Chili!Soft's Chili!ASP (www.chilisoft.net; $995; Unix/Windows NT/95) server effectively duplicates Active Server functions.

EveryWare's Tango. (www.everyware.com; $349/$995/$2,995; Macintosh-FileMaker/Windows NT/Unix-ODBC) This application allows integration with FileMaker databases on the Macintosh, third-party ODBC databases, or EveryWare's own Butler SQL Mac database. Unlike other packages, Tango supports multiple operating systems, and database query documents generated by Tango run on all platforms without modification. Tango's advanced development interface is almost completely "drag and drop" and is a good development environment for teams unfamiliar with relational database programming. A server-side language, embodied in a series of <META> HTML commands, allows execution of program logic during database calls.

Object-Oriented Databases

The arrival of the Web has quickened the steady incorporation of the object-oriented database paradigm into database design. Standard relational databases store numbers and text in tables, and they rely on external programs to manipulate the data into appropriate output. Due to this, additional programming outside the database is required to support nonnumerical objects such as graphics and audio files. In contrast, *object-oriented* design creates blocks of code including data and a set of procedures for interacting with the data; thus, individual database objects know how to behave when accessed by external programs. For example, an image in an object database might include its own procedures for conversion of GIF, JPEG, or PNG format, as well as logic guiding which conversion to use. An object might even request updates of its data across a network. This approach has obvious advantages in the multimedia environment of the Web, and it simplifies the integration of databases with object-oriented languages such as Java and JavaScript.

These systems, formerly confined to a tiny minority of database installations, are now seeing more widespread use on the Web. Object Design, Inc.'s ObjectStore (www.odi.com; Windows NT/Unix; $3,200 and up) is a Java-based, object-oriented database, written specifically to manage the text, data, and multimedia files common on Web sites. ObjectStore, along with other object-oriented databases, uses a fundamentally different way of storing information that is better suited to the multimedia environment of the Web than standard relational databases. The database comes complete with two powerful authoring tools: Object Inspector ($1,250/developer) provides a graphical interface to examine, document, and debug management ObjectStore databases; and ObjectForms ($3,500/developer) allows direct design and generation of complete HTML pages from stored ObjectStore data. ObjectStore's runtime processor interfaces directly with Microsoft, Netscape, Open Market, and other Web servers, and a request dispatcher provides load balancing for high-volume sites by directing Web requests to specific application server processes. To counter these moves by Object Design and other object-oriented developers, relational database companies such as Informix (www.informix.com) have provided support for hybrid databases that implement an object layer on top of the standard relational component. Such hybrid environments allow companies to keep the same databases, but response time of dynamic Web data is significantly slower. In the near future, it is likely that all databases will support objects as a layer running over their core relational architectures.

Examples of Dynamic Media Elements

Using the tools just described, the update team may immediately implement many forms of dynamic content. The examples given next are for individual CGI scripts, but comparable programs are easily created in Web page languages and client-side programs (see Figure 5.10). These elements provide all the dynamic content that is necessary on smaller sites, and they often complement more sophisticated content on larger sites.

Figure 5.10 Collage of dynamic media elements.

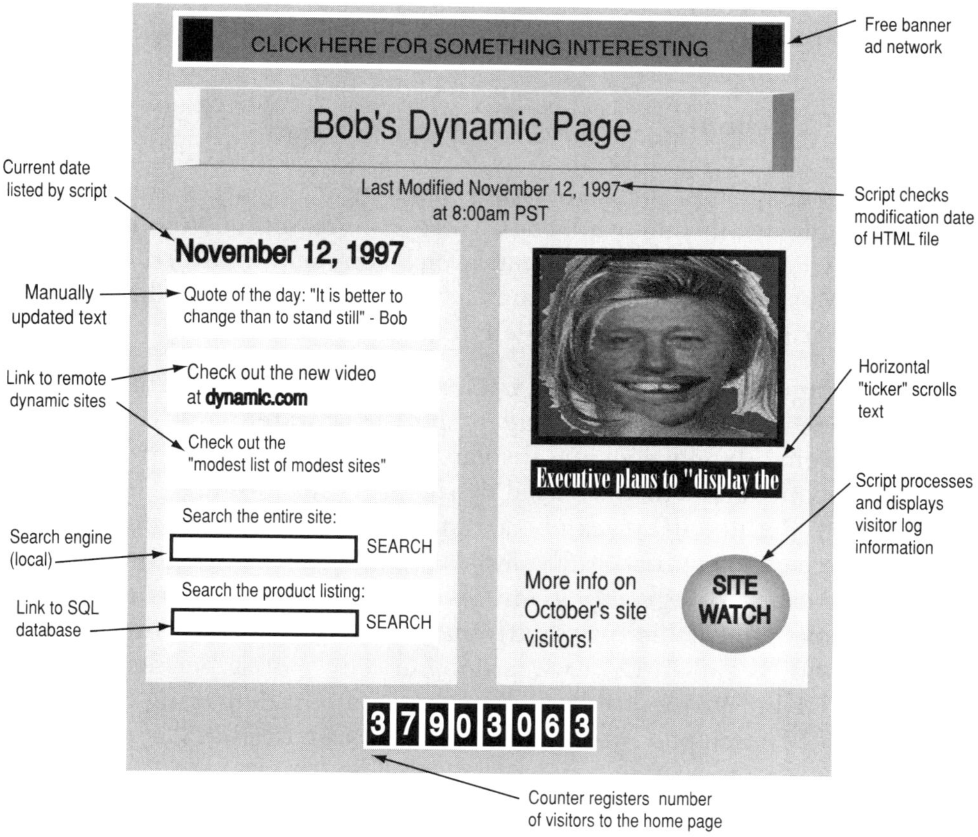

Clocks, calendars, and countdowns. Date/time programs get their information from the operating system and then create text/graphic output. More sophisticated programs organize time-sensitive information into a calendar format or "countdown" until a specified day or time. Simple date/time scripts for Unix are available at Quantum Scripts (www.q-west.com/scripts/), for Windows at NT CGI Scripts (www.geocities.com/SiliconValley/6742/), and for JavaScript at JM Web (www.geocities.com/SiliconValley/6052/java.html). Calendar programs are available from WebEvent (bio.bu .edu:80/WebEvent/) and PerlCal (128.151.21.16/wwwrlp/ perlcal/).

Page counters. These programs create a graphic numerical display of the total number of visitors to an individual Web page. Comprehensive listings of counter resources are available at Silicon Graphics (www.sgi.com/counter), Web Page Access Counters (www.markwelch.com/counter.htm), Meysoft (www.meysoft.com/scripts/scripts.html), and Matt's Script Archive (worldwidemart.com/scripts).

Page, text, image, and URL selectors. These programs select HTML pages, images, short text statements, or URLs from a larger pool and display them in random or ordered sequences. The data used by the programs originate from a predefined list or can be assembled from date/time data or access log statistics. Examples include the Random Image Picker (www.geocities.com/SiliconValley/6742/), Selena Sol's Fortune Cookie (www.extropia.com/Scripts/fortune.html), and URLoRAMA (www.middlebury.edu/~otisg/Scripts /URLoRAMA.shtml). Commercial systems delivering content based on visitor information are discussed in Chapter 6.

Scrolling text banners and tickers. These programs present text, either scrolling horizontally like a stock or sports ticker, or vertically showing entire sentences at one time.

Static scrolling text is created using animated GIFs or CGI programs, but dynamic text scrollers need Java or JavaScript for effective implementation. Examples including Animastrata (www.kiama.com/Animastrata/index.html) and NewsBreaker (www.newsbreaker.com) allow for the creation of a wide variety of vertical and horizontally scrolling text and changes to content without modifying the HTML pages. More sophisticated applets such as those from Modern Minds (www.modernminds.com) dynamically check for and post new text across a network. Other tickers such as Catchy (www.geocities.com/SoHo/2077/codec.htm) allow scheduling of multiple messages for delivery at specified times. The best resource for programs is found at Gamelan (www.gamelan.com) under Java and JavaScript.

Search engines. These specialized programs automatically index text on Web sites for rapid searches by visitors to the site. In practice, they act as general-purpose search (but not replace) systems. The queries used by site visitors are recorded to specialized access logs or fed directly into "personalization systems," as discussed more fully in Chapter 6. Some Web servers (e.g., Microsoft) contain built-in search engines, and freeware/shareware software is readily available. Additional information about search engines is available at the Search Engine Software site (www.searchenginewatch.com/software.htm), which includes reviews and ratings as well as links to the programs.

Dynamic graphics generation. Many types of data (e.g., charts and graphs) are more easily understood in graphical form. Developers working on Unix systems may use Thomas Boutell's GD graphics library (www.boutell.com/cgic/) to convert text and basic draw commands into finished GIFs. This resource provides a set of low-level routines that are called by CGI programs. Starnine Software's WebCollage (www.webcollage.com; Macintosh,Windows; $249) provides a more sophisticated commercial solution version of GD. This Macintosh and Windows NT-based tool assembles images and data from a variety of sources in real time and uses them to create unique Web graphics. Individual elements come from local files, Web URLs, or the results of calls to databases. CyberChart (www.gamelan.com) is a Java applet that collects information directly from JDBC-compliant databases and dynamically builds charts that change in real time. Sites using geographical maps may implement Cymbiont's Meridian Map Server (meridian.cymbiont.ca). This special-purpose program dynamically generates map graphics from map formats including Atlas GIS (BNA), AutoCAD (DXF), Digital Chart of the World (VPF), ESRI's Shapes (SHP), MapInfo (MIF), Ordinance Survey (NTF), and US Geological Survey (DLG). Individual maps are linked to database information and remain active during zooms and pans.

Choosing the Best Update Technology

With a wide range of software and procedures available to add dynamic content to Web sites, the update team must carefully consider which methods they will actually employ. On one extreme, a site with inadequate infrastructure might become impossible to maintain. On the other extreme, many high-end solutions costing tens of thousands of dollars are simply overkill for most sites. Next we'll list a possible scale for implementing dynamic software attuned to the size and complexity typical of public Web sites.

> **Level 1: Virtual hosting without access to programs.** For sites with minimal budgets hosted on virtual servers, the main content update method used is often manual. Additional dynamic content is included by linking to remote sites that allow rental or free use of dynamic CGI scripts. In

many cases, the ISP will provide free access to "public" scripts from basic accounts that serve the same purpose. Advanced programmers add Java or JavaScript directly to HTML pages and design downloadable media using Shockwave or Flash formats.

Level 2: Virtual hosting with programming. More expensive hosting options allow installation of programs. In this case, the update team initially installs free or low-cost CGI programs to manage individual dynamic content elements. With literally thousands of programs available, the update team is likely to find examples that suit its purpose "as is" or require relatively minor modifications. If the site is large, the developers should consider installing a free Web-based programming language such as PHP, and a relatively inexpensive database such as mSQL.

Level 3: Dedicated servers. As the size and complexity of the site increases, the update team should consider installing a commercial Web-based programming language such as Cold Fusion or MetaHTML. This will consolidate scattered CGI scripts into a single consistent programming environment that is shared by members of the team. By adding an industrial-strength, ODBC-compliant database, dynamic content is similarly organized and consolidated. Low-traffic sites might make do with CGI database gateways, but larger sites will need to use their Web server's custom API for adequate performance.

Level 4: "On-the-fly" site generation. On the largest sites, HTML templates should be replaced by complete page generation from the database. Java applets provide advanced real-time multimedia while linking directly to JDBC-compliant databases. If the site contains a mixture of dynamic and static pages, it makes sense to use a standard Web server for static pages and send dynamic requests directly to a database (like Oracle's Universal server) that supports HTTP commands. If the site contains a high proportion of nontext dynamic elements (e.g., audio, video, and multimedia files), the update team should consider an object-oriented database.

Trouble Spots

As the update team develops a strategy for developing, editing, and uploading content, certain problems routinely appear. By anticipating these trouble spots, the process of development is kept as simple and efficient as possible.

Manual Editing and Search/Replace

The safe way to support manual editing is to run a special administrative Web server with broad write permissions and restrict access to its search/replace scripts through passwords. Without this precaution, an unauthorized person could cause major problems with just a few keystrokes. Global search/replace edits of Web sites also cause trouble if the term in question appears in unexpected places. For example, consider a search that replaces "January" with "February." If a hyperlink somewhere on the site points to "January.html," the search/replace will change it to "February.html"—without changing the name of the file. Due to this, search/replace scripts should initially be run in a read-only mode. If no surprises are present, the changes should be written. Most search/replace programs also allow restricting their effects to particular directories or filenames, which will help to reduce this problem.

Document Versions

The update team will need to define which set of documents are most recent and will be used to overwrite older documents. High-end development packages often provide document version control, but update teams not having access to these systems will need to establish their own policies. Most sites fall into one of two categories:

Online editing. For groups with high-speed continuous access to the public Web server, content contained on that server is the most current. Therefore, these groups conduct significant amounts of editing on line. In this case, updates always pass from the developer platforms directly to the public servers, and editing of existing HTML always starts with a download from the public site to a staging server.

Staging editing. Sites with low-speed modem connections to the Internet frequently find it more useful to adopt an opposite strategy, making their staging server hold the most recent content. Using this approach minimizes time online to transfer completed documents. In this case, the public server is always treated as an outdated relative to the staging server, and no editing is done while online.

Web-Based Programming Languages

Most Web-based programming and markup languages allow execution of operating system commands, which cause major problems if misused. Standard security precautions, such as disabling operating system access through the language, are a necessity for public Web sites. Information on security is available at Matt Kruse's Server-Side Includes Tutorial (www.netexpress.com/~mkruse/www/info/ssi.html) or the Webcom Guide to Server-Side Includes (www.webcom.com/~webcom/help/include.shtml).

Detecting Obsolete Content

Few things make a Web surfer wince more than the appearance of a "new" or "just in" graphic on a page that has not been recently updated. More than simple neglect, it indicates to the site's audience that the managers have literally forgotten about the timeliness of their content.

Manual recordkeeping. Many smaller sites simply mark obsolete content "cleaning days" on a PaperNet or EmailNet calendar. To initiate manual checks, the update group should write a list of page modification dates and mark their expiration dates on a calendar.

Page modification dates. By listing the oldest pages on the site, or pages created during a specific time period, obsolete content is identified. Modification dates are also provided by many linkchecker programs (Chapter 3) and site management tools (Chapter 6).

Creating custom HTML tags. When individual media elements on a page have different obsolete dates, their expiration dates are determined by several methods. If content is marked by a standard "new" graphic, the update team searches for the graphic's filename. One useful way to allow communication is to put commentary on the Web page itself. The HTML comment tag <!— comment —> allows arbitrary text to be placed invisibly on a page. If several individuals update the same pages, one might leave a comment for another, as shown here:

```
<!— To Jane: don't remove the image below this until
May 24, 1998. Sincerely, Bob —>
```

This is also a good method to mark cryptic programming links through server-side includes or other programs so they aren't accidentally taken out. For example:

```
<!— Important stuff below —>
<img src="/cgi-bin/radix.pl">
<!— OK to delete after this location —>
MEDIA ELEMENT
```

```
<img src="file.gif">The Image</a>
<!—Web Team 44 last modified 10/10/96, obsolete
03/09/97—>
```

In order to make embedded comments useful, the update
team must agree on a common format for writing them. It
is a good idea to invent a unique term for the team's comments (e.g., Web Team 44) that is selected by search/
replace functions in HTML editors and management software. If Web-based programming languages are also being
used on the site, care must be taken not to accidentally generate program directives in the comments.

Cached obsolete pages. Updates to Web pages are not
useful if users don't see them! Unfortunately, bandwidth
limitations across the Internet have led to old copies of Web
pages being *cached* on end-user hard disks, ISP networks,
and online services. Caching reduces redundant file
requests and lowers Internet traffic, but it also prevents
updates from being seen. Fortunately, it is relatively simple
to force old content to be updated by adding a pragma
directive into the <META> tag within the HTML file.

```
<META HTTP-EQUIV="Pragma" CONTENT="no-cache">
```

If the page is being generated from a database or CGI
script, all that is necessary is to make the program print the
following text (example shown for a Perl script where \n is
the newline character):

```
print "Content-type: text/html \n";
print "Pragma: no-cache" \n\n";
```

In the next chapter, concepts developed for processing dynamic content are expanded to include the update team and audience. The first part shows how workflow and collaborative software helps to organize rapid and focused communication between members of the update team. The second half of the chapter explores content personalization software that lets the site's audience participate in dynamic content delivery.

ADVANCED UPDATE TECHNIQUES

Large dynamic sites present particular problems that require more sophisticated systems than those discussed in the previous chapter. In this case, the update team consists of several individuals who must coordinate their efforts, which increases organizational demands and may require installation of special project management software. Large sites also contain more content, which may make it harder for visitors to find the information they are looking for. To answer this problem, advanced sites frequently implement systems providing personalized access to content. In all cases, the necessary software is far more sophisticated than the simpler update systems described in Chapter 5. This chapter examines these sophisticated, integrated approaches to Web updates, which are shown in schematic form in Figure 6.1. Installation and use of these systems takes more effort than simple update technology, but results in a Web site that is more easily updated by its developers and accessed by its audience.

Figure 6.1 Collaborative and workgroup software.

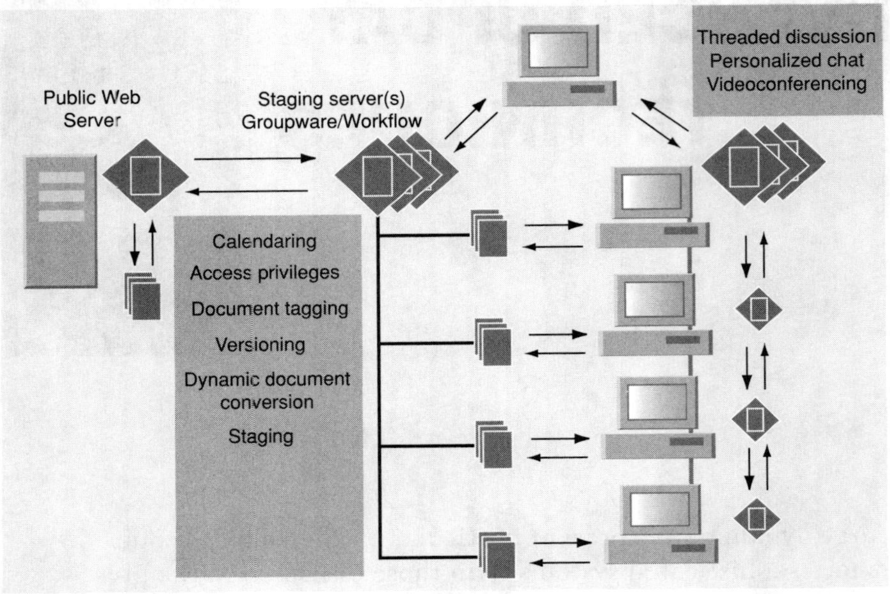

Collaborative Software

Once the update team has established a method for developing dynamic content, the team will also need to develop a comparable strategy for organizing internal communication. Chapter 2 introduced EmailNet, a simple strategy for organizing the update team based on the exchange of messages. As the size and complexity of the Web has advanced, collaborative software has been developed to focus communication within workgroups and organize content development. Properly used, *collaborative software* helps the update team's Editor avoid many problems associated with complex Web sites. Traditionally, Internet users have participated in email-based *mailing lists* and Usenet-style *threaded discussions* running under *NNTP*

(*Network News Transport Protocol*) to organize working communication. This chapter discusses support for these communication modes, as well as additional collaborative features. While many update software packages are designed for Intranets, emphasis is placed on using them to organize staging and production of public Web sites.

Mailing Lists

Mailing lists provide formal, automated methods of distributing messages within a workgroup. In the one-to-many mode, the mailing list owner/operator sends messages received by all list members. Lists running in the many-to-many mode extend these privileges and allow any list member to send messages to the entire list. The first mode is useful when the Editor or Producer of the site needs to inform everyone of new policies, deadlines, or meeting dates. The second mode is best for brainstorming content and developing ideas through communal input. Mailing list activity may also be summarized in periodic digests. Administrative functions include the ability to add and remove list members, control individual postings, and specify document collections available to members.

Starnine Software's ListStar (www.starnine.com; $499; Macintosh) provides a set of templates that simplify setup of standard list operating modes (e.g., moderated, announcement, email-on-demand, and mail robots). It can handle medium-sized lists, but it runs slower than comparable software running on Unix or Windows NT servers.

L-Soft International's Listserv Lite (lsoft.com; $450–$2,000; Unix, Windows NT/95) is a commercial version of the original freeware package dating from the 1980s. Listserv is a highly flexible program loaded with a huge number of features for creating and managing lists, users, digests, and indices. Higher-end versions of the program allow linking to a database and advanced administration options. The program may be purchased outright, or the update team may purchase yearly licenses starting at $525.

The Shelby Group's Lyris (www.lyris.com; $495–$4995; Unix, Windows NT) is an extremely fast and efficient mail server that is optimal for high-volume lists. While some knowledge of the Perl programming language is necessary to use all its features, its Web interface makes installation and routine maintenance fairly easy. Lyris provides discussion/forum support; an auto-responder *mail robot* capability for answering standard questions; and specialized functions for handling "bounced" or incorrect email addresses entered in the list.

Threaded Discussions and Conferences

Threaded discussions form an alternative approach to managing group collaboration. Instead of email messages, a central server creates a virtual billboard and manages a running commentary, or newsgroup, centered on a particular subject. Group members may read the previous discussion, or *thread*, and post their own comments at any point within it. Unlike the often chaotic environment of mailing lists, threaded discussions provide an audit trail of the working group's communication that may be used to document the update team's progress. Email attachments sent to the thread allow working documents to be exchanged during development.

Until a few years ago, threaded discussions were found exclusively in Usenet (see www.dejanews.com) and proprietary software packages. Now, most productivity programs support some kind of threaded discussion. With increasing availability of new protocols on the Internet, some commercial programs have moved beyond text-only exchanges and allow discussions using audio, video, and multimedia. Instead of simply posting documents to the discussion thread, team members may hold conferences in real time and write to a central virtual *whiteboard*.

Microsoft NetMeeting (www.microsoft.com/netmeeting; Windows NT/95) is built into Internet Explorer 4.0 and supports real-time collaboration using audio, video, file transfer, chat, document/application sharing, and whiteboards. The system supports video cameras and microphones, and NetMeeting calls can be placed through Microsoft Outlook and Exchange. NetMeeting constitutes a core application for third-party development, and many collaboration/discussion products are currently being developed for the system.

HotOffice Technologies (www.hotoffice.com; $24.95/user/month; Windows NT/95) provides basic networking, email, virtual meetings, and electronic forums with only a single Windows computer and Internet connection. The HotOffice server is remotely hosted by HotOffice, and usage is provided on a monthly per-user basis. Designed to work with Microsoft NetMeeting and related products, HotOffice is a good solution for geographically scattered groups relying on dialup Internet access for communication.

Farallon's Virtual Office (www.farallon.com; $49.95; Windows NT/95) converts each computer into a mini-Web server representing each office member as a local Web site. A variety of conference software applications allow real-time interaction by screen sharing, file exchange, Internet phone, and text-based chat. An in/out basket provides storage for documents being used by the group.

AltaVista Forum (www.altavista.com; $495–$2,395; Unix, Windows NT) contains many options and features, including password protection, built-in chat, calendars, and a 60-day free trial. It provides access to documents and discussions with multiple levels of administrative control.

Meta Info's News Channel (www.metainfo.com; $795; Windows NT) provides a set of tools for integrating Usenet news feeds with internal conferences and discussion groups. The program closely follows Usenet group organization, and it is designed to integrate Usenet with local workgroups.

Lundeen & Associates' WebCrossing (webx.lundeen.com; $995–$11,000; Macintosh, Windows NT, Unix) is a high-end conference tool that uses a distributed server to provide load-balancing and traffic management for large conferences with hundreds or thousands of participants. Basic systems with one discussion group cost approximately $1,000, and additional discussion/chat forums may be added incrementally. The developer's version allows creation of customized interfaces, control of visitor access to conferences, and support for hyperlinks between discussion threads and Web pages.

Personalized Chat

Until recently, Internet-based chat systems were rarely used for anything beyond casual conversation. Despite its similarity to conference calls, chat software did not provide the organizational tools necessary for maintaining goal-oriented communication. Drawing from the example of America Online's Instant Messenger (www.aol.com), several companies have recently added new *personalization* functions to their chat software. Each time members of the chat group goes online, they are presented with a list of people who are part of their group. By examining the list, they may quickly determine who is available for discussion and place a virtual call to notify them of the meeting. Once in the chat room, members join the main discussion or break off for private conversations. Members who don't have time to participate may make themselves invisible to the chat and call functions while continuing to work online. With its simple structure that effectively mimics real-life conversation, personalized chat forms an alternative to more expensive workflow systems.

Excite's Personal Access List [PAL] (www.excite.com; Macintosh, Windows) is a good choice for small groups in mixed computing environments. The server is hosted remotely by Excite and users currently register at no charge. The PAL software provides a bookmark-like list of individuals showing who is currently online. List members may exchange instant messages with group members or make themselves invisible if desired. Messaging proceeds in an email-type environment.

Mirabilis' ICQ (see Figure 6.2; Windows NT) software provides personalized chat features that operate in real time or through an email-style interface. Like other systems, ICQ allows creation of lists

Figure 6.2 Control panel for personalized chat using Mirabilis (www.mirabilis.com) software.

showing who is online and message/document exchange. Clients maintain a history of messages sent and received that may be used to support simple threaded discussions. Clients are available for Windows and Macintosh systems, but the server runs exclusively under Windows NT.

PeopleLink's (www.peoplelink.com; no charge; Windows NT/95, Macintosh) free software integrates personalized chat with advertising and allows banners on screen. The program is available at no charge, but its built-in advertising banner system makes it unsuitable for most internal development groups.

Groupware and Workflow

The most advanced collaboration software introduces additional management tools necessary for organizing large projects incorporating several team members. These *groupware products* provide a development environment for *workflow*—the production of custom development/staging systems for organizing dynamic site updates among several individuals. In addition to email and threaded discussions, workflow tools usually include one or more of the following features:

Calendar. This feature allows the team's Producer or Editor to schedule discussions, assign individual jobs, and establish milestones for the group. Individuals in the group receive their own custom calendars and may indicate when certain jobs have been completed. Advanced programs allow the team leader to determine the impact of changing individual deadlines on the completion times for the overall project.

Access privileges. This software option allows the administrator to rigorously control access to documents within the working group, making the documents read-write, read-only, or completely invisible to select subgroups. Access is controlled through password protection or by automatic recognition based on Internet address or other criteria.

Document tagging. This feature allows individuals in the workgroup to label files for specific action. Document tags might indicate who is responsible for the document's completion; what needs to be done to the document; information on the document's modification history; and a summary of jobs left undone (e.g., posting to a public Web site).

Staging. Groupware providing this feature divides the development process into a series of distinct authoring, editing, and publishing steps—each with its own collection of documents. Web-specific packages often provide direct support for document assembly from other files; graphics and navigation features; and automatic submission for editorial review. Some packages create one or more prepublication Web sites and automatically post completed pages to the public sites as they appear.

Databases and libraries. Most groupware allows the Editor to add documents, programs, and other resources to a virtual library shared by the workgroup. Individual team members can "check out" a library document or program for personal use and return it when their work is completed. Advanced groupware allows direct access and display of information from standard SQL and ODBC-compliant databases.

Auditing. This feature allows the Editor to examine steps taken by individual team members during the development of a particular document. Audits may follow the document's development or actions taken by members of the group. This feature helps the supervisors keep track of ongoing work.

Software Enabling Workflow

In the past, groupware consisted of proprietary client/server packages running exclusively on corporate networks. Currently, most products are integrated into Intranets and provide added support for Internet standards including SMTP/POP email, the *Lightweight Directory Access Protocol* (*LDAP*), MIME multimedia extensions, and HTTP/Web access. By bringing the development environment into the Web, these products establish a seamless connection between workflow and the final dynamic product. Many traditional groupware packages contain new features allowing the update team to develop a workflow-style "back office" for dynamic Web sites.

Starbase (www.starbasecorp.com; $95; Windows NT/95) has developed a Web interface to its client-server project management system called StarTeam Web Connect. Using Web Connect, an update team may utilize groupware features including version control, threaded discussions, document management, and audit logs. In a field of expensive solutions, the Starbase package may provide a reasonable alternative for small Web development groups.

Lotus Domino (www.lotus.com; $1,000–$3,000; Unix, Windows NT/NetWare) is an open-standards, Web-enabled version of Lotus Notes. Designed especially for groups using Lotus Notes who want to publish to the Web, it hybridizes the standard Notes groupware product with a Web server and advanced Web-specific tools. The Domino development environment uses standard Notes forms and templates, and the resulting Web pages may be accessed through the Web or the proprietary Notes client. Extensive support is provided for email exchange and collaborative discussions during development. Groupware/workflow features include file access control, defining readers, developers/editors, and support for Internet security protocols such as SSL. Domino also supports Notes' *replication* system. When multiple servers are in operation, one server will automatically update content residing on other servers to reflect any changes. This is particularly useful for scattered group members and "road warriors" who make transient network connections and spend much of their time working offline. Each time they log onto the Internet, their local copy of Domino automatically uploads and downloads changes made by other team members. Domino also supports traffic balancing across several servers. Even with its Web-based interface, Domino is still very much a proprietary product. Web documents are generated on-the-fly, but it is difficult to serve static Web pages along with the dynamic ones. The development process is dramatically different from most Web/Internet applications, and the software has a steep learning curve. Domino also cannot directly access relational databases (though the Notes environment itself is similar to an object-oriented database), and it requires an intermediate step that moves data into the Domino Storehouse. For groups that already use Notes, the Domino systems is a no-brainer; others may want to explore more Web-centric solutions.

Lotus !InstantTeamroom (www.lotus.com; $15/month per user; all platforms) is a modified Domino server for rental through national ISPs such as Netcom (www.netcom.com), developed as an alternative to the high cost of purchasing dedicated groupware. This system allows the ISP to sell end-user accounts featuring a basic collaborative Web environment with document tracking and security features. Individual accounts, or *seats*, in the Teamroom environment are rented at about $15 per user per month, making it affordable for very small development groups. By using the Domino !Instant Host and !Instant Host SDK, developers may create their own custom Teamroom-type applications and host them on participating ISPs.

Microsoft Exchange/BackOffice (backoffice.microsoft.com; $1,000–$3,000; Windows NT) is a collection of clients and servers that integrates groupware with database and Web publishing functions. The Microsoft Exchange server provides the core for groupware-style integration. Using a relational database, it maintains messages, deadlines, and lists of group members that may be delivered to the Outlook and Schedule+ client. The Outlook client allows project scheduling and collaboration through standard Internet protocols, and the Schedule+ client handles calendars. The key strength of the Exchange platform is its direct support and tight integration with other BackOffice products, including Microsoft's Web server, Windows NT, and SQL database. Like Netscape's SuiteSpot, it provides NNTP Usenet-style News service and allows direct, two-way access to Usenet newsgroups. In order to use the full set of features, companies will need to upgrade from Office95 and program their own custom workflow environments. The seamless integration of the product with Windows95 combined with a defined upgrade path from MS Mail will make it an obvious choice for shops committed to Windows, but the lack of cross-platform support for Macintosh and Unix makes it less useful in mixed computing environments.

Novell GroupWise (www.novell.com/groupwise/products/webaccess; $1,600 for 10 users, $13,340 per server; Windows 95/NT) is a welcome addition for groups using Novell's Netware products. The software provides excellent support for document staging, Web-enabled threaded discussions, calendaring, task assignment, and document sharing. Gateways allow Web integration with fax, voice, and pagers. GroupWise is an excellent choice for companies already committed to NetWare that want to avoid running an additional layer of Internet protocols on their networks. Due to its reliance on Netware's proprietary system, it is less useful for companies already using the Internet for communication.

Bulldog Software (www.bulldog.ca; $20,000; Unix, Windows NT) produces a general-purpose workflow management system suitable for team development and updating of dynamic sites. Built to use the Informix Illustra (www.informix) object-relational database, it can map documents, audio, video, and multimedia files of all kinds to workflow projects. Content management and workflow are supported through a Web-based client. Strengths include support for standard workflow functions including defining projects and tasks. Bulldog integrates file collections into "products"—collections of assets used to create a completed Web site. Individual assets are managed by a checkin/checkout system available to each team member.

Groupware Specific to Dynamic Sites

Unlike the general-purpose products listed previously, the following programs have been specifically designed to provide workflow/staging for dynamic Web sites. Additional features include dynamic generation of HTML from databases; custom graphical environments for developing Web pages; and focus on staging, editing, and publishing environments specific to Web development. With relatively limited markets, most packages aim at the high end of dynamic site development and provide robust support for sites supporting high traffic and thousands of individual pages.

Whistle Communications' InterJet (www.whistle.com; $1,995–$3,495; all platforms) provides an integrated solution for small groups that need to install an office Internet connection and organize their development group. The package provides a compact computer with built-in Internet connectivity (modem or leased-line), firewall, routing, and email. Additional software gives office computers immediate Web access through the IntraJet, and allows the use of Internet programs even when the Internet connection is inactive. The standard package comes with a trial version of NetObjects' Fusion (www.netobjects.com) to support graphical HTML authoring. Once documents are created, they may be loaded onto the IntraJet's local staging server, which automatically copies them to a second site hosted on a remote ISP. The unique combination of an Internet connection, router, firewall, and staging server makes the InterJet an outstanding choice for small sites trying to keep things simple while introducing Internet access and collaborative software.

Netmosphere Action Plan (see Figure 6.3; $499 for five users; Windows 95) is a Java-based project management system that utilizes the ActionPlan group scheduler and HotSheet for developing calendars, document exchange, and real-time communication via the Web. Using Netmosphere, the update team's Editor assigns work deadlines for each member of the project. Tasks are assigned based on resources becoming available (e.g., purchase of new equipment), and milestones are set to track progress against goals. Filters allow the effects of the project to be modeled when individual team members leave the group or resources are unavailable.

CurrentIssue's (www.currentissue.com; $1,000; Windows NT/95) modular package enables dynamic document delivery using Microsoft's Active Server technology and ODBC databases. Like other team development systems, CurrentIssue separates content from templates, and provides for document/media management. Macro functions allow parameter-passing to dynamic objects, which are automatically updated on the Web site. Unlike some other packages, it is easy to import existing static Web sites into CurrentIssue, and remote users may directly edit and update dynamically created Web pages or email messages. Custom dynamic objects supplied

Figure 6.3 Project management using the Netmosphere (www .netmosphere.com) package, showing calendar and task scheduling interfaces.

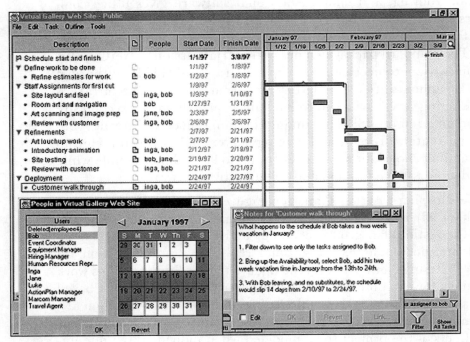

with CurrentIssue include database access, fill-out form management, calendars, discussion groups, and advertising management.

Radnet's WebShare (www.radnet.com; $2,195; Windows NT) provides a complete Web-centered groupware environment building on Netscape SuiteSpot and Microsoft BackOffice. The Radnet server utilizes an object-oriented development and relational database to control access and document sharing, and it serves on-the-fly documents directly through Web servers. The Designer application ($995) allows graphical development of dynamic pages served through the WebShare. The software also supports threaded discussion, calendars, document tracking, and programming needed to create custom workflow environments. Like Domino, Radnet supports automatic replication (through its WebShare Mobile product). Updates to the Radnet server are automatically copied to remote users running their own stripped-down copies of the main database.

Wallop Software's BuildIt (www.wallop.com; $2,495; Windows NT/95) is designed as a meta-application that allows developers to use their current HTML authoring tools within a collaborative development environment. Support is provided for Web authoring programs, including Microsoft Office97, Adobe Photoshop (www.adobe.com), SoftQuad's HoTMetaL PRO (www.sq.com), and Symantec's Visual Café (cafe.symantec.com). BuildIt includes an extensive set of management tools for broken-link analysis, Cascading Style Sheet (CSS) support, and Web template libraries. Wallop recently integrated the MKS (www.mks.com) Web Integrity program into its system. This tool creates a virtual staging process that does not require a dedicated staging server. Update workflow is divided into an unlimited number of Surf, Edit, and Approve stages; and each stage has a preview mode for viewing changes before they are forwarded to the next level. BuildIt also includes support for database authoring environments, including those supported by NetDynamics (www.netdynamics.com) and Allaire's (www.allaire .com) Cold Fusion. BuildIt is a good option for update teams that want to integrate Web development with existing workflow software. Due to its strong reliance on Windows, BuildIt is less suitable in mixed computing environments or for teams that do not have legacy project management tools.

Netscape Communicator/SuiteSpot (www.netscape.com/comprod/ server_central/; $4,995; all platforms) is a 10-server platform that provides an open-standards, Web-based collaborative environment. Access to SuiteSpot is exclusively through Web browsers, though Netscape recommends using its own Communicator client for maximum effectiveness. Document management uses LDAP directories, and additional groupware functions are provided by the Mail server,

Usenet News server and Calendar server. The Collabora server includes security and access controls, and it provides native support for HTML, Java, and JavaScript documents. Large discussion groups may be monitored with search and notification services built using individual content preference files. SuiteSpot also includes LiveLink from Open Text Corp. (www.opentext.com). LiveLink is a custom workflow development environment that provides tools for collaboration and team management, a custom search engine, and data libraries. Graphical interfaces are used to design Web pages, bulletin boards, and email notification. Using LiveLink, the update team's Editor controls access to documents and examines audit trails. SuiteSpot is ideal for groups that want to use the Web for all their collaborative projects, and who need software that also supports large-scale Intranets and Extranets. With its exclusive reliance on standard Internet protocols, SuiteSpot is almost platform independent.

Vignette's StoryServer (www.vignette.com; $30,000; Sun Solaris, Unix) is the "Cadillac" of Web groupware, and it implements a publishing model ideal for online newspapers and magazines hosting multiple dynamic sites. This high-end tool is used by several major sites on the Internet, including C|Net (www.cnet.com) and Time-Warner's Pathfinder (www.pathfinder.com). StoryServer provides a complete production environment for large update teams facilitating submission, editorial review, staging, and workflow. The program uses commercially available relational databases to store project information and Web page templates. Following an object-oriented database model, page templates link HTML documents with the programs needed to add dynamic content. Default templates provided with StoryServer detect browser types, manage lists of HTML documents, and track users through the Web site. StoryServer also stores page component templates (e.g., navigation toolbars) that are used to assemble custom page templates. Additional features include extensive support for database-Web links, separation of content from page templates, and a Web-based scripting language (based on Tcl) for template control. In addition to development and staging, StoryServer provides management tools that greatly improve the performance of high-traffic dynamic Web sites. StoryServer Web sites access databases through native libraries that allow faster turnarounds than ODBC gateways. External programs are supported through custom APIs rather than slower CGI. To reduce the speed penalty associated with generating dynamic HTML on-the-fly from the database, StoryServer caches commonly requested pages as static HTML. In operation, frequently accessed pages will be available without consulting the database, greatly reducing the load on the Web server.

Interwoven's Teammaker (www.interwoven.com; $40,000; Sun Solaris) creates an overlay for other management tools by implementing a Web-specific staging system. Web development is treated as having four levels: authoring, editing, administration, and publishing. To implementing staging, Teammaker creates a series of virtual copies of the site that are accessible through standard Web browsers. Members of the production team at each level add and modify files, forwarding them to the next level for review. The administrator may roll back files or portions of the site to earlier versions as needed, and may have this information echoed to the public site. Teammaker does not provide individual management tools (such as linkcheckers), but it functions with them.

Dynamic Document Conversion

Web sites that are primarily created for the publication of "legacy" documents originally written in word processor or desktop publishing formats have special update requirements. Examples of such sites include product information archives, educational sites offering online courses, and corporate sites repurposing internal information. If standard document conversion programs are used, the update team must build and maintain HTML-based archives parallel to the existing documents. To eliminate this step, some document workflow systems dynamically translate word processor files directly to HTML on the fly, as shown in Figure 6.4. Most of these tools were developed for corporate Intranets but are equally useful for public Web sites.

Documentum's (www.documentum.com; $20,000; Unix/Windows NT) client-server document management system recently added the ability to dynamically construct HTML from word processor, spreadsheet, audio, video, Java, and Active X files. The RightSite product, accessed through a proprietary client or through the Web, allows the update team to index files and link individual URLs to one or more documents. When visitors access the link, an HTML page is built on the fly from the specified elements. The software also provides control for access privileges and tags for assigning versions to documents or document collections.

Infodata Systems' Virtual File Cabinet [VFC] (www.infodata .com; $50,000; Windows NT) allows end users with Web browsers to

Figure 6.4 On-the-fly assembly of HTML files from legacy documents.

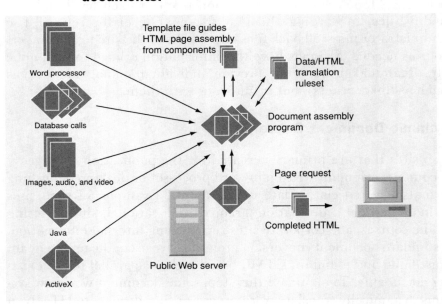

search, access, and share documents across preexisting document management systems. VFC accesses information written in HTML, SQL, ODBC, JavaScript, text, graphics, audio, video, and CAD/CAM files. Existing documents are parsed and converted to HTML on-the-fly. The package uses an object-oriented database and includes an authoring environment aiding in integration with other document management systems. Features include predefined methods for updating database content across the enterprise, detection of obsolete information, search/replace across multiple databases, and integration of mainframe and legacy databases with the Web.

Choosing a Management System

Choosing the best software for managing the update team's work is one of the hardest decisions the site developers will make. Due to its central position in the update process, the software package selected will have a direct impact on efficiency. Next we'll discuss issues that should be addressed by the update team during the decision process.

Cost

Sites with small budgets and large numbers of contributors may elect to work with the free and low-cost options provided by standard mailing lists and threaded discussions. Geographically scattered groups might also consider renting ISP-based groupware such as Lotus Instant Teamroom or HotOffice. Free personalized chat is a possible alternative for small groups. Development groups with larger budgets should purchase custom development environments. Even if legacy systems are available, it may be better for the update team to purchase a system specifically designed for dynamic Web sites. Since development and publishing occur in the same environment, learning curves are lower and it is easier to support mixed computing environments.

Amount of Content

Development groups responsible for small amounts of dynamic content may effectively use threaded discussions or mailing lists to organize their work. Groups that regularly update large amounts of content or manage time-sensitive material will need to implement calendars, deadlines, and real-time discussions to keep the information moving. Sites that are updated by their audience (e.g., classified ad sites) often have smaller organizational requirements than those receiving new material from the update team. In the former case, the update team acts more as a curator than as a developer of original content. Monitoring user input may require custom software, but the small changes made to the site by the update team will not require an elaborate staging system.

Update Method

Groups in which individual members independently create dynamic content work through calendars and regular email. In contrast, if content is developed by several writers and editors, adding mailing lists and discussion groups will be necessary to support the normal give and take of content development.

Content Delivery Strategy

Groups with sites supporting periodic content updates need to explicitly organize production schedules using calendars and submission deadlines. In contrast, groups with sites supporting user-contributed or asynchronous updates of content will likely need to install a high-end software package that tracks and tags responsibility. Sites producing broadcast content may require the team to augment standard workflow with additional software designed for assembling a broadcast stream.

Agents and Content Personalization

After the update team has organized content development and staging, the next stage is to organize delivery to the end user. Standard Web sites provide information through a "supermarket" approach where all visitors travel through the same network of pages and directories. As Web sites become larger and more complex, it makes sense to adjust the content and interface to each user's interest. This is particularly true for dynamic sites. On successful dynamic sites, most visitors will be returning for a repeat visit, and they will focus on new material relevant to their interests. Personalization software is designed to provide this function. Web sites containing personalization may alter the appearance of the home page, number of mouse clicks separating specific content from the home page, and advertising presented during surfing. Personalization makes it easier for users to find useful information hidden in the vast expanses of the Web, and it ultimately enables the development of one-to-one marketing based on long-term relationships between producer and consumer.

Virtually all personalization software today uses raw information to create user *profiles*. These shorthand descriptions summarize the complexities of user behavior in a succinct and useful way. Profiles may be based on *demographics* (the user's position within standard measures, including gender, income, and marital status) or *psychographics* (the user's stated and implicit lifestyle preferences). Since psychographic profiles focus on lifestyle and don't require the sensitive information needed for traditional demographics (e.g., income and marital status), they are particularly well suited to the anonymous user environment of the Web. Once profiles are mapped to a specific demographic or psychographic group, they are linked to content or advertising likely to be of interest to them. A schematic showing the process is provided in Figure 6.5. The next sections of this

Figure 6.5 Mechanisms used to personalize content delivered by dynamic Web sites.

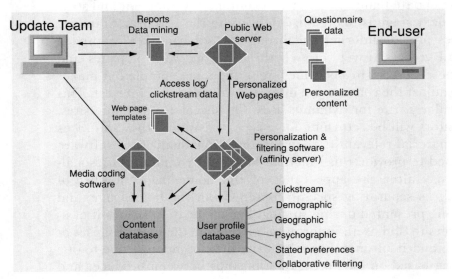

chapter discuss this emerging feature of the dynamic Web in greater detail, illustrating how site developers may incorporate it in their general update strategies.

Passive Profiling Software

Visitors to Web sites automatically and unconsciously provide information about their interests as they visit and navigate through Web sites. Profiles developed in this way include user movements between Web sites, navigation paths (or clickstreams) taken through individual sites, queries entered in search engines, and product/service purchases. The resulting information, when added to a database, is used to create a model of visitor interests.

Image Communications WebThreads (www.webthreads.com $895–$14,995; Unix, Windows NT) focuses on paths taken by individuals through a site. After the ThreadTrack program compiles a path, this information can be used by the WebTailor application to implement personalized content. An interesting feature of the package supports user participation by allowing site visitors to customize their visits with graphics they select from a directory.

Starpoint Software, Inc. (www.starpt.com; $7,500; Unix, Windows NT) allows one-to-one content personalization through a specialized affinity server developed by the company. Starpoint's Affinity Server uses the company's Content Stream analysis to profile the user, check for any existing information already on file, and deliver the most appropriate content based on this information. Individuals may be characterized through pages they request, demographic, geographic, or psychographic data. The delivered content may consist of custom Web pages, banner advertising, or product information and pricing. Management of the system is conducted through a Java-based interface that provides access to user profiles and content decision rules. Versions are available for the Web and Marimba Castanet (www.marimba.com) push channels (covered later in the chapter).

Aptex's SelectCast (www.aptex.com; $25,000; Unix, Windows NT) for Ad Servers is based on algorithms used to detect credit card fraud and evaluate loan applications in the financial industry. SelectCast analyzes passively compiled information collected from Web access logs and translates it into *vectors* (mathematical constructs) that are clustered into naturally occurring groups and averaged to create a composite profile for targeting advertising and products. Versions are available for targeting advertising or content. A version of SelectCast called Ultramatch is currently being used by InfoSeek (www.infoseek.com). Ultramatch combines keywords users type into the InfoSeek search engine with access statistics and ad click-throughs to build a passive user profile. The resulting profiles are mapped to affinity groups (e.g., business users) using psychographics.

Afficast's Interaction Manager (www.affinicast.com; $10,000–$30,000; Unix, Windows NT) is a Java-based server that combines a wide variety of inputs (including bookmarks and clickstreams) to construct psychographic user profiles for delivering personalized content and advertising. Profiles are enhanced by integrating information actively collected from users with passive profiling. The Interaction Manager is currently being used by the Yahoo! (www.yahoo.com) and Excite! (www.excite.com) search engines to target advertising.

IBM's Surfaid (192.195.29.133/docs/surfaid1.htm) adds a Web interface to IBM's Intelligent Miner toolkit and applies *data-mining* analysis to Web access. Data mining goes beyond traditional log and clickstream analysis by providing an environment in which the site developers may create and test a hypothesis. The Feature Discovery program analyzes user clickstreams and cluster groups into market segments with related surfing behavior. The Feature Analyzer then compares the outcome of particular actions taken on the Web site (e.g., ordering products) with specific features of the market segments. The Predictor uses this information to recommend content individually targeted to each surfer visiting the site. Surfaid users can supplement Web server logs with site registration data, customer databases, and third-party demographic profiles. To facilitate data mining, IBM maintains a central data repository of all information related to the customer's site.

Active (Registration-Based) Profiling

The easiest approach to personalization involves little more than asking visitors for their preferences. Since the beginning of the Web, sites have used fill-out registration or order forms to communicate with site operators. With the advent of new software, this information may be used to control delivery of dynamic content. Fill-out forms offer several advantages over passive profiling. Unlike vague information gleaned from site exploration, highly specific questions may be asked. The end user freely provides the information and is unlikely to be upset if it is subsequently used for agreed-upon personalization. Also, since answers on registration forms are specific, less software processing is required to extract useful information.

Collaborative Filtering

The dynamic, interactive nature of the Web allows new approaches for developing user profiles. Chief among the many methods being tested is *collaborative filtering*, which pools dynamically extracted profiles to create a consensus content recommendation. Personalized content is seen as the collective recommendations of site visitors. Unlike passive or active profiles, no comparisons are made to psychographic or demographic models. Collaborative filtering also allows visitors to directly affect personalized information through their interactions with each other. In most systems, visitors find other individuals with similar profiles and exchange information on the Web site. This allows users to control filtering simply by sending messages to each other. The end result of the technology is to convert isolated visitors into mini-communities with shared interests. Many groups see collaborative filtering as the long-term key to unique, Web-specific personalization, since it exploits the many-to-many communication mode common throughout the Internet. Due to the complexity of the software, only a few products are available.

Firefly (www.firefly.net; Passport Office $3,995, Catalog Navigator $24,950; Unix, Windows NT) is a recognized pioneer in content personalization, and its systems are used by major Web sites for applications including AOLs (www.aol.com) Greenhouse Networks, FilmFinder (www.filmfinder.com), and My Yahoo! (my.yahoo.com). Firefly's three-program package begins with Passport Office, which provides administrative control over collaborative filtering, and a server that issues and recognizes Passport profiles. A sample fill-out form

Figure 6.6 Fill-out form linked to personalize access to the Yahoo! (www.yahoo.com) search engine.

Personalize My YAHOO!

Welcome to My Yahoo. You are already registered as a Yahoo! user and ready to use My Yahoo!. My Yahoo! provides personalized news, internet, quotes, sports scores and other services. All that you need to do to use My Yahoo! is to complete the following simple personalization step.

what do you like?

Tell us what interests you and we'll suggest the categories, sites, and headline news topics which we think are useful and cool... but think of our suggestions as starting points rather than the end result. You will always be able to fine tune or even completely reconfigure your choices, if and when you wish.

NEWS	SPORTS	ARTS	ENTERTAINMENT
Business	Baseball	Architecture	
Current Events	Basketball	Fashion	Anime
Health	Golf	Fine Arts	Comic Books
Investing	Football	Literature	Movies + Film
Politics	Hockey	Museums + Galleries	Online Chatting
Technology	Soccer	Performing Arts	Personalities
	Tennis	Photography	Television

LIFESTYLES	MUSIC	RECREATION	SHOPPING
Kids	Alternative	Automobiles	Apparel
Lesbian Gay +	Blues	Cooking	Banking
Bisexual	Classical	Eating Out	Books
Parenting	Country + Western	Home + Garden	Music
Seniors	Jazz	Outdoors	Hardware
Teens	Rap + Hip Hop	Travel	Software
Women's Issues	Rock + Roll	Video Games	

TECHNOLOGY	STOCK QUOTES
Computing	(IF YOU KNOW THE TICKER SYMBOLS OF YOUR FAVORITE STOCK QUOTES,
Cyberculture	MUTUAL FUNDS, AND COMMODITIES, ENTER UP TO 30 OF THEM BELOW,
Multimedia	SEPARATED BY SPACES OR COMMAS.)
WWW Authoring	

Use these interests   Reset this form

providing information used by Passport is shown in Figure 6.6. Web site users that register for Passports thereafter receive personalized pages. The Catalog Navigator uses collaborative filtering profiles to deliver customized content. For example, a visitor considering a product may easily access community ratings of the product, as well as community recommendations for products providing similar features.

Even more advanced personalization is provided by the Community Navigator. The flagship product lets members of a Firefly community find others with similar tastes.

Firefly products integrate directly with Microsoft Active Server Pages and major commercial databases. Firefly is also co-author of the *Open Profiling Standard* (*OPS*), which enables the exchange of information between people and businesses within a framework for privacy (discussed later in the chapter).

LikeMinds, Inc. (www.likeminds.com; Unix/Windows NT) has produced collaborative filtering software designed to help content and purchasing decisions. The LikeMinds Preference Server allows businesses to implement highly specific one-to-one advertising. The product supports standard ODBC database access, and authoring tools allow the user interface to be customized. LikeMinds' software was used to create the MovieCritic (www.moviecritic.com) Web site, which recommends movie reviews (and reviewers with similar tastes). The software also supports a subset of collaborative filtering tailored to small, arbitrary groups. Given a group of individuals, the software registers their interests and combines them to make recommendations likely to be enjoyed by all.

One-to-One Filtering

In contrast to collaborative filtering sites, the goal of *one-to-one filtering* is to address the specifics of each individual independent of other visitors or clients. Sites implementing these strategies typically have long-term audiences that repeatedly visit the site for customized information, goods or services, or customer support. To accomplish this, the filtering software monitors individuals through each visit they make to the site and builds an increasingly specific model of their interests.

Open Sesame (www.opensesame.com/company/index.html; $25,000; Unix, Windows NT) uses an alternate model for content personalization. Instead of collaborative filtering, the Learn Sesame product monitors user activity to gradually build up a profile of user interests. Learn Sesame marks down pages requested by users and extracts important words from the selected content stream. The next time the user visits the site, Open Sesame displays information collected from passive profiling and asks the user to choose the information that should be added to the profile. Between visits, the software analyzes the Web site and records any new content.

BroadVision One-To-One (www.broadvision.com; $100,000; Unix, Windows NT) is a high-end product designed for Global 2000 businesses, Web content providers, systems integrators, Web developers, and software VARs. Web sites implemented with One-To-One support personalized electronic commerce, customer self-service, and interactive content publishing. Besides workflow features for the update team, One-To-One offers content targeting and "matchmaker" systems linking business reps and clients through their profiles or a human manager. Primarily designed for electronic commerce, the system allows the creation and building of unique one-to-one relations between sites and customers ordering goods and services.

Developing an Update Personalization Strategy

With enormous effort going into content personalization, it may seem to some developers that installation of these advanced systems is essential for their sites to be successful. In practice, this is far from certain. Personalization's value depends heavily upon the specifics of the content being created by the update team. For many Internet users, the main appeal of the Web is the potential for exploration, rather than passive reception of predigested material. To this end, personalization schemes that restrict content based on calculated preferences must be carefully implemented. In developing a viable update personalization strategy, the update team will need to ask some critical questions.

Is It Affordable?

Personalization software is extremely complex and expensive. High-end packages start in the $20,000–$40,000 range, and a typical large installation frequently costs over $100,000 for full development. In view of these numbers, the update team needs to demonstrate that the benefits of personalization will justify the expenses. In the future, costs are likely to drop and the benefits of personalization software will be available to larger numbers of development groups.

Does the Content Lend Itself to Personalization?

Some sites (e.g., promotion for film and television entertainment) contain material deliberately designed for broad demographic appeal. In this case, personalization may be of little use and will run contrary to the expectations of site visitors.

Should Active or Passive Profiling Be Used?

For broad targeting (e.g., banner ad presentation), a passive profile system may be effective. On the other hand, if original information is developed for a specific market, it is better to let the audience actively define their profiles through registration. Development of true one-to-one marketing almost always requires information actively supplied by the user.

Should Display of Results Be Limited, or All Inclusive?

Some personalization systems display a prioritized list of content arranged according to the user profile. Others automatically deliver the top-scoring content to the user without showing other possibilities. The update team will need to examine the intended site audience and determine if the particular demographic/psychographic group they are trying to reach will simply accept what the personalization system recommends, or will want to browse through a larger list of personalized content for themselves.

Will Personalization Be Consensus or One-to-One?

Consensus filtering is useful when individuals want to follow the tastes of their demographic groups. On the other hand, one-to-one filters may have an easier time identifying interesting new content that hasn't been around long enough to emerge in consensus demographics. One-to-one filters are appropriate for long-term relations between client and vendor, while consensus filtering helps to create a long-lived community of shared interests.

How Will User Privacy Be Protected?

Personal information, whether passively or actively collected, is inherently sensitive. Passively collected information may not reveal the identity of an individual, but still may be used to manipulate behavior in unethical ways. Consciously supplied information may be even more sensitive. Publishing personalization data or selling it to mailing lists or marketing firms without the individual's knowledge is unethical and frequently illegal. All registration forms should state clearly what the information is being used for and should provide a legal release for these uses. Individuals should also have the right to access and change existing information on request. To facilitate appropriate use of profile data, Firefly Networks, Inc., Netscape, and VeriSign (www.verisign.com) recently proposed the *Open Profile Standard* (*OPS*). Instead of cookies or custom registration systems, participating Web users will carry personalization information in an OPS on their hard disks in a format that may be accessed by Web servers. Users will have access to their OPS file and will control how individual items of information are reported to Web sites or ISPs. W3C (www.w3c.org) is evaluating OPS as part of the Platform for Privacy Preferences, and the final standard is due near the end of 1998.

Implementing a Personalization Strategy

Once a personalization strategy has been put into place, additional decisions are necessary to make it work. Many attempts at personalization do little but irritate the user by supplying content tagged as personal that appears to be trivial or irrelevant. As a far-fetched example of a personalization error, a visitor interested in discussing the philosophical consequences of the idiom, "out of sight, out of mind," might receive ads from exclusive mental institutions! The update team needs to consider which aspects of their dynamic content are suitable for personalization, and adapt software according to principles such as those discussed next.

Useful Information

The update team needs to confirm what sort of information needs to be determined in order to personalize content. Passive profiling provides very limited information and may not be sufficient to personalize most content. Extremely long registration forms or those containing vague or obvious questions are unlikely to be filled out correctly. In contrast, effective questions will make personalization a success. The following is a list of some appropriate entries on a registration form:

- Contact information (name, address, country of origin)
- Demographic information (gender, age, occupation)
- Psychographic "lifestyle" preferences
- Preferences for particular types of content
- Interest in more information (e.g., supplied by marketing rep)
- Releases controlling how the actively supplied information is used
- Releases allowing combination of passive tracking data with actively collected information

The following is a list of some inappropriate entries:

- Extremely personal questions irrelevant to the site's content
- Questions designed to elicit "slips" and other unintentional information
- Choices between disagreeable options (e.g., "Are you still a dog thief?")
- Marketing questions aimed at children

Questionnaires should not be prepared in isolation. After an initial draft is complete, others should read the form for grammar and punctuation, order of questions, and appropriateness for the audience. Other individuals in the update team should try answering the questionnaire to determine if it really collects the information the site operators are looking for.

Appropriate Tracking Technology

One-to-one personalization requires the software to automatically identify each visitor entering the site. Many groups have adopted the simple and effective strategy of giving each user a unique name/password combination that leads to personalized content. Passive identification is problematic. Anonymous identification methods tracking clickstreams or visitor IP address are not accurate enough to uniquely identify most users. At present, the *cookie* system introduced by Netscape provides the only universal solution to passive tracking. Cookies are files stored on the user's computer that may be accessed and written to by any Web server. Since they invisibly write cryptic information to the user's hard disk, their status is controversial. While security problems with cookies have frequently been exaggerated, the possibility of inappropriate use of cookie information is very real. This situation may change as the OPS privacy standard becomes more widely adopted.

Microtargeting Algorithms

Visitors supplying large amounts of personal information will expect equally personal results. For example, a personalization system that delivers the same information each time the visitor logs in is not fulfilling its intended purpose, whereas programs that take into account the content presented during previous visits when "personalizing" do fulfill their purpose. Large sites should consider advanced products such as IBM's Surfaid (its main strength lies in its back-end processing algorithms) in order to ensure useful personalization.

Security

Sites relying on demographic information (e.g., income and family size) for personalization must use strict security measures. The update team should inform the maintenance team when it plans to store sensitive information, and both teams should coordinate with each other to make it hack-proof. Some Web-based personalization software assigns coded descriptions of users and accesses this code instead of the primary information. This technology is strongly preferable to systems that access sensitive information directly.

Push Technology

Push covers a broad continuum of delivery strategies that automatically deliver dynamic content, often based on personal preferences. In simple cases, a push *channel* may consist of smarter methods of surfing and content caching. More complex push schemes collect content from various sources and deliver it to the end-user's computer on a periodic or an as-needed basis. Once the content is received, end users surf local content on their desktops instead of visiting the general Internet. With its "narrowcast" features, push is

Figure 6.7 Features of push technology.

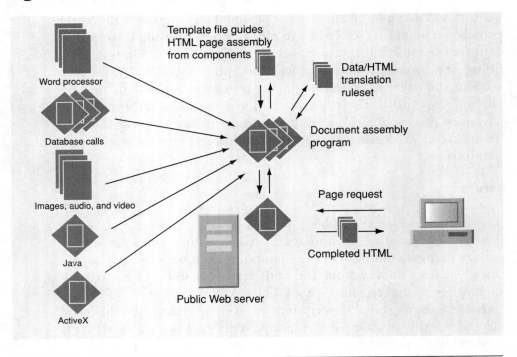

suited to updates to end users, or to managing administrative flow within the update team. Sites implementing personalization strategies such as those listed earlier in the chapter create *de facto* push channels. For groups seeking lower-cost approaches, certain push technologies avoid the cost of custom software while providing basic personalization. The features of push technology are illustrated in Figure 6.7.

Types of Push Tools

Initial attempts to create push channels involved the now obsolete "client pull" technology developed by Netscape in 1995. During

1996, the market split into two components. One group emphasized the differences between push and Web content, developing custom servers, clients, and protocols. The other group focused on adapting existing Web content for push delivery. At present, both approaches to push are in use, but pushing existing content is currently more common than creating new material for proprietary channels.

Proprietary Push Software

A large variety of proprietary—and incompatible—software protocols have been developed to enable push content. While the majority of these systems have not developed a subscriber base and have fallen by the wayside, a few have developed enough marketshare to be used in dynamic sites. In most cases, the purchase of a custom server is required, but a few function via standard Web delivery. The three most common software tools are:

Intermind's Communicator (www.intermind.com; free for non-profit, $95 commercial, $995 with ad insertions; all platforms) combines a Web-based push system with a specialized personalization system. Running as a high-end notification service, it allows the creation of push channel objects called *hyperconnectors* using a Web browser. After the hyperconnectors are uploaded to the Web server, visitors subscribe by re-downloading them to their local servers. Subscribers are automatically notified when content on a particular page changes. This approach eliminates the need for specialized push server software, though Intermind does sell a custom server ($10,000) for integrating push content with databases or search engines. Since most data is stored on the local Web server, users may automatically customize subscriptions without revealing personal information. The small amount of server-side information is kept anonymous, and Intermind has hired the firm of Coopers & Lybrand (www.colybrand.com) to audit its handing of end-user data.

BackWeb (www.backweb.com; Unix, Windows NT) uses a proprietary server and authoring environment (BALI) to create push content. Information is distributed in individual InfoPaks that include animation and pseudo-broadcast interfaces. Push content is automatically sent to the user's hard disk for local access. BackWeb also supports onscreen updates that work even if the Web browser is in the background. The BackWeb authoring environment offers considerable flexibility for developing custom channel interfaces.

Marimba's Castanet (www.marimba.com; Unix, Windows NT) environment is the most ambitious of push offerings. Written in Java, and functioning primarily in that environment, Castanet delivers both Web and custom multimedia content with equal ease. The push environment consists of a server called the Transmitter and a push client called the Tuner. Writing Tuners for given push channels takes considerable knowledge of programming, but Marimba also offers a graphical development environment called Bongo to ease the process. Information is read offline by the Tuner after being automatically sent to the user's hard disk. To simplify delivery, Marimba channels support incremental updating, which is roughly equivalent to the replication strategies found in Lotus Notes and other groupware. Each Tuner checks its state against its transmitter and dynamically updates its channel information with new information. The channel's content is added to the end user's computer (in files that could reach hundreds of megabytes in size), and the client allows offline browsing.

Channel Definition Format (CDF)

This is a proprietary push file format developed by Microsoft as part of its Dynamic HTML system (see Chapter 5). Push content is tagged within a CDF file, which describes the specific parts of a Web site that should be delivered to specific channels, and how often the channels should be updated. Upon execution, CDF information assembles push content and returns it to the users, who specify desired push channels. Changes to standard Web pages are necessary to make the system work. Advantages of CDF include support for database links and the ability to individually push media elements to a Web page. Disadvantages include working in an environment strongly favoring Microsoft's Explorer browser and the Windows operating system. To bolster the service, Microsoft provides CDF channels to major Web sites in its distribution version of Explorer.

Netcaster Push Format

This system uses a combination of HTML, Java, and JavaScript from Netscape's Dynamic HTML (see Chapter 5) to define the content and frequency of retrieval from a Web site. Netcaster push is actually a specialized form of *client pull* enabled through a JavaScript object with features similar to CDF. Multimedia-based push is supported through Marimba's (www.marimba.com) Castanet software. Advantages of the system include the ability to push Web pages without modifying their content and adherence to nonproprietary Web standards. Disadvantages include lack of fine-grained control; entire Web pages—instead of individual media elements—must be pushed to the end user's desktop.

Integrating Push into Dynamic Site Strategies

Even more than in the content personalization realm, the world of push is awash in hype. The reason for much of the enthusiasm—elimination of casual browser exploration in favor of force-feeding restricted content and advertising—is probably more interesting to marketers than the general Internet audience. Unless push content is compelling in a day-to-day format, most users quickly become tired of receiving information. The update team should analyze its own content for relevance and real interest according to the questions given next.

Does the Content Change Constantly, or Infrequently?

A regular push delivery service won't work if the content updates occur on an irregular basis. In this case, a simple email-based notification strategy may provide a better system for reaching users.

Is the Content Interesting Enough to Preempt Other Activities?

Notification systems such as BackWeb's popup alerts may seem exciting, but could simply irritate users occupied with other work. Unless the content is critical to their audience's day-to-day work, the update team should assume that push content will be accessed irregularly in an offline browsing mode. Updates designed to appear at specific times are better handled using a full Webcast strategy.

Can the Update Team Support Broadcast-Style Production?

Castanet and other high-end push schemes are centered around a near-broadcast model of delivery. Effective channel development will require developing production capabilities comparable to television—including schedules, scripts, and even online personalities. In many cases, the content may not warrant the high production costs and may be more effectively provided through a standard Web interface.

Can Content Be Personalized Enough to Be Effective?

Straight push channels download huge amounts of information, only a tiny fraction of which is usually relevant to each individual. If it is difficult to effectively personalize the content, it may be safer to let users find it for themselves on the Web.

This concludes the survey of maintenance and update technologies for dynamic Web sites. In the following chapters, the theoretical perspective is extended to an analysis of dynamic sites operating on the Web today. After a brief exposition detailing characteristics of particular kinds of dynamic sites, case studies are presented. These will show the reader how various components of dynamic site hardware and software are assembled to create practical solutions to real-world problems.

PART FOUR

DYNAMIC MEDIA STRATEGIES

CONTENT PROMOTION AND SALES

The Consumer Model

Promoting and selling goods and services over the Internet has become one of the main forces driving the development of dynamic Web sites. In a survey reported in *USA Today* (www.usatoday.com), electronic commerce in 1997 was estimated at $5.7 billion and is expected to grow to $117 billion by the year 2000. There are two main reasons for this startling growth. First, the unlimited "shelf space" in cyberspace allows support for huge, searchable product catalogs—allowing rare and hard-to-find items to be sold economically. Second, application of dynamic Web technology makes these systems easier to maintain and more responsive to the customer than comparable "real world" stores. Promotional sites with dynamically updated information are popular even when nothing is sold. The 1997 Nielsen Commerce study (www .nielsenmedia.com) indicated that only 20 percent of Internet users bought products on line—but almost 60 percent used information on the Internet to guide an offline purchase. Many individuals reluctant to use the Web to purchase nevertheless look to it as an information resource to help them make purchasing decisions.

The Internet already features several success stories. In May 1997, Dell Computer announced that its site was receiving 250,000 unique visitors a week and sales in excess of $1 million per month; it outlined a plan to shift much of its marketing efforts to the Web. Other successful sites include Amazon.com (www.amazon.com) and the Internet Shopping Network (www.isn.com).

Features of Promotion/Sales Sites

Enabling sales and promotion through the Web requires extensive application of dynamic Web technology. Internet users expect online catalogs to be up to date and site operators to be responsive to their queries. Since online shopping is a relatively new experience and generally perceived as risky, most Web users are extremely sensitive to poorly maintained sites displaying obsolete information. Large product catalogs require advanced dynamic technology to manage sales and support interaction with their customers. Secure ordering systems are necessary to transfer credit card data and electronic cash tokens between the consumer and vendor, and information obtained must be compatible with existing accounting and ordering systems. Compared with other dynamic sites, content promotion and sales solutions share the following features:

- Since catalogs typically change on a scale of weeks or months, update frequencies and percentages are lower than for other kinds of dynamic content.

- Updates usually come from a single vendor or group of vendors using the site. This centralizes the source of updates and makes it easier to create an update team to manage content.

- Catalog information is frequently available through well-organized databases and only requires installation of a Web/database gateway for use.

- Bandwidth requirements for online catalogs tend to be lower than sites in which online audio, video, and multimedia form their main products.

- For sites without the resources to operate their own commerce systems, numerous remote hosting services offer support for commerce as part of their rental fee.

At present, most groups frequently update their site information manually and have not implemented automated dynamic systems. According to the 1997 Activmedia Survey (www.activmedia.com), only 20 percent of sales and promoted sites use advanced dynamic technology to manage transactions, and only 5 percent have developed end-to-end automation. However, this is changing rapidly: 30 percent of the commerce sites surveyed expect to add an automated dynamic content system by the end of 1997.

Components of Dynamic Promotion and Sales Sites

Groups specializing in online product promotion and distribution should integrate a variety of dynamic software components. Current pricing, and correct calculation of sales tax and shipping costs need to be maintained for a global customer base. If more than one vendor supplies product information, the update team must ensure timely updates and honesty about price, quality, and performance. Sites processing sensitive information such as credit cards and personal demographics need strong security to ensure the safety of their customers. Finally, groups with dynamic sites must actively curate external links exchanged with other sites, since increased traffic leads directly to sales. As with many other areas of the Internet, there is an often confusing array of options available for setting up and maintaining dynamic storefronts.

Product Catalog

The core of each dynamic promotion and sales system is a database containing detailed product descriptions. The database should be organized in a way that facilitates both searches by users and modifications by the update team. Most commercial software designed for smaller sites provides a built-in database. Examples of commercial catalog software are listed in Table 7.1. For large sites that integrate legacy databases, products such as Intelligent Environments' Amazon (www.ieinc.com; $2,495; multiple platforms) system allows existing infrastructure to be used for online commerce.

Table 7.1 Commercial Web-Based Catalog Software Packages

Catalog Software Package	What It Does
Microsoft's Merchant Server http://www.microsoft.com $4,999; Windows NT	Integrates its Merchant server into its Enterprise site server to create a comprehensive environment for Windows NT-based commerce systems.
IBM's Net.Commerce System www.internet.ibm.com/ commercepoint $4,995; Unix, Windows NT	Storefront authoring environment for Netscape servers. Connects to ODBC and IBM's own DB2 database format. Support for SET and price display can be controlled for consumer vs. wholesale purchases.
iCat's Electronic Commerce Suite www.icat.com $9,995; Mac, Unix, Windows 95/NT	Storefront development system supporting InternetSecure, Credit Card Network, Mac/PC Authorize, CyberCash, First Virtual, and Central Technologies accounting systems.
EveryWare Tango Merchant www.everyware.com $1,995; Mac, Windows NT	Provides a visual storefront development environment coupled with complete support for electronic commerce. The

Table 7.1 *Continued*

Catalog Software Package	What It Does
	system directly supports EveryWare's Connected Accounting software for back-end processing.
ICentral Incorporated ShopSite www.icentral.com Unix	Dynamic system designed for frequent changes in products and prices in large catalogs through a point-and-click interface to an SSL-capable "shopping cart" style system. Works with credit card verification systems and First Virtual.
Mercantec www.mercantec.com $1,080	Shopping cart metaphor supports a large number of back-end systems for product catalogs, credit cards, cybercash, orders, fulfillment databases, accounting services, and shipping (including UPS and Federal Express).
Global Business Communications www.globus.com Unix	Java-based software package for Web sites supporting distribution and retailing. Product databases can be generated directly from imported MS Access, DBase, or Excel.
NetConsult Communications www.netconsult.com $5,000; Windows NT/Unix	Software enabling a front-end catalog system with a large set of back-end processing features. The catalog works with an integrated Sybase SQL database.
The Vision Factory Cat@log www.thevisionfactory.com $4,995; Unix, Windows NT	Provides tools for storefront creation and processing options including VeriFone vPOS, CyberCash, and First Virtual.

Product Classification System

In addition to the basic catalog, additional classifying software helps customers find what they are looking for. Most databases allow keyword searches (e.g., product name and catalog number). Many also allow searches using *attributes,* basic features that are shared by several products and vary in a consistent way. Examples of attributes include price, color, and model. Object-oriented databases (Chapter 5) are often used to store attributes, since they manage this information in a more intuitive way than relational database tables. To implement attribute searches for large catalogs, high-end object systems such as the Krakatoa system from Cadis Software (www.cadis.com) are necessary. This system allows the developer to create arbitrary attributes and assign them to existing database information. Since attribute searches allow comparison shopping, they are likely to become increasingly common as the size of online catalogs increases.

User Interface

Most commerce systems use CGI or other external programs to create fill-out order forms linked to product descriptions. An example of a fill-out form from the authors' Kaleidospace site is shown in Figure 7.1. The order forms have the advantage of familiarity, but the customers must fill out a new form each time they select new products. To overcome this problem, most dynamic order systems support the *shopping cart* metaphor. At the beginning of a session, visitors check out empty carts and add items to them as they continue to explore the site. At any time, they can "open" the carts to see what they have already bought, and add or remove items. At the end of the session, orders are confirmed and paid for during a "check out" process. While powerful and well-suited to Web catalogs, shopping carts may be difficult for new Web users to understand.

Secure Servers

Most commerce packages handle sensitive information using the digital SSL (Secure Sockets Layer) authentication systems developed by

Figure 7.1 Kaleidospace (kspace.com) artist page order form.

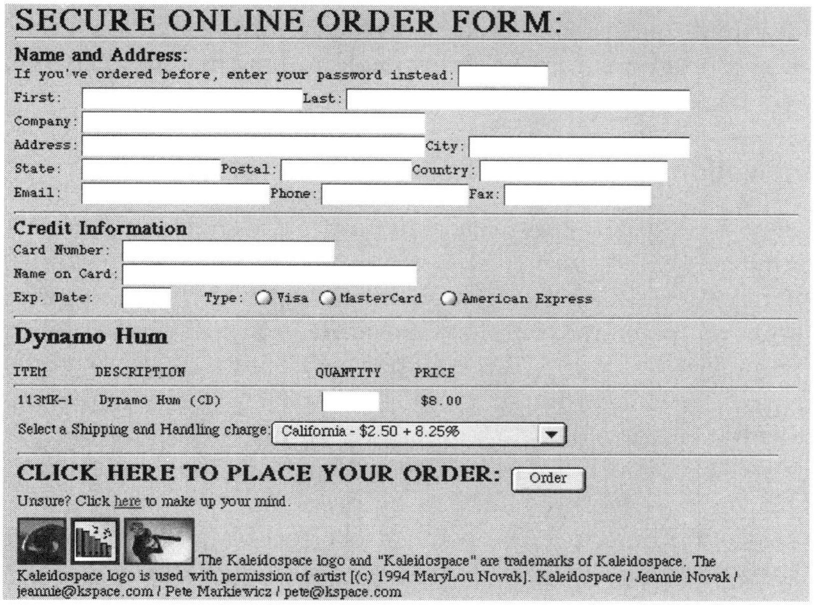

SECURE ONLINE ORDER FORM:

Name and Address:
If you've ordered before, enter your password instead:

First: Last:
Company:
Address: City:
State: Postal: Country:
Email: Phone: Fax:

Credit Information
Card Number:
Name on Card:
Exp. Date: Type: ○ Visa ○ MasterCard ○ American Express

Dynamo Hum

ITEM	DESCRIPTION	QUANTITY	PRICE
113MK-1	Dynamo Hum (CD)		$8.00

Select a Shipping and Handling charge: California - $2.50 + 8.25% ▼

CLICK HERE TO PLACE YOUR ORDER: [Order]

Unsure? Click here to make up your mind.

The Kaleidospace logo and "Kaleidospace" are trademarks of Kaleidospace. The Kaleidospace logo is used with permission of artist [(c) 1994 MaryLou Novak]. Kaleidospace / Jeannie Novak / jeannie@kspace.com / Pete Markiewicz / pete@kspace.com

VeriSign (www.verisign.com) and S-HTTP (Secure HyperText Transfer Protocol) for handling sensitive information. A few programs, such as IBM's Net.Commerce (www.internet.ibm.com/commercepoint; $4,995; Unix, Windows NT) system, support the new *Secure Electronic Transaction (SET)* protocol. Orders processed in this way are relatively safe, but the maintenance team's real job is hardly over once orders are collected. Since over 90 percent of recorded information thefts are "inside jobs," the development team needs to enforce security at all levels in the organization. Groups that don't want to deal with these problems may opt to sign up for a secure transaction service offered by their ISP. In choosing secure transaction software for promotion and sales, the development group should use development and programming resources as a guide. Commerce software varies from low-cost, CGI-based fill-out forms to complex adaptive systems designed to integrate with corporate mainframes costing hundreds of thousands of dollars. Many of the less-expensive packages require the services of programmers experienced in the Perl programming language, and high-end systems may require equally high-end hardware. Installation of CGI-based programs may be unavailable for sites running shared virtual servers (see Chapter 3).

Payment Validation and Management

Most businesses already capture credit card payments using proprietary online software. Since these systems do not interface with the Web, their use requires an extra step on the part of the site operators. Standards for credit and debit authorization include VeriFone vPOS (www.verifone.com), IBM's CommercePoint (www.ibm.com), and ICVerify's MacAuthorize and PCAuthorize (www.mktmkt .com/ic.html). Advanced Web commerce software has automatic built-in credit card validation, and it accepts/rejects sales in real time. This increases site dynamism by providing immediate feedback to customers, and it reduces time and effort by the business. An alternative to standard credit card processing is provided by CyberCash (www.cybercash.com). To initiate a transaction, the buyers indicate the products they want to purchase. The merchant returns an electronic invoice for confirmation. When both sides confirm the sale, encrypted credit/debit card information is forwarded directly to CyberCash, along with encrypted information identifying the merchant. The advantage of the CyberCash system is that the merchant never needs to read or store credit card numbers on a local system. Businesses handling credit cards and/or electronic cash should set up merchant accounts. Examples of Web-aware companies offering merchant accounts include Cardservice International (www.cardservice.com). Groups that don't qualify for merchant accounts may have to restrict sales to checks and money orders.

E-Cash and Micropayments

Due to the perceived dangers of the Internet, several groups have developed systems that completely avoid transferring card numbers.

First Virtual (www.firstvirtual.com) provides consumers with an ATM-style Virtual PIN number. To make a purchase, the customer sends email to the merchant with the PIN number. First Virtual returns an email confirmation before charging the customer's account. E-cash systems from DigiCash (www.digicash.com) come closer to true digital money, allowing Web users to buy virtual money and place it on their own computers in a software "wallet." Upon purchasing a product, the e-cash software notifies the e-cash bank and charges the visitor's credit card. By using this method, the only numbers transmitted online refer to the particular transaction and cannot be used by hackers to make additional purchases. Some e-cash systems also support microtransactions—payments ranging down to fractions of a cent for goods and services. Despite the promise, e-cash has taken off slowly and 1997 users numbered in the tens of thousands—versus hundreds of millions of credit card users.

Back-Office Order Fulfillment

Managing sales requires moving information from the Web to existing order processing and accounting systems. The development group's current software should support Web access. Sales information from the Web also needs to reach systems used for accounting, tax preparation, and sales reports. Many Web-based commerce packages output results in database or spreadsheet formats suitable for import into these programs, and a few provide live links to the software.

Customer Databases

Using the technology described in Chapter 6, passively collected customer tracking information is always supplemented with actively provided sales information. Both are combined to create a customer database that will allow the site to be dynamically modified to maximize sales. Database information may be used for personalized marketing, bonus programs, and to push new product announcements to registered customers.

Customer Service/Help Desk

Software providing chat, conference, or Internet telephony is used to provide live support desk information to customers as they shop. Live interaction may be coupled with quick access to product information and brochures. Systems are also being developed that allow telephone-style conversations through the Web, and that tie Web queries directly to phone response by customer representatives. On some sites, it may be useful to let customers talk to each other as well as to the help desk; collaborative filtering systems (Chapter 6) allow users to recommend products to each other, and chat rooms turn a virtual billboard into a true hangout.

Case Study: Luminous Dataworks' MoviePeople

URL: moviepeople.hollywood.com (see Figure 7.2)

Contact: Scott Vanderbilt

Email: scott@lumdata.com

Size of Web site (pages): 1 HTML page (all others generated by database queries)

Pages with dynamic content: 100%

Weekly visitors: 1,600,000 hits; 140,000 unique IPs

Site online: June 1997

Dynamic content online: June 1997

MoviePeople is an example of a promotional service designed to sell advertising space and to encourage offline movie-related purchases. Part of Hollywood Online (www.hollywood.com),

MoviePeople is a specialty database that allows visitors to search for particular actors, directors, and feature films. The site's relatively simple function is an extremely popular one, and an ever-growing list of films makes the site highly dynamic.

Infrastructure

The high-volume servers hosting the MoviePeople site were originally stored in house on the Hollywood Online's internal LAN. As traffic grew, it was necessary to move the server out to a T3 line set directly on the ISP's NAP, or Network Access Point (Chapter 2). MoviePeople is powered by a Dell PowerEdge 4100 with 256

Figure 7.2 MoviePeople (moviepeople.hollywood.com).

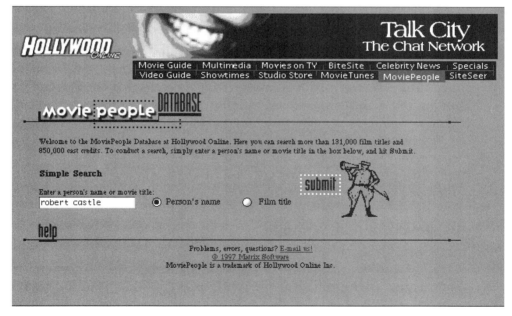

megabytes of RAM and a single 9-gigabyte hard drive running Windows NT. A proprietary Web server integrated directly with the database is used to search and process user queries.

Team Structure

The developers modeled their maintenance and update groups after film production and had close connections to the arts and entertainment supported by Hollywood Online. Working within a predefined budget, the team managers developed a series of custom programs for use within the site. The division of labor within the team is simple compared to many other dynamic sites; job responsibilities are divided between administration and database entry.

Site Maintenance

The maintenance team has developed proprietary, inhouse methods for log analysis and site management. Access logs are collected and analyzed to determine DPOs (distinct points of origin) and page turns (ad impressions). The site experiences occasional sharp traffic increases associated with film-related events. To manage the traffic spikes, the maintenance team relies on direct server monitoring and does not employ specialized load-balancing or other tools. Since searches output tables with text information, performance decay under high traffic is less than graphic-heavy sites. The maintenance team backs up the servers with 4-mm DAT tape drives and stores information on development servers.

Dynamic Content Strategy

MoviePeople is designed to provide a steady supply of information concerning high-profile actors and feature films. Such content attracts a large general audience, and the main goal of the developers is to create a site that encourages repeat visits through dynamic content. The information on the site originates in an Xbase set of tables that is licensed from a third party. Tables are added to the database on a regular schedule following a periodic publishing model. A custom Web application was programmed to serve the data, and no Web/database gateway was necessary. The database creates pages on the fly and integrates advertising banners with search results. Information is also combined with non-Web documents such as word processor files. Adding the regular updates is a major challenge for the developers, since their typical monthly throughput is 750 megabytes of data or more. The near complete reliance on a database allows rollback of the site to display older information simply by restoring archived database files. Rollbacks, however, are unlikely occurrences; information turns over too quickly for archives to be of much value. Obsolete information is removed manually and is not archived on the site. An example of search result output is shown in Figure 7.3.

Interface

MoviePeople is a relatively new site, and no interface changes have been necessary since it went on line in 1997. Since the purpose of the site is to search a database for text listings of actors and films, graphics are kept to a minimum. The basic interface was standardized using a manually produced template and is maintained by the server/database system through on-the-fly page generation. Information in the logs has only a marginal effect on the way in which dynamic content is presented to the audience.

Future Plans

MoviePeople has not revealed long-term plans, but possibilities include access to more film-related information (e.g., detailed actor and director biographies), and links to audio and video archives of films discovered in searches. With time, the site is likely to move from its indirect promotional status and provide links allowing visitors to order video copies of films discovered in the database.

Figure 7.3 Example of MoviePeople search results.

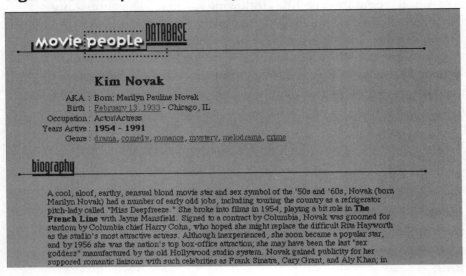

Case Study: Ostry Internet Solutions

URL: www.ostry.com (see Figure 7.4)

Contact: Bernd Hilmar

Email: service@ostry.com

Size of Web site (pages): 70 pages on main site; approximately 1,000 client pages

Pages with dynamic content: 10%

Weekly visitors: 30,000 hits; 2,000 unique IPs

Site online: September 1996

Dynamic content online: November 1996

Ostry Internet Solutions (OIS) is a Web development group located in Vienna, Austria, that has created dynamic content for its

Figure 7.4 Ostry Internet Solutions (www.ostry.com).

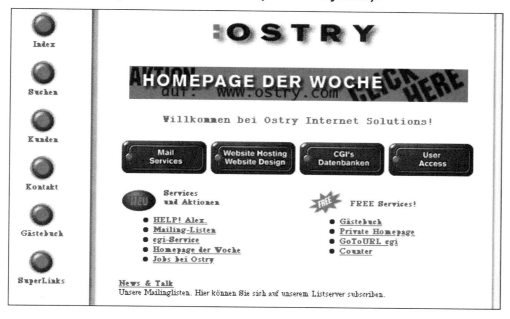

own site and for its sales clients—including an office supply store, an online kitchenware catalog, and a gateway for a used car database. The client sites function in concert with OIS's main site, sharing common hardware and software platforms. OIS also operates a search engine called Multisubmit (www.multisubmit.at) aimed at the Austrian- and German-speaking visitors who form 99 percent of their audience. OIS has taken the unusual step of implementing dynamic sites using Macintosh-based Web servers coupled to an ACI 4th-Dimension (www.aci-4D.com) relational database.

Infrastructure

The OIS site is served from a Macintosh PowerPC 9600 running at 200MHz with 96 megabytes of RAM and 2 gigabytes of disk space. The site communicates with the Internet through a T1 line. A

Webstar server from Starnine (www.starnine.com) capable of supporting secure transactions powers the site. Email is supported through the Apple Mailserver (www.apple.com) and sendmail (www.sendmail.org). Static Web pages are delivered by a Windows NT server.

Team Structure

Site maintenance and updates are organized around an online catalog model. Despite the small size of the site, OIS has established formal positions for Producer, Editor, and Webmaster/Administrator. An organizational flowchart of the site is used to assign maintenance and update jobs, which are assigned through PaperNet, email messages, and during conferences using personalized chat software via SoftArc's FirstClass (www.softarc.com) bulletin board system. According to the developers, Mac-based bulletin board software such as FirstClass and Spider Island (www.spiderisland.com) provides a viable alternative to more expensive groupware on Windows and Unix systems.

Site Maintenance

Site activity on the Macintosh server is monitored using KeepItUp and AutoBoot (www.vl-brabant.be/mac/) shareware. These applications help to overcome the Mac's crash-prone behavior relative to Unix and Windows NT. KeepItUp monitors the Webstar server and restarts it when it quits. If it can't be restarted, it reboots the entire system. AutoBoot detects "bomb" messages and restarts the Mac. When they are out of the office, the administrators use Farallon's Timbuktu (www.farallon.com) to administer the system. The program provides full access and a copy of the remote Mac's screen on the administrator's computer. Log analysis is supported by LogDoor, a custom 4th Dimension database application. User queries are routed through a Maxum Phantom (www.maxum.com) search engine and stored for analysis. Combining this information with log data provides a simple method to dynamically adjust the site to visitor traffic. The directory structure of the site has been modified to accommodate changes in content and interface. The site is backed up through standard SCSI tape drives.

Dynamic Content Strategy

Content is derived from original documents, repurposed word processor information, user-contributed information, and dynamic content served directly from a 4th Dimension database. Since the Windows NT server delivers static pages, Mac traffic is entirely confined to dynamic pages generated by the 4D database. OIS uses the NetLink/4D (www.foresight.com/) gateway, which is also used on the Windows NT server. Other dynamic elements (e.g., client response forms and mailing lists) are created using Maxum's (www .maxum.com) NetCloak and NetForms programs. Updates to company and client sites follow an incremental strategy, and new information is posted as it becomes available. Automated dynamic media elements (such as page counters) are created through CGI scripts, some of which link directly to the 4th Dimension database. Email response from customers is supported through NetForms. Outdated content is discovered through manual inspection of the site, user messages, and by running search/replace queries in HTML editors. Old information is archived rather than being removed. An example of an order form in the OIS system is shown in Figure 7.5.

Interface

Frequent interface changes are made on the OIS site in order to show activity to regular clients. Three updates occurred in the first year of site operation, and more are expected in the future. Interface adjustment decisions are based on visitor origin. Since the site serves many German- and Austrian-speaking visitors, parallel pages in

Figure 7.5 Example of language-specific order form on the OIS Web site.

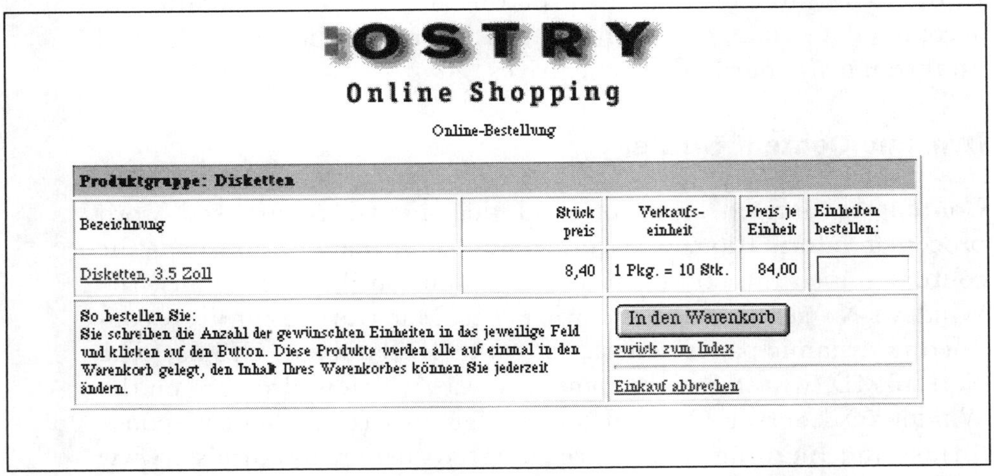

┊OSTRY

Online Shopping

Online-Bestellung

Produktgruppe: Disketten				
Bezeichnung	Stück preis	Verkaufs- einheit	Preis je Einheit	Einheiten bestellen:
Disketten, 3.5 Zoll	8,40	1 Pkg. = 10 Stk.	84,00	

So bestellen Sie:
Sie schreiben die Anzahl der gewünschten Einheiten in das jeweilige Feld und klicken auf den Button. Diese Produkte werden alle auf einmal in den Warenkorb gelegt, den Inhalt Ihres Warenkorbes können Sie jederzeit ändern.

In den Warenkorb

zurück zum Index

Einkauf abbrechen

English and German are maintained as part of the interface. To standardize its interface, OIS uses a mixture of manually generated HTML templates and Cascading Style Sheets (CSS).

Future Trends

OIS expects the proportion of dynamic pages onsite to triple to 30 percent toward the end of 1997. Despite increasing traffic, the developers have no plans to migrate from the Mac-based system, and instead look forward to improvements in Apple's System 8 and the forthcoming multitasking Rhapsody operating system.

Case Study: PJW Associates' Claims Information Network Site

URL: lossnet.com.au (members only; see Figure 7.6)

Contact: Paul J. Willemse

Figure 7.6 Claims Information Network Site (lossnet.com.au).

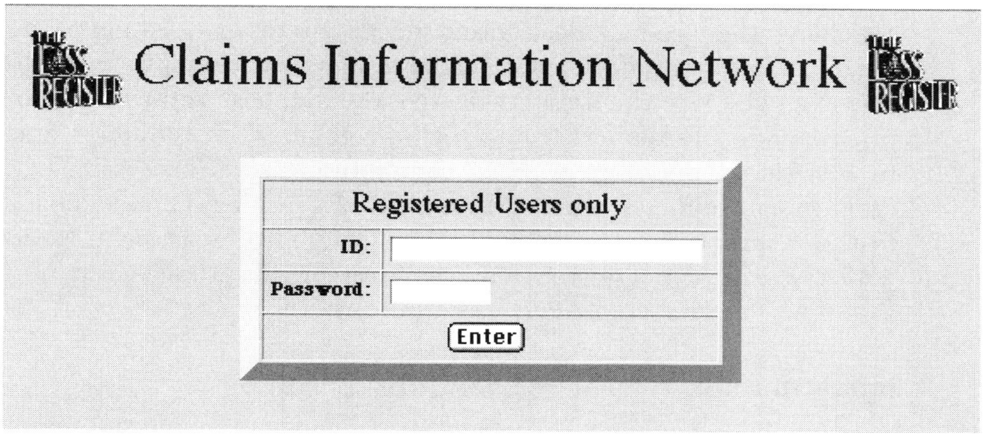

Email: admin@lossreg.com.au

Size of Web site (pages): 1 HTML page (all others generated by database queries)

Pages with dynamic content: 100%

Weekly visitors: 150,000 hits; 150 unique IPs

Site online: February 1997

Dynamic content online: February 1997

The *Claims Information Network Site* (*CINS*) provides an unusual variation of the standard sales and promotion model. On this members-only system, insurance claims adjusters use dynamic Web technology to complete claim forms, approve replacement items, and order replacements via a shopping cart system. The replacement for a lost, stolen, or destroyed item is selected from a database containing information about common items lost in thefts and fires—including TVs, VCRs, radios, and appliances. To use CINS, the insurance adjuster enters a description of the item provided by the customer. Consulting its information, the database returns all products satisfying the product description. If the item in question is no longer manufactured, the system suggests a replacement similar to the original. Once the item is selected, the database returns a list of prices and local suppliers from which the claims adjuster adds items to a virtual shopping cat. After completing claims processing, an order is sent to the supplier and a copy of the invoice is emailed back to the insurance company. Other database features assist in fraud detection and help adjusters locate contractors for property repair—as well as lawyers, engineers, and other professionals.

Infrastructure

CINS operates from a PowerMac 8100/100 with 128 megabytes of RAM and 4.3 gigabytes of hard disk space. It is currently accessed through an ISDN line, though higher speed access may be available in the future. Despite the relatively slow speed of the connection, evidence of traffic congestion has not appeared in the access logs. WS4D (www.mdg.com) Web server software is used, which consists of a 4th Dimension database modified to handled Web traffic. The total integration eliminates the need for a database gateway, allowing direct programming in native 4D and resulting in very fast execution of HTTP commands. Additional Unix/NT systems are maintained and update databases for use by the data entry staff. System backups write to removable disk drives.

Team Structure

Production on CINS is organized along the lines of retail catalog publishing. Work is assigned through PaperNet and EmailNet, augmented with custom software developed in house to support collaboration. Individual job descriptions include writers, fact-checkers, media converters, and site testers who search for obsolete content. Several staff members collect data for replacement items from vendors and suppliers. An Editor heading the team makes final decisions on whether content is posted to the site.

Site Maintenance

The default WS4D server feature set provides built-in performance and traffic monitoring features. Internal routines check page download times. To keep the site running, a custom AppleScript monitors the server and restarts it when necessary. Additional log analysis utilizes programs developed in house. Since it is a membership-based site, traffic is predictable and does not show major spikes. The developers monitor traffic and adjust payment for the service based on transactions through proprietary software.

Dynamic Content Strategy

The main goal of this site is to provide extremely specific information to a specialized group of professionals. The main determinant for the update strategy is accuracy, since old or incorrect information could result in a waste of time and money. Update information from the vendors/suppliers is delivered in the form of postal letters, diskettes, and email. The update team maintains one single page of static HTML. All intermediate pages allowing database queries are dynamically generated. Dynamic page output includes HTML and JavaScript. Information is posted as it appears to staging servers, after which it is cleared for the public site. Depending on content, updates are either posted as received or at fixed periods (four times daily). The update team typically adds 100 or more items to the database every day. An insurer using the database and discovering that a replacement is unavailable may indicate this through a "backup" entry. Upon receiving the message, the developers locate a source for the item and add it to the database. Keeping the database up to date is one of the biggest challenges faced by the developers. Rapidly changing information includes product prices and status, such as whether a product is obsolete or has been replaced by a new model. To keep information current, CINS uses custom database tags to detect and remove obsolete material. Content is also checked secondarily by a team member using a search/replace program. CINS does not personalize for individual insurers, but access log statistics are used to fine-tune features of the site. Based on traffic, certain areas are emphasized or deemphasized over time. Understanding visitor access is also facilitated by tracking visitor clickstreams with the use of cookies. An example of database results on CINS is illustrated in Figure 7.7.

Interface

With a low-bandwidth connection, virtually all of the CINS interface is implemented using HTML tables and fill-out forms. Graphics are confined to a single 5-kilobyte image repeated on most pages. The completely dynamic nature of the site allows the user interface to be adjusted by direct manipulations of the 4D database. In keeping with this flexibility, there have been six interface changes since the site was launched—or about one per month. The primary motivation for interface modifications was to support new types of dynamic content.

Figure 7.7 Web/database gateway example on CINS.

Since all content is dynamic, no changes to file or directory structures have been necessary.

Future Plans

CINS will be implementing several new services and features, many of which are centered around making the service faster and personalizing the service for individual insurers. Another goal is providing vendors/suppliers with direct site connections so they may update their own product information. Long term, the site will likely evolve from simple sales to a "matchmaking" service integrating the insurance companies and vendors into a tight online community.

The case studies shown here demonstrate several features of real-world dynamic sites promoting or supporting electronic commerce. All of the sites described began with an existing database and developed their own middleware solution to support their sites. In some cases, such as the MoviePeople site, dynamic content is purely promotional and sales dollars come from advertising banners posted on each Web page. When online catalogs are implemented, they may share common hardware and software platforms—as in the OIS example. Despite the perception that commerce sites must be huge, neither OIS nor CINS run high-end servers. Both groups get along comfortably with Macintosh-based database systems, and CINS effectively conducts business with an Internet connection comparable to a 56k consumer modem. CINS points out additional interesting trends. While the site provides a searchable product catalog, it has been tailored to an extremely specific niche market that must join CINS to participate. This illustrates that online sales may benefit from strategies that target a specific audience, which OIS also does with its support for multiple languages. By integrating buyers and sellers into the same system, the CINS strategy is moving away from simple commerce toward a virtual marketplace of vendors and buyers. Such sites—deriving most of their content directly from users—form the subject of the next chapter.

USER-DRIVEN SITES

The Community Model

One of the most popular and unique types of dynamic sites on the Internet allows visitors to add to the site's content or interface. These sites contain dynamic content that directly reflects the Internet audience, rather than the interests of the developers. In other media, this might be seen as a recipe for mediocrity, but user-driven sites comprise the single most popular area of the Web. Examples include search engines such as Yahoo! (www.yahoo.com), discussion groups such as the Usenet gateway DejaNews (www.dejanews.com), and chat sites such as Talk City (www.talkcity.com) and the Web Broadcasting System (www.wbs.com), which allow visitors to interact with each other as well as with the site. Other sites facilitate interactions between buyers and sellers and provide a forum for artists and entertainers to promote their work. User-driven content also includes classified ads, collaborative storytelling, opinion polls, virtual music jams, and graffiti walls.

Features of User-Driven Sites

A key difference between user-driven sites and other dynamic models is that the developers act in a facilitator (rather than creative) role. The update team may design interfaces and schedule events, but it is up to the visitors themselves to provide content that keeps the site interesting. The requirement for user input results in several unique features, discussed next.

Prosumer Content

By providing information on the site, the audience takes on two seemingly opposing roles: producer and consumer. This hybrid *prosumer* role was originally predicted by author Alvin Toffler and is crucial to the success of user-driven sites. The typical prosumer is not a professional developer and the information will reflect a different orientation than standard promotional or marketing content.

Real-Time

Most user-driven sites operate in real or near-real time, allowing individuals to post and respond to messages as they appear. Since CGI or other external programs typically mediate user posts, there are greater demands on hardware and software than with less interactive sites. The demands of real-time chat programs may approach the requirements of Webcasting (Chapter 10), since users maintain continuous or near-continuous connections to the site during their conversations.

Proprietary Software

Like online games and auctions (Chapter 12), real-time user input frequently requires installation of proprietary software. Sites that only allow text postings can often use HTML-based fill-out forms. In contrast, custom clients are usually needed to support interface features difficult to implement in standard HTML, including instant screen refreshes, paging systems, real-time animation, audio, and video. With the rise of Java, some groups are moving away from standard clients to invisibly downloaded applets that perform similar functions.

Editorial Input

Since content is provided by "nonprofessionals," it may not be up to the standards of spelling, grammar, punctuation, and style found on other sites. The developers may need to edit posted material directly, or place it in a context where it is readily understood. The developers also need to develop an interface that presents the user contributions effectively. A good example of this is the DejaNews site mentioned earlier. While it operates in much the same way as standard Usenet, its Web interface attracts visitors who are confused by standard Usenet read/post systems. In particular, the search engine on the site is much easier to understand and use than comparable commands in Usenet-specific programs.

Calendar Information

User-contributed information is frequently time sensitive. For example, classified ads may need to appear before a certain date, and be taken down after that time. Older information on the site needs to be dated so that users can place it in the right perspective. Good user-driven sites usually supply several ways of finding calendar-based information, including sorted lists and database searches for content posted at particular dates and times. If the site runs paid classified postings, a calendar system is necessary to determine when to remove the ad, as well as bill for the time the ad ran on the site.

Content Liability

Public forums have the potential for many forms of abuse. Examples include harassment of individuals in chat rooms, defamation of character, solicitation of illegal acts, and inappropriate conversations with minors. In most cases, it is the responsibility of the site administrators to manage these problems. User-driven sites must have systems in place for reporting abuse and shutting out the problem individual. Since user-driven sites frequently cater to a general audience, it may also be necessary to rate the site using PICS (www .w3.org/pub/WWW/PICS/raters.htm) or other systems.

Links to Other Sites

Many individuals contributing to user-driven sites also maintain material elsewhere on the Web, including personal home pages and contact information. Most user-driven sites encourage visitors to provide access to their own resources, and to use the main site as a forum for promotion and publicity. In the extreme case, the user-driven site becomes a tool for finding other sites.

Components of User-Driven Sites

Programs supporting chat and threaded postings were discussed previously in Chapter 5, along with groupware and collaborative software. Many of these same systems find direct application on user-driven sites. In addition to these programs, more specific technology for enabling user content may be found in general directories such as Forum One Software Products and Reviews (freenet .msp.mn.us/~dwool/webconf.html), (www.prosody.com/ForumOne/ products.htm) and the Gamelan Java Chat Index (www.gamelan .com/pages/Gamelan.net.chat.html). Following is a series of user-driven site components.

Fill-Out Forms

Most user-driven sites implement fill-out forms to manage registration, updates of personal information, comments, and even access to threaded discussions. Forms may be used to register users for members-only areas and serve as an interface for external chat and posting software. Forms may also be used to report problems with the site or inform the developers of individuals causing problems within the community. Most sites process forms information through CGI programs that test the data and process it for inclusion in databases or email messages. In some cases, the forms are generated as part of a larger document management system and feed directly into databases. Sites that retain user information sometimes give members the option of modifying their information through password-protected fill-out forms.

Discussion Forums

Forums provide ongoing discussions with a recorded history that anyone may access prior to making a contribution. In addition to the systems discussed in Chapter 5, several other packages should be considered by the developers. Groups operating virtually any site could adapt the free set of scripts for chat and bulletin boards at Matt's Script Archive (www.worldwidemart.com/scripts/wwwboard.shtml). At the low end of commercial software, Virtual Publisher (www.virtualpublisher.com; $75–$500; Windows NT/Unix) produces several CGI products for adding interactivity, including chat software, bulletin boards, classifieds, trivia questions, and opinion poll surveys. Other discussion-based systems include Lundeen's Web Crossing (webx.lundeen.com; 0–$199; Unix, Windows NT), DigitalFacades Xpound! (www.xpound.com; $1,195–$4,995 ; Windows NT, Unix), and Post On The Fly Conference (www.homecom.com/conference; $495; Windows NT/Unix).

Classifieds

Sites supporting commercial exchanges frequently allow visitors to post announcements of goods and services for sale. Classified sites showcase material ranging from used equipment to job résumés. As with chat, many freeware and shareware CGI-based classified programs are available from the CGI Resources Index (www .cgiresources.com). Commercial packages for classified ads are rare, but most discussion groups may be modified to support classified content. To support classifieds it is a good idea to provide ad-specific search functions based on pricing, geographic location, and product attributes like size or model year.

HTML-Based Chat

Many freeware CGI script packages provide a simple form of user-to-user chat based entirely in HTML. Examples of such systems include FreeChat (zippy.sonoma.edu/kendrick/nbs/unix/www/ freechat; Unix), which supports HTML text with icons representing individual chatters. Administrative functions include defining a variety of user levels (registered, sysop), access to icon databases, and the ability for individuals to exchange private messages outside the main discussion. Go.com (www.go.com; $50/month license; all platforms) provides a relatively inexpensive commercial alternative. This remotely hosted service provides public and private messages, user profiles, interactive games, graphic avatars, email, and instant messaging—without using Java or plug-ins. IChat (www.ichat.com; $595 for 25 concurrent users; Windows NT) provides a sophisticated text-based chat environment that also provides a notification service. Higher-end systems include Webmaster's WebMaster (www .webmaster.com; $495 for 1000 users; Windows NT/95) chat client and server software. This Java-based IRC client manages thousands of simultaneous sessions.

Surveys and Polls

To further the feeling of an online community in the user's mind, many sites host opinion polls, tests, puzzles, and surveys. Standard CGI programs are easily developed for this purpose. Poll results allow each individual to see how other site visitors think and feel about issues. In this way, they help to convert a bulletin board into a regular hangout for visitors. They also provide a method to explicitly ask the audience content-oriented questions that might be raised by sales figures and access log statistics. In extreme cases, poll and survey input can be run through collaborative filtering software (Chapter 6), and material on the site is prioritized by the community as a whole.

Autobots

To keep conversations going, many sites implement automated programs that initiate and participate in ongoing discussions. These programs also function as virtual help desks within the ongoing discussion. *Autobots* may be implemented as CGI programs (Chapter 5) or through special scripting environments such as The Palace's Iptscrae (www.thepalace.com) language. Examples of functioning chatterbots may be found on sites such as Blue Platypus (www .blueplatypus.com). A few sites have implemented *adbots* that talk about products, though their effectiveness seems far from certain.

Virtual Worlds

While the *Virtual Reality Modeling Language* (VRML) was widely expected to convert the 2D world of the Web to a 3D environment, in 1997 most advanced systems use other means to provide a graphical sense of place to user-driven sites. Products including Ligos Software's VRealm Builder (205.131.23.2/ligos/) and Chaco Communications' Pueblo (www.chaco.com) show potential but have yet to gain significant audiences. The non-VRML Palace (www .thepalace.com; $2,995, 100 users; Macintosh, Unix, Windows NT) is currently the most common visual chat environment on the Web. Originally a non-Web client/server combination, it is currently being reimplemented in Java. Palace visitors use graphical avatars to move between rooms created with static graphic backgrounds. Skunk New Media's IsoView (www.skunkmedia.com; $2,995, Unix, Windows NT) and NetDive's CUChat (www.netdive.com; $499 for 60 users; all platforms) also provide a Java-based, cross-platform chat environment resembling The Palace.

Case Study: Artist Direct's Ultimate Band List

URL: www.ubl.com (see Figure 8.1)

Contact: Steve Rogers

Email: info@artistdirect.com

Size of Web site (pages): 10,000

Pages with dynamic content: 90%

Weekly visitors: >1,000,000 hits; 250,000 unique IPs

Site online: November 1994

Dynamic content online: November 1994

Artist Direct, an outgrowth of record label American Recordings' (american.recordings.com) pioneering work on the Web, provides several services to the online music world. The best known of these is the Ultimate Band List (UBL), one of the oldest and most popular music search engines on the Internet. Beginning as a posting board where unsigned bands could list their latest albums, it has grown into a comprehensive search service that includes radio stations, music professionals, record stores, clubs, concert venues, music news, and current music charts. The bulk of UBL content is posted directly by musicians, fans, labels, and industry professionals, and it is organized into a card-catalog style directory for effective searching. UBL also runs features on selected artists and offers con-

Figure 8.1 Ultimate Band List (www.ubl.com).

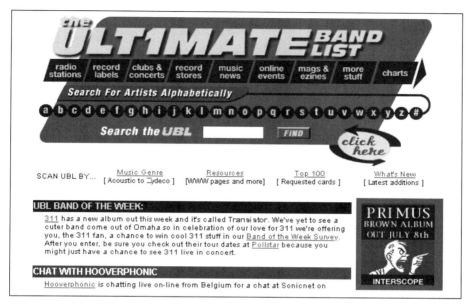

tests supported by labels and radio stations. Musicians with products sold through CDNow (www.cdnow.com) have links on their UBL pages leading directly to an order form for purchasing.

Infrastructure

The UBL server is a Sun Ultrasparc running Solaris on a high-speed network hosted remotely by an ISP. Standard Web server software is linked to a series of custom database and program applications developed in house. Reasons for this arrangement are partly historical, and partly due to the superior performance of Sun's relative to NT workstations.

Team Structure

The update team has defined specific jobs necessary for maintaining UBL, including collecting content, converting to Web format, testing of content online, and detecting outdated material. Since most of the content is automatically submitted by users to the database, maintenance and policing the site for incorrect information forms a major part of the work. Daily team interaction is organized through a mix of PaperNet documents, email messages, and face-to-face consultation. Despite the size of the site, the group does not use specialized management software or groupware to organize updates.

Site Maintenance

Many routine UBL maintenance functions are performed by the hosting service storing the server. The developers check the server using operating system-level tools, but no proprietary load-balancing or traffic management software has been installed. Instead, increases in traffic have been handled by upgrading the speed and capacity of the Sun workstation and by moving it directly onto the ISP's high-speed backbone. Additional speed was provided by upgrading the system's memory to prevent slowdowns caused by *paging* and other virtual memory processes. Backups are run through standard tape drives.

Dynamic Content Strategy

User-driven input forms the bulk of the site's content. As shown in Figure 8.2, the visitor supplies information in a series of fill-out forms that successively create a card describing the musician or group and their work. Information from the forms is sent to the site's custom database, one of the oldest continuously operating search engines on the Web. Page output formats include HTML, Java, and JavaScript, as well as links to audio and video files. Old content is flagged using a non-Internet calendar program that alerts the update team when

Figure 8.2 Sample user content contributed to UBL.

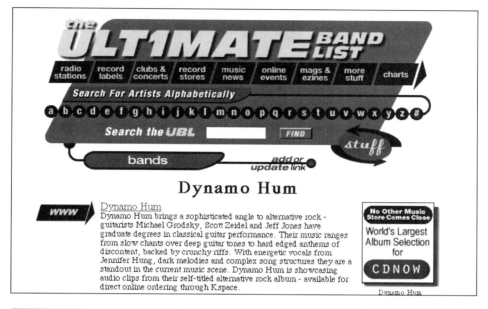

particular media elements have expired. In the future, Artist Direct will probably move its search engine to a commercial database and incorporate obsolete markup tags directly in UBL pages. Much of the old content retains its value, so it is archived on the site rather than completely removed. Artist Direct also integrates user-driven information submitted to UBL with promotional data sent by record labels and other advertisers. Nonuser information is accepted as text-only documents, audio, or video samples. To enforce this policy, the update group actively educated its contributors in marketing and publicity about media formats, thereby saving the update team considerable work. Server-side includes (Chapter 5) are also used to integrate dynamic media elements into UBL documents, while other information is added manually.

Interface

In its relatively long history on the Web, UBL has received four facelifts. Reasons for making interface changes include advancements in HTML/Web browser technology and improving navigation. The original, text-only interface has been supplanted by a combined navigation toolbar/search engine. As shown in Figure 8.2, the complete unity of search and navigation links into a single graphic object leaves the rest of the page free to display search results and advertising. Another strong reason for interface changes was product branding; UBL is one of the few recognizable brand names that originated on the Web. The initial site did not promote UBL as a distinct brand, but more recent versions emphasize it. Other changes include major reworking of file/directory structures and upgrading older static Web pages to dynamic, database-delivered form.

Future Plans

A key future project for Artist Direct is a *matchmaking* service designed to link touring musicians and venue operators. Within this Extranet, touring bands will post their planned tours, and booking agents will enter offers for particular venues. This method will streamline booking for major bands and will replace a "roomful" of wire-bound notebooks currently used by bands and agents. Artist Direct would also like to develop an inhouse sales system for consumers purchasing music discovered in UBL, closing the loop between user promotion and user sales.

Case Study: World Merchandise Exchange's Womex Online

URL: www.womex.com (see Figure 8.3)

Contact: Glenn Reyer

Email: marketing@womex.com

Size of Web site (pages): 1200

Pages with dynamic content: 18%

Weekly visitors: 200,000 hits; 35,000 unique IPs

Site online: July 1996

Dynamic content online: July 1996

Womex Online provides a Web-specific matchmaking service that links buyers and sellers handling large amounts of retail merchandise. Though technically a commerce site, it has evolved to

---

Figure 8.3 Womex Online (www.womex.com).

---

become a marketplace for user-driven content. The service focuses on the international trading community and acts as a facilitator by listing information supplied by its members. Items exchanged are usually durable goods destined for the mass merchandise market such as toys, electronics, and giftware. Womex actively solicits new retail clients, and helps them make the transition to the Internet. Large customers connect directly to Womex through a private Extranet that improves the reliability of information exchange relative to the public Internet. This very large site processes a high volume of information and maintains a thriving virtual community of buyers and sellers.

Infrastructure

The Womex servers are dedicated systems remotely hosted by a major ISP. The overall network consists of two Hewlett-Packard (HP) Unix K400 dual-processor computers running HP Unix, linked with 20 Windows NT servers. Each system has 256 megabytes of RAM, and the network has a combined disk space of 750 gigabytes. Web server software includes server products from Netscape, Microsoft's IIS server, and Oracle's integrated database/Web server. Visitors and general users connect to Womex through T1 lines leading to the public Internet. Clients that develop a closer relationship with Womex connect directly through private T1 lines forming the company's Extranet.

Team Structure

When designing its service, Womex felt that existing real-world production models did not apply as well to its system as did the matchmaking systems developed by companies such as America Online (www.aol.com). Accordingly, Womex set up its development group along an administrative model similar to online services. A head Web Administrator manages a large maintenance and update group including writers, editors, media conversion specialists, copy editors, fact-checkers, upload specialists, site testers, and traditional MIS personnel. Ensuring timeliness and accuracy of content is a particular concern, and multiple fact-checkers are necessary to cope with the high volume of contributed postings.

Site Maintenance

Server monitoring is accomplished with a mix of locally created utilities and HP Openview (www.dmo.hp.com/edserver/edserver.html). Increases in traffic are managed using load-bearing software running on the HP servers. Access to the site exhibits little variation, probably because Womex clients are distributed throughout the world and access the servers at all hours. Traffic is analyzed using a combination of access logs and tracking cookies. The complete network is backed up on a regular basis using a series of tape drives. The rapid growth of the service has required several major modifications, including mass changes of filenames, content movement between Web servers, and a steady conversion of static pages to dynamically generated pages.

Dynamic Content Strategy

The chief goal of the Womex site is to provide a matchmaking forum linking buyers and sellers in the import/export business. As such, dynamic content needs to support the creation of an online community as much as it provides a classified-type description of goods. The site update team processes widely divergent forms of content submitted by clients, including new products, industry news, and shipping schedules. Womex manages this complex update environment using Wallop Software's BuildIt (www.wallop.com). This comprehensive system provides complete control of site structure, document versions, staging servers, and editorial review prior to posting. Information updates are managed through a checkin/checkout system applied to all software and documents. Development begins on a primary server, and it passes through two distinct staging servers prior to public posting. Media types supported include HTML, Java,

JavaScript, and on-the-fly database-generated pages. Content is personalized for clients using a proprietary inhouse system. Obsolete material on the site is easily recognized through custom tags generated in the BuildIt environment and is removed from the site.

Interface

At present, the Womex Online interface is adjusted manually based on user traffic. Three major interface changes have been made since the service began, largely to support multiple browsers and to improve navigation within the service. Since Womex has many long-term members, interface changes also serve to increase member interest in the site and create a perception of an active and progressive company. Wallop's BuildIt was used to develop each new version of the site, and the information was subsequently transferred to the public Web server.

Future Plans

Womex expects to double the current percentage of on-the-fly pages served during its next year of operation. Content will become increasing personalized, and Womex is continuing to develop an advanced automated personalization system that would also provide content for push channels. In the future. Womex hopes to begin supporting direct sales of merchandise on its site.

These case studies show the effectiveness of the user-driven model for dynamic sites. The Ultimate Band List expands on the database gateway model for delivering Web content by opening it to public contribution. The end result is a site with unique and popular information that supports *one-to-many* advertising and sales. The Womex site extends the model by actively encouraging members to use the site as a forum for commercial exchange. In this case, user information consists of *one-to-one* transactions rather than postings intended for a larger audience. The Womex site is also unique in using a commercial document management system developed for the Web. Despite the wide variety of programs and utilities covered in Chapters 3 through 6, the majority of dynamic sites continue to utilize proprietary systems for development. It is likely that this situation will shift in the near future when older sites started in the pre-dynamic era are joined by new startups created specifically to take advantage of commercial software. Both examples also illustrate a common theme for all dynamic sites discussed in this book: Time and personnel resources are more limiting than hardware and software.

PERIODIC MEDIA SITES

SITES
The Publishing Model

O ne of the most powerful metaphors for visualizing the Web has been a global publishing system, one that emulates the text and graphics layout of printed documents while providing worldwide distribution at almost no cost. With this in mind, individuals and groups have flocked to the Internet to create thousands of online books, magazines, newspapers, bulletins, and guides published on a periodic basis. Periodic media formed the first form of dynamic content on the Web. Not content to showcase content that mimics their printed counterparts, these publishing sites incorporate audio, video, multimedia, and interactive controls. The simple mechanism used to hyperlink Web documents has also given rise to "content aggregators"—sites that select and organize news stories on other sites into shorthand bulletins. Other examples of periodic sites include episodic Web entertainment sites such as the psychologically oriented serial in Ferndale (www.ferndale.com) and the Web's first online soap opera, The Spot (www.thespot.com). Popular and easy to implement, publishing sites now form a major portion of information available on the Web.

Features of Periodic Media Sites

Periodic media sites are best defined by the mode of dynamic updating they require. Instead of constantly pushing new material onto the Web site, periodic media site update teams organize information into regular issues, dailies, or editions. This attracts visitors that regularly return to collect new information as part of their own daily schedules. In practice, most groups do not update the entire site at once, but add the information to the site as it becomes available. Online publishing design further regulates the appearance of updates by integrating them into regular features, editor columns, or topic-specific articles. Unlike other sites (e.g., product catalogs), these sites credit site content authors; the presence of a byline is important to the audience, since it implies editorial input as opposed to mere fact reporting. The following provides a breakdown of additional features common to many editorial sites.

Complement to Real-World Publications

Many publishing sites were started by existing newspapers, magazines, and media companies in order to establish a beachhead in the online world. Since financial models for printed and online content are very different, Web-based publishing is frequently designed to complement the existing printed articles instead of duplicating or replacing them. A smaller number of publishing sites are specific to the Web, but have in turn spawned printed versions as well!

Page-Oriented Information

Despite the availability of advanced media, the backbone of most publishing sites is periodically renewed information provided largely in text format with some graphic supplements. While audio, video, and multimedia may be available, these formats are not critical to most of the content. This model allows small media sites to be competitive, since the update teams may utilize simple and inexpensive HTML edits to update site content.

Editorial Vision

Online publishing sites frequently borrow another aspect of real-world publishing—a strong editorial voice. Unlike sites posting user input, publishing sites exert tight control over style and content following traditional editorial practices in newspapers and magazines. Content is further broken into objective news reports and subjective opinion, a division that is frequently not evident on other kinds of dynamic sites.

Predictable Traffic Variations

Dynamic sites developed using the periodic model often experience major changes in traffic, but the changes occur in a well-understood pattern. While the maintenance team must allow for increases in traffic, the predictability of these changes makes the site easier to manage. Traffic fluctuations are generally less than tenfold, much less extreme than in sites that cover unique online events (see Chapter 10).

Archives

The periodic model for content updates provides a natural organization for storing old information in archives. Most publishing sites maintain back issues of site content, which are integrated into searchable databases installed on the site. Content-aggregation sites may depend on the continued integrity of these links.

Components of Dynamic Periodic Media Sites

The online publishing model has heavily influenced the development of dynamic site programs, most of which were implicitly designed to support periodic online media. Therefore, it is not surprising that major dynamic Web systems are frequently sold to support virtual newspapers and magazines. Software examples include Vignette's StoryServer (www.vignette.com), Wallop Software's BuildIt (www .wallop.com), InContext's Site Command (www.incontext.com), and other programs discussed more fully in Chapter 6. For more examples, consult the IETF Working Group for Distributed Web Authoring and Versioning (www.ics.uci.edu/~ejw/authoring/). All periodic publication tools must support a set of dynamic components, including those discussed next.

Calendaring

This is the single most important aspect of periodic publishing. Development tools must assign production deadlines for dynamic media elements and organize the production team around these goals. Calendar software is needed to notify the update team of milestones in the production process. If content from various sources must appear on a specific date, the calendar software should help to synchronize contributions from different authors so they are ready at the same time.

Editorial Staging

The editorial voice common to most periodic media sites requires that content be staged for review. The site management system needs to provide mechanisms for tagging documents for editorial review and a protocol for the editor to advance a document to the next stage in production. Most software also supports a single high-level administrator (e.g., editor-in-chief) who provides global update approval and triggers posts to the final site.

Page Layout

With text and graphics forming the mainstay of most periodic publishing sites, effective two-dimensional design and layout become very important. Most groups will need to utilize advanced HTML editing, allowing precise placement of media elements on the page. Graphic design and style are generally under greater scrutiny in periodic media sites (unlike those showcasing products or encouraging user interaction). Groups hoping to attract large audiences will need to hire graphics designers familiar with creating attractive and legible online documents. Page layout should be designed so that individual media elements (such as complete articles) are updated without disrupting the surrounding page code or graphic interface.

Archives/Back Issues

For large sites, a serious management problem arises in association with archiving thousands of old articles in a consistent fashion. The management software should provide a naming system so that documents stored in archive directories or databases may be accessed and searched in a consistent fashion. On large media sites, storage requirements may become enormous in only a few months. Most software provides a cut-off mechanism, after which older editions are stored offline or erased.

Feedback

Communication between the publisher and reader has always been important in printed media, but the Web advances this interaction to a new level. Compared to the print world, response to articles is typically very high, and most users now search for answers from online media as opposed to printed editions. Interaction is the first step in building a community around the editorial voice of the site, and it will establish a dedicated base of online subscribers in the long term.

Case Study: Intertec Publishing's Internet Review

URL: www.internetreview.com (see Figure 9.1)

Contact: Matthew Giles

Email: mgiles@mindspring.com

Size of Web site (pages): 2,000

Pages with dynamic content: 15%

Weekly visitors: 25,000 hits; 2,500 unique IPs

Site online: September 1996

Dynamic content online: October 1996

Internet Review has served the commercial real estate industry since 1991. Providing industry publications, databases, and other resources to industry professionals, Internet Review originally ran as a

Figure 9.1 Internet Review (www.internetreview.com).

proprietary online service. Acquired in late 1995 by Intertec Publishing, Internet Review has now moved its publication to the Web. The current site supports the full text of Intertec's family of commercial real estate publications: Commercial Real Estate South, Midwest Real Estate News, National Real Estate Investor, and Shopping Center World. Content on these sites is frequently updated, and the developers employ cutting-edge techniques to keep their information current.

Infrastructure

The Internet Review Web server is a dedicated system hosted on a remote ISP and accessed at T1 speeds. Hardware consists of an Intel dual-Pentium processor with 64 megabytes of RAM and a 2-gigabyte hard disk. The system and supporting tracking and analysis software run under Windows NT.

Team Structure

Not surprisingly, the Internet Review development team is organized around a newspaper production model. The team credits its pre-Web experience with helping it to respond faster to many organizational issues than it would have otherwise. During concept development for the Web site, the team created an organizational flowchart and assigned positions for writers, editors, copy editors, and site administrators. Editorial control is exerted over the style and content of articles posted to the site. During the update process, the team communicates through EmailNet, phone, fax, and face-to-face meetings. It has not been necessary to install specialized groupware to manage the update process. As with many other sites, the main challenge faced by the developers is time management rather than physical resources.

Site Maintenance

Specialized programs are not used to monitor server performance, but access logs are analyzed using WebTrends (www.webtrends.com).

The site has experienced a steady increase in traffic since it was founded, but traffic spikes are rare and have not posed a problem. User preferences are recorded using Netscape's cookie system and are combined with log data for comprehensive user tracking. Periodic system backups are accomplished using standard tape drives.

Dynamic Content Strategy

Goals for the online version of Internet Review are to promote content to the specialized market and provide access to relevant databases of information through the Web. Dynamic pages encourage repeat visits and let users know that the site is active and curated. Content destined for the site originates in original documents, graphics, repurposed word processor files, and information served from a database. Internet Review currently utilizes Microsoft Access (www.microsoft.com/access) and Microrim's RBase (www.microrim .com) software to store and link information to the Web. Once converted to the appropriate format, information is loaded onto a staging server on the company network for review prior to final posting. Individual dynamic media elements are created through a mixture of CGI scripts, database calls, and manual editing. Document flow is organized using Inlet Software's CurrentIssue (www .currentissue.com) management system. Output format may include HTML, Java/JavaScript, database-generated pages, and rotating banner ads. The update team creates HTML pages and does not use a high-level graphical authoring environment, finding current programs slow and too proprietary for their work. Searchable archives are actively maintained on the site. Keyword searches are available for back issues, specialty databases, reviews, and profiles related to the real estate industry. Perhaps due to the regular organization of site content, the update team does not use automatic methods to detect obsolete articles. Instead, old material is removed manually based on external calendar dates and user input. Despite a newspaper-style layout, the update team recently adopted a more incremental posting strategy for the site. The reasons for doing this were suggested by the team's previous online research and experience. Unlike a true newspaper model, this site relies heavily on incremental postings, ensuring that site visitors learn something new each time they return to the site. The update team feels that reliance on incremental postings also keeps the site's content ahead of its print media competition.

Interface

The Internet Review has had one major interface change since its launch. Initially, the home page listed broad topics, but individual features and research articles were located deeper in the site. After careful analysis of access statistics, the site operators moved feature articles and research directly onto the front page. The new interface improved navigation and also increased interest in the site. These changes did not necessitate an internal reorganization of the site's files and directories.

Future Plans

The developers anticipate a steady interest in the site content as their target audience becomes increasingly Internet aware. To support this, they expect to increase the percentage of dynamic pages on Internet Review and allied publications from 15 percent to 50 percent during the next few months. As the market matures, they expect a continued movement away from a standard periodic model to a more loosely organized issue that posts late-breaking information as it happens.

Case Study: HotNews.com

URL: www.hotnews.com (see Figure 9.2)

Contact: Justin Higgins

Email: webmaster@techplanet.com

Size of Web site (pages): 10

Pages with dynamic content: 100%

Weekly visitors: 200,000 hits; 13,000 unique IPs

Site online: July 1997

Dynamic content online: July 1997

HotNews.com is a relatively new media site that functions as an information and news aggregator. Divided into a small number of pages, it lists late-breaking stories reported on other media sites along with short capsule descriptions of each article. By organizing

Figure 9.2 HotNews.com (www.hotnews.com).

the online news of the day, it performs an editorial role similar to digest magazines. Unlike a paper digest, however, HotNews.com does not have to reprint the articles; instead, it simply provides a hyperlink to the original site. This useful and somewhat controversial model extends the normal publishing model in a way that exploits the unique features of the Web. An all-dynamic site, HotNews.com demonstrates general strategies for organizing content that essentially exists elsewhere.

Infrastructure

The HotNews.com Web site is located on an inhouse network and runs on a high-performance Windows NT platform. Details of the exact configuration of hardware and software are proprietary.

Team Structure

As an online media site, HotNews.com takes its production model directly from the newspaper world. Specific job descriptions have been developed for the update team including a copy editor, writers, content editors, and an individual responsible for removing outdated material. Information is shared during content development through email messages and conferencing software.

Site Maintenance

Analysis of access logs is provided by WebTrends (www .webtrends.com) and is actively used in design and updating. As a new site, HotNews.com is experiencing exponential traffic growth and frequent fluctuations in traffic, but to date it has not required the installation of performance monitoring software. To avoid problems caused by traffic fluctuations, the development team assumed extremely high traffic from the very beginning and purchased its hardware and software accordingly. At present levels, traffic spikes do not rise high enough to slow down the site.

Dynamic Content Strategy

As a new publishing site on the Internet, HotNews.com utilizes dynamic content to encourage repeat visits and to keep up with competing sites. The chief job required for the update team is to locate articles relevant to the site audience. During production, the update team surfs for interesting and topical articles to list, and writes short original summaries of their content. This information is loaded into Stormcloud Development's WebDBC (www.stormcloud.com) database/gateway system. Final pages are dynamically generated directly from the database. WebDBC software has many advantages, including automatic support for keyword searches of content and attributes. For example, site visitors may use WebDBC to locate all articles in a particular category or request the five most recent articles on a topic. Pages generated by the database may also include other dynamic elements such as rotating banner ads and bulletin-board-style postings. The primary distinguishing factor among media aggregation sites is timeliness of the posted links, and HotNews.com makes a strong effort to keep its information updated as quickly as possible. Despite linking to sites that post information periodically, HotNews.com itself has moved to an incremental posting strategy. This gives it an edge in the all-important area of fresh content relative to other sites. Content posting is also strongly influenced by access log analysis. To select material for posting, the update team examines recent logs to determine which articles are generating the most click-throughs to the media sites.

Interface

In keeping with its summary position, HotNews.com uses a very simple interface that has not changed since the site was launched. Individual pages list articles relating to science/technology, national/international news, business, sports, and arts/entertainment. High-contrast large fonts are printed over a black background for maximum onscreen readability. This color scheme is inverted relative to most online newspapers, which use black text on white backgrounds. This inversion helps visitors to clearly distinguish HotNews.com pages from its linked sites. This prevents confusion in the user's mind, which could ultimately lead to problems with the primary content sites. To further distinguish its product, Hot-News.com can supply it within a push channel using Microsoft's CDF protocol.

Future Plans

With a completely dynamic interface, HotNews.com is not likely to undergo major structural changes in the near future. If they do occur, modifications are more likely to be tied to legal/political rather than technological issues. By making deep links into other media sites, HotNews.com and similar aggregation services cause the linked sites to receive traffic that bypasses their home pages. While not discounting this additional traffic, some groups are concerned that deep links weaken their branding and make advertising less effective.

These case studies embody trends found throughout the online publishing world. Internet Review is a good example of how a small site targeting a niche audience provides effective dynamic content. Despite the modest size of the publication relative to giants such as C|Net (www.cnet.com), the developers found it useful to use a document management and staging system. The simpler layout and content of the HotNews.com site does not use document management, but it has gone to significant lengths to drive page production through a database. Both of these strategies allow the developers to handle larger amounts of material that would be impossible to organize with an all-manual approach. It is also noteworthy that the sites use an incremental strategy to post content. In the case of HotNews.com, this is understandable. While sites it links to may make content available on a daily or weekly basis, their update schedules are random relative to each other. This makes an incremental strategy almost inevitable. In the case of Internet Review, the advantage is not so clear. The site does divide content into apparent editions, but individual columns may be posted as soon as they appear. The given reason is competition with print, and this strategy may predict a gradual disappearance of true periodic posting in favor of an incremental strategy.

EVENT AND WEBCASTING SITES
The Broadcasting Model

One of the most rapidly evolving groups of dynamic sites focuses on hosting or listing online events. Originally, the relatively static nature of HTML caused developers to supply information via a publishing model, and events took the form of journal entries. With the rise of streaming audio and video in 1995–1996, event sites moved closer to a *Webcast* model, providing a continuous stream of dynamic content. The proliferation of Webcasting resulted in a specific kind of event site—a dynamic guide listing ongoing and future events. While the rush to emulate traditional broadcast media continues unabated, many development groups have expanded on the Webcast model by linking real-time content streams to data served from the Web. These hybrid sites form the topic of this chapter.

Features of Event Sites

All event sites are driven by the occasional or one-time nature of their content. Depending on the speed and duration of the event, radically different technologies are necessary. For example, a NASA site reporting on a 10-year space mission may easily supply information through HTML pages, while a site focusing on the President's State of the Union Address may be delivered in real-time audio. Site operation is also influenced by the number of events supported. Managing a single broadcast stream presents a challenge different from listing airtimes for Webcasts scattered throughout the Internet. The following sections summarize the features of event sites most likely to affect strategies for maintenance and updates.

Multimedia Support

Event sites typically use audio, video, and streaming animation technology to present their information. In contrast to text and graphic formats, the storage and processing requirements for audio and video formats are high, necessitating faster (and more expensive) hardware and software. Audience members need the fastest connections possible to access the event stream and frequently must install specialized helpers and plug-ins to augment their Web browsers.

Real-World Parallel

Many event sites link to happenings in the real world and change their content in direct parallel with the progress of the corresponding physical events. This puts significant day-to-day constraints on updates not encountered with other forms of content. In some cases (e.g., Web-based storytelling sites such as KAPOW at www.kapow .com), a physical event may actually be created to reinforce the online occurrence.

Unicast and Multicast

Many Web sites delivering streaming media operate in a *unicast* mode and provide VCR-type access to all points of the content stream. Similar to ordinary Web access, unicast functions in a one-to-one mode. Other sites (usually supporting large audiences) *multicast* identical content to a large number of viewers. This many-to-many model is similar to traditional broadcast media. Small unicast audiences can be supported through standard client/server systems, while true multicast (see the MBONE FAQ at www.research.att.com/mbone-faq.html for more information) will require new technology to function efficiently on the Internet.

Small Audience Size

Sites covering slow events using standard Web technology handle traffic volumes comparable to other dynamic sites. In most cases, this will be in the thousands to tens of thousands of daily visits—quite small relative to the audience of a nationally televised program. Due to the enormous demands Webcasting imposes on hardware and bandwidth, most sites restrict their audience even further—to hundreds or even dozens of viewers. The problem becomes more severe as the Webcast tries to emulate high-fidelity audio or video broadcasting. The flip side of small audiences is that developers may effectively support events with only a small number of viewers. Compared to radio or television, niche broadcasting on the Web is cheap.

Quality Limitations

The vast majority of consumers are limited to 56k or 28.8 modem speeds. At this bandwidth, audio approaches the quality of a good FM radio station, but video is restricted to grainy, jerky images a few inches across. Figure 10.1 shows an example of a high-end video image—a far cry from full-motion, full-screen video! Under these conditions, the appeal of streaming media is restricted and cannot hold audience interest for very long. In order to be effective, streaming media is usually combined with standard Web pages providing additional information about the event.

Figure 10.1 Video frame sizes characteristic of the Internet.

The Ghost of Gramercy Place

Experimental Film

Movie Excerpt (1.1 mb; QuickTime)
Click above to view the movie excerpt.

Relating the experience of two ghosts, one a member of a cruel and noble family, the other a servant who poisoned her during a time of war and destruction. The lead character describes the transformation of her wailing from cries of anger and frustration to empathy with those she oppressed and the material world.

Life History

Event sites often have a specific life span. After the site's event occurs, the associated content may be archived or removed entirely from the Internet. Sites not managed in this way run the risk of announcing events (e.g., movie premieres) that have long since ended. Even if the site hosts regular events (or simply lists events held elsewhere), it must dynamically alter the type of content it presents before and after each event. Sites providing event listings often run a mini life cycle in which the update team posts publicity for upcoming events, links to ongoing events, and archives for completed events.

Components of Event Sites

With the possible exception of online gaming (Chapter 11), event sites require the most specialized software of all dynamic sites. The advanced media protocols used for most Webcasts require the installation of proprietary servers and specialized clients. To support audio and video links to the real world, the developers must master aspects of broadcasting technology. Once an event has begun, the maintenance team must manage site performance without interrupting ongoing audio or video streams. Some of the tools necessary to support this level of dynamic control are reviewed in the following section.

Traffic Management Software

By attracting visitors at specific times, event sites experience rapid traffic changes that may either be gentle (e.g., a site covering a bicycle circumnavigation of the world) or sudden (e.g., sites supporting yearly holidays or awards). As an example, bandwidth requirements for democracy.net (www.democracy.net) typically jump one hundred-fold during its live webcasts—far greater than the two- to fivefold changes typical of non-Webcast sites. Some development groups, such as the network supporting the Mars Pathfinder (www.nasa.jpl.gov) site successfully managed hit rates thousands of times higher than normal. On the other hand, nearly all the sites covering the 1997 Academy Awards (e.g., www.mrshowbiz.com; www.oscars.com) ground to a halt during the television broadcast. To be successful, event sites need to install load-balancing software and real-time performance monitors such as those described in Chapter 3. In planning for particular events, the developers may elect to run load-simulation software and verify that the hardware and software can handle the expected traffic.

Support for Media Streams

Event sites frequently must interface their equipment to audio and video systems designed for traditional broadcast. These systems deliver media streams instead of discrete files and documents. Instead of a standard staging process, the developers will need to create a system capable of accepting, converting, and uploading information as fast as it becomes available from the stream. The following sections provide examples of media stream types commonly used on event sites and representative programs designed to manage the demands of rapid conversion to Web format.

Wordcasts

These systems deliver streams of text or highly compressed versions of spoken conversation. Wordcasts have significant advantages, since relatively low-end equipment handles much larger audiences than audio- or video-based systems. Wordcasters (www.wordcasters.com) provides a real-time text transcript of audio events. The customer provides an audio feed (e.g., through a phone line); the Wordcast system transcribes the text and posts it live to the Wordcasters site. Clients using a Java-enabled browser may view and respond to the real-time text transcript. Compared to other media, Wordcast events support large audiences. More sophisticated Wordcasts are supported using compression software from Voxware, Inc. (www.voxware .com; Macintosh, Windows NT/95). This unique system uses VoiceFront technology to achieve extremely high compression ratios (200:1) for spoken words. A minute of VoiceFront-encoded speech may occupy as little as 18k, compared to the hundreds of kilobytes typical of streaming audio systems.

Streaming Audio and Video

Due to its resemblance to traditional broadcasting, streaming audio/video has attracted widespread attention. Some of the large groups of vendors supplying (incompatible) streaming systems are listed in Table 10.1. In general, these products deliver reasonable-quality audio at 28.8 and 56k modem speeds. Delivery of video is more variable. Simple "talking head" video may be transmitted at 28.8 speeds, but more realistic motion requires ISDN or leased-line connections. Some video systems support an alternate slideshow presentation coupled with a real-time audio track. For certain content (e.g., music videos), this format is acceptable. Virtually all streaming

Table 10.1 List of Streaming Media Vendors

Streamlining Media Vendor	What They Offer
Macromedia Shockwave www.macromedia.com Macintosh, Windows NT, Unix	Expansion of popular multimedia system now allows streaming audio delivery along with multimedia. End users need to install a custom client, but no specialized server is required for delivery.
Headspace Beatnik www.headspace.com Macintosh, Windows NT	Authoring and delivery tool designed for music professionals creating interactive music presentations. Beatnik supports a wide variety of audio watermaking, JavaScript control of the plug-in, and a MIDI instrument editor.
Liquid Audio www.liquidaudio.com Windows NT	"End-to-end" system supporting streaming audio using Dolby Digital encoding, digital watermarks for copyright protection, music ordering, and direct recording to CD-R drives to create standard "Red Book" audio CDs.
Xing Technology www.xingtech.com Windows NT/Unix	Early adopter of MPEG-based streaming audio and video delivery. Provides custom client and server systems adapted for low-speed Internet connections or higher-speed videos sent over an Intranet.
Progressive Networks RealMedia www.real.com $0–$4,000; Unix/Windows NT	Integrated client and server providing support for Progressive's RealAudio and the new RealVideo format. Video may be compressed

Table 10.1 *Continued*

Streamlining Media Vendor	What They Offer
	with a variety of options, including a "slide show" format useful for low-speed modems.
Audioactive www.audioactive.com $13,800; Unix/Windows NT	High-quality MPEG audio compression using a proprietary client/server platform. The distribution contains a server, encoders, and clients—and a hardware-based encoder is under development.
NetTOOB www.duplexx.com $4,895; Windows NT	Streaming video using MPEG-1 compression, known for high image quality. Can play both audio and video files encoded in a variety of formats. Does not require a special server for content delivery.
VDOnet www.vdo.net $1,000–$9,000 (50 streams); Windows NT	Proprietary client/server video streaming system popular with many large broadcasting companies. Basic server streams archived video, and high-end VDOLive system provides real-time video from live events.
Vosaic MediaServer www.vosaic.com Unix, Windows NT	Integrated system including client and server. Allows users to manage live audio streams with a VCR-style interface—including pause, rewind, and fast forward. Provides log analysis and integrated with Vosaic MediaBase database.

audio/video products require proprietary client downloads and PowerPC or Pentium-level processors for effective use. For more information, consult Sound and Video Formats (www.nic-bnc.ca/publications/netnotes/notes24.htm) and Audio Resource Guides (www.comlab.ox.ac.uk/archive/audio.html).

Streaming Multimedia

These protocols integrate streaming audio and video with computer-generated data such as animation and interactive controls. In a rapid move to the top, Microsoft's Netshow (www.microsoft.com/netshow; free; Windows NT) has become the front runner in the streaming multimedia race. Included at no cost in Microsoft's Site Server (www.microsoft.com/siteserver), it uses the company's Active Streaming Format (ASF) to deliver multimedia. The FS option provides full-motion, full-screen video using *MPEG* compression, but use requires T1 (or higher!) speed connections. Macromedia's Shockwave (www.macromedia.com; $995; Macintosh, Windows) environment, coupled with Flash ($199), provides comparable features to Netshow and supports the enormous installed base of applications and tools created for Director. Upgrades of The Palace (www.thepalace.com; $2,995; 100 streams; Macintosh, Unix, Windows NT) chat server to the new PalacePresents format lets developers create moderated, auditorium-type events. Within each chatroom, moderators may command the speaking floor, add streaming audio/video, and point to external Web links relevant to the show. Use of PalacePresents requires purchasing the newest version of The Palace server.

Media Management

Groups developing slower-paced event sites may utilize many of the management tools described in Chapter 6, but those providing streaming audio and video require specialized systems. FreeRange Media's Java-based Lariat (www.freerange.com; $995; Unix, Windows NT) system is designed specifically for Progressive Network's RealMedia (www.real.com) platform. Lariat is a Java-based tool designed to orchestrate live media events, online concerts, and Webcasts. Management tools include listener personalization, viewing menus for end users, and an automated system for mass encoding of streaming media files. Vosaic (www.vosaic.com; Unix, Windows NT) provides a similar product within its MediaSuite package adapted for its own video technology. A high-end solution is provided by Silicon Graphics' Mediabase (www.sgi.com; $2,000; 10 streams; Unix). Working with SGI Origin Servers, Mediabase creates a searchable database for audio and video files in multiple formats. It also supports a variety of capture and playback options for Mac, Windows, and Unix client programs, and it is compatible with major relational database platforms.

Case Study: Luminous Dataworks' ShowTimes

URL: showtimes.hollywood.com (see Figure 10.2)

Contact: Scott Vanderbilt

Email: scott@lumdata.com

Size of Web site (pages): 1 HTML page (all others generated by database queries)

Pages with dynamic content: 100%

Weekly visitors: 1,600,000 hits; 140,000 unique IPs

Site online: June 1997

Dynamic content online: June 1997

Figure 10.2 ShowTimes (showtimes.hollywood.com).

ShowTimes is an online event guide within Hollywood Online (www.hollywood.com) that lists the dates, times, and locations of feature film presentations. It is the official site of the National Association of Theatre Owners (NATO) and provides listings for over 7,000 theaters throughout the United States. Users enter their zip code or city/state and search for theaters showing films in their area. Clickable buttons lead to road maps and descriptions of the theaters. Each film listing is linked to a brief synopsis, reviews, and RealAudio-encoded interviews with the film's cast and crew. This complex site is routinely updated on a daily and weekly basis.

Infrastructure

ShowTimes runs on an HP NetServer LH Pro with 192 megabytes of RAM and a 24-gigabyte hard disk. In order to handle the high volume of traffic processed by the server, the hardware is located directly on a Network Access Point (NAP). Additional servers within the Hollywood Online domain serve streaming audio clips.

Team Structure

Specific job descriptions within the ShowTimes update team include loading content into the main database, and detecting and removing outdated content. The "uploader" position incorporates some editorial control. Groupware and workflow functions are provided by custom software developed in house especially designed to manage the mix of table-style data (e.g., theater addresses) and multimedia (e.g., images, audio, and video).

Site Maintenance

The maintenance group at Hollywood Online routinely collects access logs and analyzes them to determine DPOs (distinct points of origin) and page turns (ad impressions). Individual users are identified using Netscape's cookie technology coupled with log data. As might be expected, the site experiences occasional sharp traffic increases associated with film-related events. To manage the traffic spikes, the maintenance team relies on direct monitoring of the servers and does not employ specialized load-balancing or performance tools. Regular system backups use standard 4-mm DAT tape drives.

Dynamic Content Strategy

The heart of ShowTimes is a database/gateway system built from scratch. Information comes from preexisting Zip Code and ADI (Area of Dominant Influence) databases acquired from several sources. ADI information divides the country into about 200 consumer markets based on population. Original text and multimedia are also generated by the update team. Pages such as the example in Figure 10.3 are dynamically constructed from the database and

Figure 10.3 Dynamically constructed page on ShowTimes showing theater information.

include HTML, JavaScript, and rotating banner ads. Since film schedules have little value after the show is over, old information is deleted rather than archived. Most of the ShowTimes database is replaced every week, and the content visible on site is modified on a daily basis. The rapid turnover of time-sensitive data presents the biggest management problem for the update team. In addition to the main schedule database, ShowTimes incorporates a smaller set of tables that do not change as often.

Interface

Global interface changes to the ShowTimes site are effected through manually generated templates that are processed by the database to generate dynamic pages. The current interface is the third to be developed in less than three months. Changes were introduced into the original design to improve navigation and enhance visitor interest. Due to its database-driven design, no files or directories were directly affected by theses changes.

Future Plans

ShowTimes provides a type of information that is of interest to its audience on a regular (e.g., weekly) basis. For this reason, the developers plan to implement push technology using Microsoft's CDF protocol to deliver personalized movie listings to regular users.

Case Study: Virtual Netcasting Corporation's L.A. Live

URL: www.lalive.com (see Figure 10.4)

Contact: Zack Zalon

Email: livemaster@lalive.com

Size of Web site (pages): 200

Pages with dynamic content: 100%

Weekly visitors: 750,000 hits

Site online: August 1996

Dynamic content online: August 1996

L.A. Live, operated by the Virtual Netcast Corporation (VNC) in Los Angeles, is a promotional site that features multiple live Webcasts. More than a streaming media site, it provides promotion and content personalization leading visitors to the music they want. L.A. Live also runs a public chatroom and provides a "virtual postcard" service.

Figure 10.4 L.A. Live (www.lalive.com).

Infrastructure

The L.A. Live server is located on VNC's inhouse network and consists of a Sun UltraSparc with 256 megabytes of RAM and a 16-gigabyte hard disk. A 10-megabit link connects the server to the general Internet. The high memory and disk capacities (substantially greater than most dynamic sites) are necessary for storage and processing of real-time audio and video data. Installed software includes a Netscape Web server supporting SSL commerce transactions and a RealMedia streaming audio/video server. Additional hardware is used to record, digitize, and transmit live conference information from the event to the server.

Team Structure

L.A. Live follows a television production model for organizing maintenance and updates of dynamic content. Jobs within the update team include content collectors, writers, and Web administrators. The team communicates primarily via EmailNet combined with face-to-face discussions. Since a well-defined policy for updates has been established, it has not been necessary to create an editorial position for final approval of postings.

Site Maintenance

Most maintenance follows standard procedures for Unix workstations. Site statistics are compiled and analyzed using the popular Analog (www.statslab.cam.ac.uk/~sret1/analog/) package, which works efficiently with large log files. System images are stored to tape drives and to backup hard disks. Storage to hard disks offers fast retrieval, increased capacity during events, and a mechanism for "hot swaps" in the event of a disk crash.

Dynamic Content Strategy

L.A. Live is departing from the standard Webcast model to provide a more personalized experience for its audience. The service supports multiple simultaneous Webcasts and personalizes content for the particular musical taste of site visitors. In order to reach these ambitious aims, L.A. Live has developed a proprietary site management program that is used to control the generation of navigation elements, advertising banners, insite links, and audio/video media. Individual pages (see Figure 10.5) are developed in standard HTML, with hyperlinks to dynamic media elements generated through the program. All dynamic content is generated with reference to user statistics. Access is analyzed on a daily basis and compared to earlier results to establish trends. This allows L.A. Live to direct visitors into taste-defined areas of the site where content, advertising, and

Figure 10.5 Dynamically generated event page on L.A. Live.

navigation is specifically targeted to each individual. Personalized content may optionally be provided through a push channel using Netscape's Netcaster system. Use of inhouse management has made establishing a separate staging server unnecessary. Obsolete content is detected and removed via custom software tags created by the proprietary management system.

Interface

L.A. Live has had one major facelift during its first year of operation. Interface changes were prompted by a desire to support different browser types, improve navigation, and attract user interest. During these upgrades, it was necessary to reformat older pages to be consistent with the new style, and convert static pages for dynamic delivery.

Future Plans

L.A. Live plans to expand the number of events it covers and also anticipates creating a new interface. Future media support will depend on which streaming media vendor becomes the dominant provider; Progressive Networks RealMedia is seen as a likely winner. L.A. Live may also experiment with integrated media packages such as Microsoft Netshow.

Case Study: UltimateTV

URL: www.ultimatetv.com (see Figure 10.6)

Figure 10.6 UltimateTV (www.ultimatetv.com).

Contact: David Cronshaw

Email: info@ultimatetv.com

Size of Web site (pages): 2,500

Pages with dynamic content: 90%

Weekly visitors: <1,000,000 hits; 250,000 unique IPs

Site online: December 1994

Dynamic content online: December 1994

UltimateTV began its existence at the end of 1994 as TV Net, one of the first informational resources for commercial and international television on the Internet. During the next three years, it changed names, servers, and operating systems, and expanded into a popular listing guide for TV shows and local stations scattered throughout the world. The site's dynamic content includes show promotions and advertising, feature articles written by columnists, and its rapidly changing list of television show schedules. UltimateTV's event listings complement an extensive set of chatrooms, discussion forums, and bulletin boards aimed at TV fans and professionals in the television industry. The site also operates an online store for TV-related memorabilia. More recently, UltimateTV has begun linking to streaming video sites and "freeze frame" television signals located on other event sites on the Internet. To support access to these systems, UltimateTV has created an online help desk describing installation and use of streaming video software. Management of this complex site requires considerable effort by the update team, and some of the methods used may be surprising in light of other sites considered in this chapter.

Infrastructure

UltimateTV runs on a Sun Netra i145 workstation located on the 10-megabit network of a regional ISP. The system has 64 megabytes of RAM and a 2-gigabyte hard disk. Netscape servers are used to manage Web traffic. A second Pentium workstation running BSDi Unix (www.bsdi.com) handles many of the online chat and discussion forums. The system does not directly support streaming audio and video, but instead provides access to streaming sites elsewhere on the Internet.

Team Structure

Although UltimateTV's founder, David Cronshaw, came from the television industry, many of the methods used to organize maintenance and updates are typical of newspaper and magazine publications. The diverse and extensive content updates are handled by a mixture of email, live conferencing, and custom programs. Job divisions include an editor-in-chief, various content developers, writers, and a server administrator. The group uses Microsoft Scheduler+ (www.microsoft.com) to handle time-sensitive postings to the site.

Site Maintenance

UltimateTV routinely manages heavy server loads, and events such as the Emmy Awards (www.emmys.org) cause major traffic spikes. With no custom performance or load-balancing software installed, the server operation is monitored directly through Unix operating system commands. The maintenance team has also dealt successfully with "potty mouths" who attempt to disrupt discussions in its chatrooms and bulletin boards. Custom programs were developed to identify and lock out unwelcome visitors in the original HTML-based rooms. Newer chat software available from companies such as ichat (www.ichat.com) provide similar abilities. The maintenance team has also handled numerous changes in hardware and software. Since going online, UltimateTV has been hosted on a virtual server,

Figure 10.7 Link to video "freeze frame" on a remote site within UltimateTV pages.

moved to a dedicated BSDi Unix workstation, moved again to a Sun workstation, and finally transferred to a high-speed LAN offered by a regional ISP.

Dynamic Content Strategy

During its long history, UltimateTV has developed many methods to produce and distribute dynamic content. About 90 percent of the raw information provided on the site is submitted by email, with the remainder arriving by fax. As shown in Figure 10.7, content is also supplied by linking to streaming media on remote sites. On early versions of the site, this information was coded entirely in static HTML. During 1995 and 1996, a large collection of CGI programs were developed in house to directly generate dynamic content. At present, the site is updated through a mixture of manual editing and CGI scripts connected to page templates. Perhaps because of its long experience with Web content, the UltimateTV update team has not needed to install document control software or a centralized database. The timeliness and accuracy of updated information thus depends on the experience and meticulousness of the update team.

Interface

In keeping with "old" Web sites, UltimateTV has undergone numerous interface changes since its inception. The original service went online before basic page features such as backgrounds and centered graphics were available. During subsequent upgrades, much effort has gone into determining how many links to list on the home page. Initial analysis of access logs showed that visitors preferred a large number of topics listed on the home page. As the size of the site increased, the home page threatened to become unmanageable. The current interface solves the problem by listing topics and subtopics along a sidebar running on the left of the screen. Information within each subtopic appears in the page body in a newspaper-style format. During its steady growth, UltimateTV has made some changes to its file structure, but the basic layout of directories has been preserved.

Future Plans

One of the near-term goals of the developers is the purchase and installation of a high-end site management system. While the group has successfully run the site without a centralized system, software-based document management will ease the task of the editors. Other anticipated changes include replacing the current collection of custom CGI scripts with a commercial database. UltimateTV may begin offering streaming video of its own, but it will probably outsource delivery to a video network such as InterVU (www.intervu .net) rather than installing its own video server.

The sites considered here illustrate several common requirements for managing online events. The complexity of running sites using multiple media types has forced the developers to invent their own proprietary management software. In two of the sites just described (ShowTimes and L.A. Live), a document management system was created from scratch to manage dynamic content. While UltimateTV did not create a management program, its large collection of CGI scripts function in an equivalent fashion. UltimateTV also differs from the other event sites in having adopted a publishing model for content delivery. Although this approach puts fewer demands on infrastructure, it calls for a more complex update team that ShowTimes and L.A. Live require. Groups running the sites previously discussed find it necessary to complement streaming media with text and graphics, reflecting the low appeal of current Webcast content. For now, streaming media remains a novelty that augments—but does not replace—Web-based event information.

ONLINE GAMES AND AUCTIONS
The Competition Model

A great deal of attention has recently been focused on Internet games and auctions. With billions of dollars spent annually for arcade and cartridge games, the business case for real-time multiplayer competition over the Internet is compelling. Auctions provide similar potential for sales. Until recently, the combination of a limited Web interface, slow network response, and difficulties in tracking individual players made the Web a less-than-attractive medium for gaming. This situation is rapidly changing. Pioneering companies such as ClassicGames.com (www.classicgames.com) and Lightning Entertainment (www.ltng.com) support board and card games over the Internet through proprietary clients. Faster-paced multiplayer gaming systems such as those within the Total Entertainment Network (www.ten.com) and Multi-Player Games Network (mpgn.com) are moving from closed systems to all-Web interfaces. Auction sites such as OnSale (Figure 11.1) have sold millions of dollars' worth of goods during 1996 and 1997. The following discussion considers the game and auction world as part of a broader group of dynamic sites that exist to provide competitive interactions between their users. It does not consider non-Web aspects of gaming (e.g., design of proprietary game client software) or game archives maintained on the Web (e.g., HappyPuppy at www.happypuppy.com).

Features of Sites Supporting Games and Auctions

Sites that support games and auctions fall under the user-driven model (Chapter 8) but have additional features that make them unique, including a very high-paced interaction level. On most sites running chat or threaded discussions, messages are posted on a scale of minutes to hours. By contrast, games and auction sites support interactions between users on the order of minutes to fractions of a second. Furthermore, this interaction is competitive rather than cooperative. Game players typically post challenges to other users and attempt to beat them at a particular task. Posted information may be in the form of spatial coordinates (e.g., player movements in a two-dimensional world) or text (dollar amounts posted in gambling or auction bids). The characteristics of the design of game and auction sites are discussed next.

Interface Design

Game sites rely heavily on interface design to stimulate interest in competition. On some sites, the interface mimics traditional objects such as playing cards and checkerboards. These environments are easily developed using current dynamic Web technology. Access to competitive information forms a second aspect of game and auction design. In order to play, users need information about the range of available games, location, number of players, their current status in the game, and the reward/prize offered to the winner. Dynamic programming is necessary to implement these demanding interface features.

Figure 11.1 OnSale (www.onsale.com).

Ranking

Game players have a very specific notion of online community; they wish to see their performance ranked against other members. Rank can consist of scores, money available for bidding, or playing level. In order to implement ranking, the developers must collect information from individual games, sort it, and push the results to everyone. Ranking may also be used to allow or deny users access to a particular competitive event.

Player Communication

In most computer games, users compete strictly on a "win or die" basis. More elaborate multiplayer games and online auctions may allow a greater range of communication between the players. Examples of player communication include gaming invitations and the exchange of shared strategies. Player communication may be enabled through email and personalized chat.

Proprietary Software

Development groups typically program auction or gaming systems from scratch. This includes the design of a dynamic interface, server programming for rapid response, and metering systems that tally winnings or charge for playing time. Tracking users and monitoring time online for payment may also require proprietary software.

Hardware and Bandwidth

Real-time interactivity involving multiple users places serious demands on hardware and bandwidth. Groups developing gaming sites will typically need to use the fastest hardware and Internet connections they can afford. In addition, the development and staging system must support frequent uploads of new information without disrupting the continuity or speed of games in progress.

Components of Gaming and Auction Sites

Since the Web has only recently provided the dynamic tools needed to create competitive game and auction sites, most early developers created custom software operating according to a client-server model. Use of proprietary programs originally helped to differentiate between vendors, allowed a greater freedom in interface design, and simplified payment systems. With the increasing diversity of dynamic Web software, it has become possible to develop sites that use dynamic Web technology to enhance these services or, in some cases, replace them. Software components typically used in Web-based game designs are described in more detail next.

Multimedia Clients

Games with sophisticated visual animation and audio may be created in streaming multimedia environments such as Macromedia's (www.macromedia.com) Shockwave and Flash programs, or mBED's Weblet (www.mbed.com) system. Newer systems utilize client-side programming languages that provide automatic download and configuration of a game client. Slower game play suitable for auctions is supported through JavaScript, and DHTML specifications (Chapter 5) from Netscape and Microsoft provide a similar capability. Faster systems may require programming ActiveX applications or Java applets.

Game/Auction Servers

Despite the ubiquity of games in older Bulletin Board System (BBS) software packages, there are currently few options for "canned" Web sites offering competitive interaction. Most Web-specific efforts have used the Virtual Reality Modeling Language (VRML) environments, which unfortunately has to date precluded effective gaming due to its slow operation. Auction sites often use more conventional software, and a few companies have developed integrated packages. Popular choices include Web Ducks' OpenSite (www.webducks.com; $299; Unix, Windows NT) auction system, which supports real-time bidding. OpenSite installs as a series of extensions to standard Web servers allowing setup and administration of interactive auctions. A higher-end auction product is offered by WebVision's AUCTIONnet (www.webvision.com; $30,000; Unix), a vertical-market system designed to support all aspects of bidding at the individual or business-to-business level.

Membership and Tracking Systems

Game sites require databases that store user accounts and identify the user at login. Such detailed control is necessary to score performance in games and auctions, and to implement billing schemes based on time or access to particular services. To develop a system, the database must receive information from access logs or cookie-based tracking systems. Game companies have expressed interest in pay-per-play micropayment systems (Chapter 7), but at present most provide free membership or charge monthly/yearly subscriptions. Gaming sites frequently use customer accounts to help personalize site visits.

Case Study: Auction World

URL: www.a-world.com (see Figure 11.2)

Contact: Fardin Golzar

Email: customerservice@a-world.com

Size of Web site (pages): ~400

Pages with dynamic content: 95%

Weekly visitors: 90,000 hits; 9,000 unique IPs

Site online: March 1997

Dynamic content online: March 1997

Auction World provides promotional bidding on a large variety of goods and services. With a simple interface, it supports online auctions that may be personalized to customers' needs and interests. The auctions run at a moderate pace, taking several hours to days to complete. Prizes are provided by sponsors who process orders for winners after the bidding is completed.

Infrastructure

Auction World runs on a single-processor Pentium P166 with 128 megabytes of RAM and a 4-gigabyte hard disk provided by the host-

Figure 11.2 Auction World (www.a-world.com).

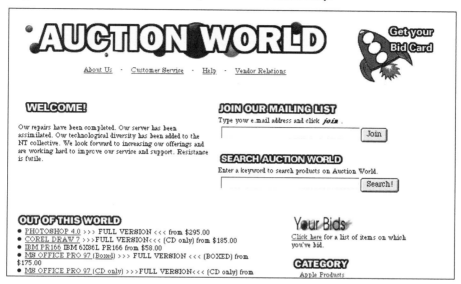

ing ISP. Software includes Windows NT 4.0, Microsoft's Internet Information Server 3.0, the WebDBC 3.0 (www.stormcloud.com) database gateway, and Microsoft's Access 7.0 (www.microsoft .com/access). The site is backed up through a remote service. Secure online transactions are enabled using VeriSign (www.verisign.com) digital certificates combined with the IIS software.

Team Structure

The dominant production model for Auction World is a retail/catalog publishing model. During team development, the group designed job positions for data collectors, site testers, and server administrators. Communication between team members is through email exchange, personalized chat, and components of a proprietary site management program developed in house. To date, the maintenance team reports "no challenges" in managing the site.

Site Maintenance

Statistics for site traffic are provided by the hosting ISP. Cookie tracking is also implemented and is combined with access statistics to monitor user movement through the site. During the time the site has been online, the maintenance team has transferred it between Web servers and changed the operating system from Unix to Windows NT.

Dynamic Content Strategy

The goals of Auction World are to provide a dynamic bidding experience for its patrons and in doing so, promote the companies who provide products and services. Content is added to the site directly through the Web DBC environment and user-driven interfaces including button choices and fill-out forms (Figure 11.3). To keep the site up and running 24 hours a day, Auction World follows an incremental posting strategy. Over 95 percent of its content is dynamically assembled from a database and delivered on-the-fly in HTML and JavaScript formats. The remaining pages are updated using manual HTML editing, CGI-based media elements, and rotating banner ads. The site combines information contained in member accounts with access statistics to personalize the content, providing members with the exact items they have shown interest in each time they visit. Obsolete content is detected using a document management system (developed in house) that automatically flags information past its expiration date.

Interface

The Auction World interface consists of bright elementary colors and light page backgrounds to increase friendliness, and is deliberately kept simple in layout to move the visitor's attention to the products up for bidding. Two interface changes have occurred since the site went online, serving the primary purpose of increasing interest in the site.

Future Plans

With nearly the entire site delivered from a database, Auction World has reached a milestone in its dynamic interface. The clean design and layout of the site has attracted interest from other companies, which have solicited Auction World to help them develop their own sites.

Figure 11.3 Products and current bids on the Auction World site.

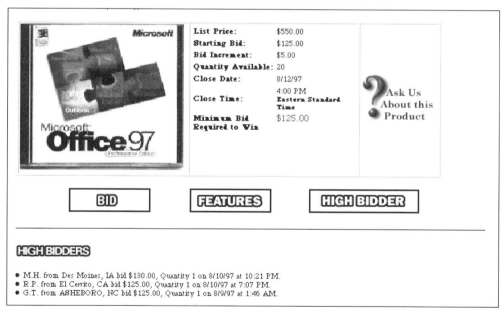

Case Study: Prizefight

URL: www.prizefight.com (see Figure 11.4)

Contact: Carol Perletz

Email: info@prizefight.com

Size of Web site (pages): 200

Pages with dynamic content: 90%

Weekly visitors: 300,000 hits; 1,000 unique IPs

Site online: January 1997

Dynamic content online: January 1997

Prizefight is an online auction site containing a user interface that employs strong elements of game competition. Online players compete for promotional prizes and services donated by sponsors in a highly interactive Web environment with second-by-second updates comparable to proprietary game software. Examples of prizes available through participation in the auctions include computers, whitewater rafting adventures, golf accessories, and rollerblade sets. There is no charge for the service. Users log on with nicknames and email addresses, and enter an auction by clicking on a rotating set of prize images. Players accumulate virtual Prizefight money by competing in first-level "Jersey" auctions. During the auction, visitors see bids placed by themselves and others. Winners then use their accumulated Jersey earnings to compete for the real prizes in Vermont auctions. The all-Web design of this system is one of the most dynamic interfaces currently on the Web.

Infrastructure

The Prizefight server is a dedicated Pentium system hosted remotely by an ISP on its 10-megabit network. The current server has 48 megabytes of RAM and a 2-gigabyte hard disk running Windows NT. The system runs a Microsoft IIS server, and additional copies are present on the half-dozen or so staging servers used to prepare content. NT offers several advantages relative to Unix for this group, not the least of which is the ability to do meaningful development on laptop computers when the group is away from the office. To implement the site's dynamic operation, the developers programmed their own custom real-time database (written in C) to manage the Prizefight player and sponsor data.

Team Structure

The development group is organized along a model similar to that used in retail/catalog publishing. Working together in a common

Figure 11.4 Prizefight (www.prizefight.com).

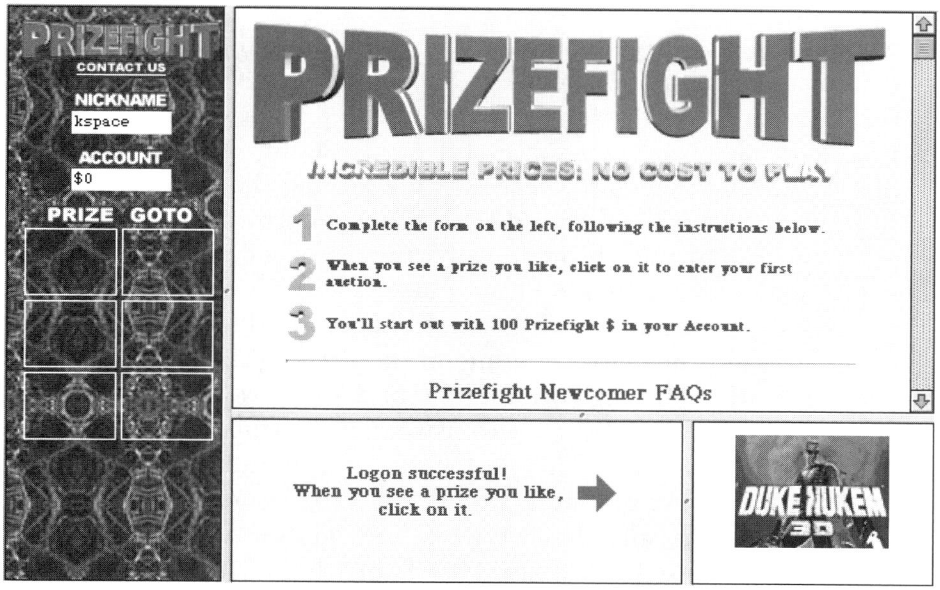

environment, the group's primary coordination is through direct discussion and EmailNet. Specific jobs have been created for collecting information, converting content to Web format, uploading content, testing the site for broken links, and general site maintenance. Editorial control is exerted over user information posted to the site.

Site Maintenance

Access statistics to the site are provided by the ISP hosting the server and include standard Web access logs and individual user tracking via cookies. A third level of stats is collected within the custom database program while players are making their bids. This information is used to uniquely identify individuals within bidding events. By requiring a (free) membership, Prizefight has a developed, stable worldwide following and does experience sudden traffic spikes.

Dynamic Content Strategy

As an auction site, the key goal for implementing dynamic content is to provide specific, personalized information for visitors, including the number of items for sale and updated data on bidding. The Prizefight site has been successful in attracting heavy usage from players around the world, necessitating around-the-clock updates of content. Information received from sponsors providing promotional prizes is submitted through word processor documents, printed pages, and graphic files A second layer of user-driven information consists of new accounts, individual bids on products posted to the site, and real-time chats. Staging on the Prizefight system follows a complex path including both incremental and periodic updates. The developers have created an extensive set of utilities for preparing data before it is folded into the public site's database. Information includes auction close dates, product prices, images, prize descriptions, and advertising. Each type of information is formatted and merged into a single database that is proofed on the local staging server. Once uploaded, a final step merges the new information with the existing database. The current server has the capacity to efficiently handle about 800,000 player accounts. The high performance of the system is partly due to the decision to code applications directly in C, rather than using a scripting or generic database language.

The prep cycle may run a week or more before the data is folded into the public database. In addition to the custom software, the developers use Photoshop, Word, Excel, and other standard packages to assist in the preparation of images and text. The update team stages new information on one of the local servers, uploads it to the central server in secondary directories, and then does a "hot switch" over to the new files in real time. The dynamic pages consist of visible and invisible frames loaded with JavaScript code. During operation, the frames update and communicate with each other to support the bidding process, providing a second-by-second update comparable to video games (Figure 11.5). Dynamic information is delivered in a way that masks long network delays. For example, some frames present buffered chat messages while waiting for the Web server to return information. After bidding is complete, Prizefight corresponds with winners through customized email responses. Manual scans are used to detect and remove obsolete content. Since bidding information does not have long-term value, old content is removed from the site and not archived. If absolutely necessary, system backups can be used to roll back the Web site to an earlier version.

The rapid flow of information characteristic of an online auction causes particular challenges for the developers. One of the biggest issues is efficiently uploading product and promotional data without disruption of any ongoing events. The developers spent a significant amount of effort arriving at a system that would tolerate uploads from the update team while actively being used to support auctions.

Interface

During the site's time online, the developers have made two interface changes to accommodate new content and improve user navigation. Analysis of access statistics have been extremely helpful in maintaining the Prizefight interface. For example, the analysis recently led the developers to plan a second, less-demanding version of the auction program for people with less-capable browsers and poorer connections. Statistics are also helpful for finding interface bugs. In one case, a programming problem that locked users into a loop was detected by comparing the ratio of logins to plays. Initially, the bug appeared to increase the number of users, and only the combination of access data with cookie and internal tracking information revealed that the new users' data actually represented the same individual logging in several times in a row.

Figure 11.5 Real-time bidding event on the Prizefight Web site.

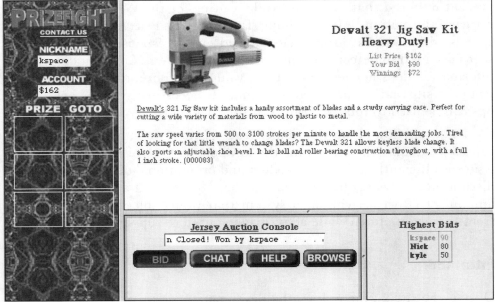

Future Plans

Prizefight expects to maintain a stable proportion of dynamic to static content during the next 12 months. Likely future innovations include increasing personalization and support for even greater interactivity during the auction process.

Case Study: Total Entertainment Network (TEN)

URL: www.ten.net (see Figure 11.6)

Contact: Charles Cooper

Email: charles@ten.net

Size of Web site (pages): 4,500

Pages with dynamic content: 25%

Weekly visitors: 825,400 hits; 444,800 IPs

Site online August 1995

Dynamic content online: January 1997

TEN is one of the pioneers of online, multiplayer games. Beginning with a proprietary network, TEN has expanded to provide Internet access to a large number of multiplayer games. Users join TEN for a flat monthly subscription and download proprietary gaming clients to join in the action. The site has tens of thousands of active members, and a significant fraction of these are online at any one time. A portion of the TEN site offers instructions, news, calendar/event information, and advertising; complementing the real-time user interaction mediated through the proprietary game client. A site within the site (FileFactory) provides PC demos, shareware

Figure 11.6 Total Entertainment Network (www.ten.net).

games, user maps, and walkthroughs. TEN actively solicits files from site visitors to add to this archive.

Infrastructure

The TEN servers are located on an inhouse network. High-end Sun workstations with 256 megabytes of RAM and between 2 and 10 gigabytes of disk storage are used. In order to manage the extremely high traffic generated on the site, a pair of T3 connections to the Internet is maintained. Traffic includes standard Web interaction, large (tens of megabytes) file downloads, and information from proprietary gaming clients. Netscape enterprise servers are used to handle Web requests. A Digital Linear Tape (DLT) system is used to back up the network.

Team Structure

Managing a high-traffic site such as TEN requires significant organization in the developer group. In creating the site, the operators developed specific job descriptions and an organizational flowchart constrained within a specific budget goal. Individual jobs were defined for producer, content collectors, editors, media conversion specialists, editors/copy editors, linkcheckers, obsolete content detectors, and Web administrators. The team communicates through face-to-face communication and email messages, and also uses Novell Groupwise (www.novell.com) and Microsoft Project (www.microsoft.com). Additional workflow control is provided by a suite of Intranet programs created in house. Even with software support, the developers consider coordination of their efforts and work delegation their main challenge in maintaining the site.

Site Maintenance

To monitor server performance, TEN's maintenance team uses custom scripts developed in house. Access logs are analyzed remotely by

I/PRO (www.ipro.com), and the maintenance team also checks terms typed by users in local search engines. Access statistics information is echoed to some portions of the site, such as FileFactory's 10 most popular downloads page. Moderate (twofold) traffic changes are experienced but, due to the high overall traffic of the site, these are quite significant. Outdated content is removed when noticed by the developers or visitors, and it is also found via manual scans of the pages. Maintenance is more complex than many sites, since traffic comes through standard Web protocol and from proprietary game clients adapted to run on the Internet.

Dynamic Content Strategy

The update team follows a software/CD-ROM publishing model for Web-based content, which comes from original text, written documents, and files uploaded by users. Content is posted incrementally as it appears, and adjustments are frequently made according to visitor preference. Multiple staging servers are used to prepare content for online publication. Approximately 25 percent of the pages on the sites contain dynamic elements. Dynamic content is managed through database calls, automated CGI programs, and manual editing. Output supports HTML, Java/JavaScript, Dynamic HTML, bulletin-board postings to pages, and banner ad rotation. Personalized interaction is provided via personalized email analysis of terms typed into the local search engine. Outside the Web, the proprietary game client provides extensive interaction between game players, including admission, scores, and rankings. Since many games require rapid response from users, the system provides bandwidth checks to determine if a user's connection is fast enough to play.

Interface

Since going online, TEN has made five user interface changes. Reasons for the changes include improving navigation, attracting new users interested in the highly competitive gaming area, and improving compatibility with Web browsers. Interface is maintained through manually produced page templates, cascading style sheets, CGI scripts with fill-out forms, and assembly directly from database templates. The interface changes have also involved several behind-the-scenes changes, including directory structure modification, filename alterations, page format standardization, and server/operating system relocation.

Future Plans

The operators expect the percentage of dynamic content to increase by 15–30 percent over the next 12 months. Long term, it is likely that the increasing power of dynamic media will allow games currently mediated through proprietary clients to run directly through the Web interface.

The three sites analyzed in this chapter show significant differences in their approach to competitive sites. On the TEN site, dynamic content provides information and access to games—rather than to the games themselves, which run through proprietary software clients. On Auction World, bids are moved on a time scale comparable to regular Web communication. This allowed the designers to use standard HTML in most of the design, ensuring maximum compatibility and a clean page layout. Prizefight has taken a more ambitious approach to interface design, and has created a real-time dynamic site with response times measured in fractions of a second. While this interface has some problems (text animation flickers not unlike early computer games), it clearly represents the cutting edge of dynamic site development. Prizefight runs nearly as fast as conventional computer games, and its success bodes well for proprietary game systems moving to an all-Web interface. It is likely that when TEN begins offering Web-based multiplayer games, it will incorporate many of the dynamic innovations found in Auction World and Prizefight. Both of the latter sites required extensive and complex back-end programming to implement. In each case, the developers wrote their own proprietary site management and groupware/workflow applications to keep up with the rapid changes in the dynamic content. This indicates that groups wishing to create similar sites will need heavy-duty programming experience and must be willing to go through an extensive design/debugging process.

ONLINE CLASSROOMS AND VIRTUAL UNIVERSITIES

The Education Model

During the early history of the Web, the vast majority of sites were built and maintained by universities and other educational organizations. With the development of dynamic sites, today's focus is shifting from promoting offline education to developing true virtual classrooms. In the business word, computer-based training software is exiting from proprietary CD-ROM systems and migrating to the Web. According to a recent study by International Data Corporation (www.idcresearch .com/f/idcf.htm), the computer training market is expected to expand from $90 million in 1996 to almost $2 billion by the year 2000—about 15 percent of the total training market. As Internet access becomes commonplace, universities and companies may provide material to students regardless of their geographic location. The Internet's ability to create communities is also a powerful impetus to education. Dynamic Web-based discussion groups, chat, and even groupware all have direct applications in education and training, and may provide a level of instruction impossible with CD-ROMs or live classrooms. Connectivity also benefits instructors who may share media resources and information between themselves as well as with their students.

This chapter presents case studies of educational Web sites employing dynamic content. As such, it does not consider the variety of non-Web audioconference/videoconference systems used for distance learning in the past. For a more comprehensive list of resources, consult sites such as The Comprehensive Distance Education List of Resources (talon.extramural.uiuc.edu/ramage/disted.html) or the Distance Learning Resource Network (www.fwl.org/edtech/dlrn.html).

Features of Educational Sites

Educational Web sites (also referred to as "distance learning" resources) emphasize the transmission of knowledge between instructors and students, usually over an extended period of time. This requirement necessitates a different type of dynamic Web site than is needed for storefronts or Webcasts. Less reliance is placed on automated dynamic response and more on "human origin" content. While companies specializing in computer training are falling over each other to adapt extensive training systems to the Web environment, many sites get by using simple manual update technology. Developers frequently have access to resources distributed throughout a high-speed network within a university system, further aiding development and maintenance.

Online education sites may be divided into several groups. The correspondence-style model is adapted from computer-based training systems and provides self-paced course work. Students do most of their learning in isolation and interact primarily with the computer. When students encounter difficulties, they contact a virtual help desk for discussion assistance. The instructor-based model relies on dynamic development of course material posted by an instruction. Emulating the traditional classroom, sites following this second model begin with connectivity software and recruit instructors to develop content for online courses. Each method has advantages and disadvantages for particular markets. Students do much of their learning in shared environments allowing interaction with students and instructors. Both approaches are useful. For businesses teaching specific employee skills, the enhanced correspondence course is often appropriate. Educators wishing to reach a dispersed student body, or groups interested in providing education to individuals outside the traditional real world of schools, usually opt for the second more dynamic approach. A final class of sites provides access to information used by instructors in developing the course work.

Components of Dynamic Educational Sites

Dynamic sites offering educational resources and classes utilize several types of media elements in their presentation and interaction with their audience.

Membership System

Even when courses are free, most groups maintaining educational sites collect information from students through questionnaires. This information is used to identify the community of students and teachers within the site, and allow or restrict access to educational resources. Since students may be revealing sensitive information in their registration data, security measures are developed by the maintenance team.

Instructor Membership

For sites providing virtual classrooms, a parallel mechanism is established to recruit teachers. Since Internet access and competency are automatic requirements for instructors, it makes sense to put instructor registration on line. Instructors will need to coordinate their teaching efforts, so membership-based discussion and collaborative systems are also useful.

Course Calendars

Educational sites require strict control over the time at which course work is prepared and submitted to the site. Students need a way to rapidly locate course material and identify deadlines for testing and graduation. Live interactions, such as chat and threaded discussion, require a mechanism for notifying participants.

Course Development

As the sophistication of the Web interface and dynamic content grows, instructors need authoring tools that insulate them from programming details. A number of companies have moved to answer this need. Examples include DigitalThink (www.digitalthink.com), which develops Web-based correspondence-style courses for companies and individual students. Another company specializing in course development is Centra (www.centra.com), whose Symposium software ($35,000; Windows NT) provides a standard Java-based environment for developing courses using conferencing, text-based chat, and shared whiteboards.

Personalization Tools

Students match their current skill levels to the range of instruction provided. In a simple case, course requirements are displayed on the site for easy access, and students have access to instructors to decide whether a course is appropriate. More complex personalization software might take the students' registration data and dynamically present them with course work appropriate for their levels. While such a system does not exist yet, it would be extremely valuable for large educational sites offering classes to very large audiences.

Case Study: SUNLINK

URL: www.sunlink.ucf.edu (see Figure 12.1)

Contact: Matt Renfroe

Email: sunlink@mail.firn.edu

Size of Web site (pages): 1150

Pages with dynamic content: 25%

Weekly visitors: 3,000 hits; 150 unique IPs

Figure 12.1 SUNLINK (www.sunlink.ucf.edu).

Site online: July 1996

Dynamic content online: September 1996

SUNLINK represents a "back-end" educational site designed to promote information exchange between instructors. Funded by the Florida Department of Education, SUNLINK provides a shared database of materials available to K12 educators through library media centers. Originally distributed on CD-ROM, the SUNLINK database has been retrofitted to the Web site. The site provides access to this database over the Internet. While the site is technically an educator's Extranet, many of the media listings may be of general interest to educators elsewhere on the Internet. Operating as a dynamic Web site, SUNLINK must track and update media listings from libraries scattered throughout the state, present simple ways of finding resources, and facilitate contact between educators. The site developed for this has features common to most educational sites, and is described in greater detail next.

Infrastructure

SUNLINK operates on a PowerMac 7200/120 with 32 megabytes of RAM and 1 gigabyte of disk space. Despite the use of relatively slow server hardware, access speeds are comparable to other sites. The Web server connects to the general Internet through a T1 line, providing sufficient bandwidth for current and anticipated future traffic. As with almost all Mac-based Web sites, SUNLINK uses Webstar from Starnine Technologies (www.starnine.com). At present, the site runs as a database and does not support direct delivery of audio or video resources.

Team Structure

SUNLINK's production uses a Webmaster model, under which a single individual is responsible for all maintenance, site design, and content updates. The SUNLINK administrator is also responsible for actively soliciting content for the site, and also has editorial control over postings. Coordination with primary content providers is achieved through a mixture of YellNet, PaperNet, and EmailNet (Chapter 2).

Site Maintenance

Localized on an inhouse academic network, the SUNLINK Web server is monitored directly. With local access, no special software is necessary to determine whether the site is online. Access logs are processed using the Analog 2.0 (www.statslab.cam.ac.uk/~sret1/analog/) shareware program. No attempt is made to adjust content based on visitor traffic, which tends to be constant and does not show sudden spikes of activity. While the interface of the site has been changed in the past, it has not been necessary to adjust the basic file or directory structure of the server since the site came online in 1996. System backups are supported locally through CD-R drives.

Dynamic Content Strategy

Dynamic content keeps the SUNLINK site interesting for its audience, who often visit the site repeatedly looking for current information. Information about media resources is received from K12 educators located throughout the state and is loaded into the database for further access. Page updates are handled via manual text editing, and dynamic page elements use Maxum's (www.maxum .com) NetCloak and NetForms software. This system allows the SUNLINK administrator to personalize pages based on date, time, address, and browser type. Using this software has circumvented the need for a full database. This speeds up the operation of the site relative to a database page delivery system. SUNLINK also hosts two distinct search engines allowing users to explore both the SUNLINK Web pages and media database. As shown in Figure 12.2, media resource information is accessed graphically through pages displaying maps of various Florida counties. Outdated information is detected and removed manually, and most old information is archived rather than thrown away.

Interface

Since much of SUNLINK's content is entered manually, keeping the interface consistent over time is a major challenge for the administrator. Since going online, the SUNLINK site has undergone two Web facelifts designed to improve navigation and increase the interest of regular visitors. To simplify interface maintenance, NetCloak software is used to create specialized page templates (or macros)

Figure 12.2 Graphical interface to the SUNLINK media database.

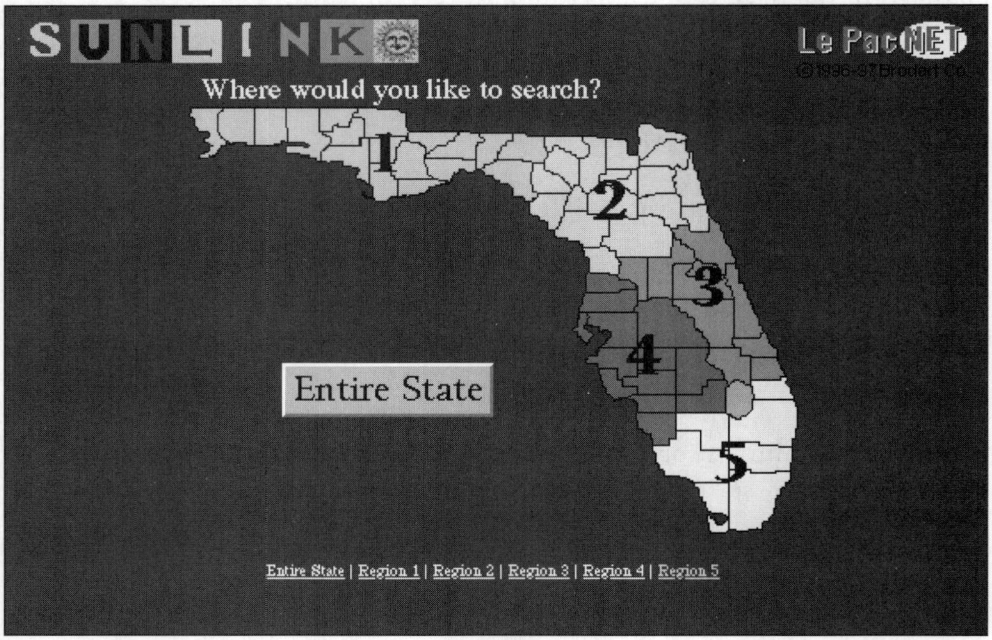

that allow common interface elements to be automatically replicated across the site.

Future Plans

The SUNLINK Web site plans to incorporate greater interactivity in the future, including chat/forum areas. The percentage of pages with dynamic content is expected to double in the remaining months of 1997.

Case Study: Spectrum Universal's Virtual University

URL: www.vu.org (see Figure 12.3)

Contact: Paul Leighton

Email: campus@vu.org

Size of Web site (pages): ~600

Pages with dynamic content: 65%

Weekly visitors: 750,000 hits; 20,000 unique IPs

Site online: April 1995

Dynamic content online: July 1996

Spectrum Universal has a long history of providing online educational content. Beginning with online courses and workshops through modem bulletin boards in the early 1980s, more than a half-million people from 128 countries have participated in their online classes. Spectrum was one of the first educational groups to move to the Web, and it continues to actively recruit teachers and students online. Currently, the Spectrum Virtual University serves

65,000–70,000 adult learners from around the world during a typical semester, and this number is expected to increase substantially by the end of 1997. As a pioneering educational site supporting an instructor-based system, the Virtual University illustrates the requirements for supporting public education on the Internet.

Figure 12.3 Spectrum Virtual University (www.vu.org).

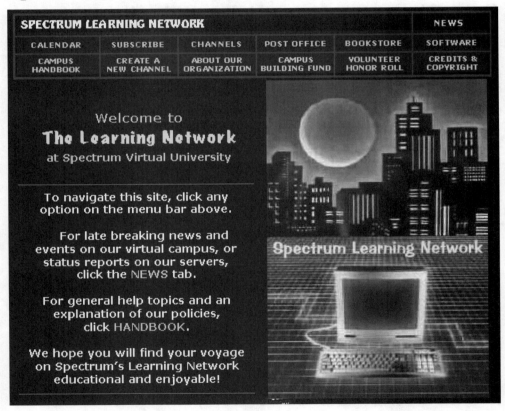

Infrastructure

The Spectrum Virtual University is hosted remotely on a shared T3-level network. Hardware consists of a Sun workstation with 64 megabytes of RAM and a 2-gigabyte hard drive running the Solaris operating system. The site uses a modified version of Apache compiled with the Nod_perl and SSL modules. The current configuration was established after several experiments with alternate hardware and software.

Team Structure

Maintenance and updates are organized around a model closely resembling television production, which complements the channel-based model used for information delivery. As with many growing sites, Spectrum has had to adjust its team structure in recent times. While a detailed personnel plan formed part of the original design of the site, rapid growth of content has necessitated a new division of labor for update team members. Currently, the team includes an overall producer, content collectors, writers, editors, media conversion specialists, and a Web administrator. Content is provided by instructors, many of which are recruited online through fill-out forms. A copy editor position was developed to check incoming content for grammar, punctuation, and accuracy. Other online editors control the style and form of content presentation.

Team communication proceeds through a wide variety of methods. Phone, fax, and email are part of the system, along with bulletin board software developed especially for the site. A custom Virtual Conference Room was created for Spectrum by Webmaster, Inc. (www.webmaster.com) and uses a dual Java/IRC platform. Chat and billboard areas are open to all visitors. In other areas of the site, specialized administrative pages are utilized by the development team and class instructors. Spectrum has found that extensive support for collaboration is absolutely necessary for the success of the university; group management of the enormous volume of content flowing through the site presents the single greatest challenge faced by the developers.

Site Maintenance

With its early start on the Web, Spectrum had to develop its own management system. Currently, the site is maintained through a mixture of Unix operating systems commands (e.g., Unix "top" program for monitoring server processes), commercial software, and inhouse utility/commercial programs. The advanced proprietary management system is one of the features distinguishing the Virtual University from its competitors, and it enables support for the high daily traffic experienced by the site. Daily log analysis utilizes a custom utility designed in house, and monthly analysis reports are generated using WebTrends (www.webtrends.com). Access statistics play a critical role in the site's dynamic strategy. Other custom utilities validate pages, check for broken links, and monitor page download times. Since the site experiences frequent jumps in traffic, real-time monitoring is necessary for efficient operation.

To increase site performance, Spectrum exploited the fast and configurable Apache server. By compiling in the freeware mod_perl module, calls to Perl programs may be made without triggering a standard CGI interface. This eliminates the need to repeatedly launch separate copies of Perl for every CGI script, bulletin board, and other programs executing on the server. The site is backed up through a standard tape drive. Like many early Web sites, rapid changes in interface and content have necessitated major reorganizations of the site, which has been moved to a new server four times. Initially, the site was run under Unix. When NT Web systems first appeared, the site was moved to the NT platform, and then was moved back to Unix six months later! In the words of the administrator, the NT server was "slower than molasses" compared to Unix. Spectrum's experience should serve as a caution to other sites considering a Unix/NT migration.

Dynamic Content Strategy

Content for the Virtual University flows from a wide variety of sources: original documents, translated word processor/desktop publishing files, graphics, and original multimedia. The site also supports a significant level of user-driven content through its classified ads, calendars (see Figure 12.4), and discussion groups. A wide variety of media formats are supported, including HTML, Java/JavaScript, Dynamic HTML, collaborative art, bulletin boards, and banner advertising. Information is posted directly to the site using both incremental and periodic strategies. Despite the high level of content, a staging server is not used. Document control is accomplished through custom groupware developed in house. Dynamic content is enabled through a database (Chapter 5) and manual HTML editing. A significant fraction of content is generated on the fly directly from the database. A search/replace program is used to detect obsolete content, but the update team also relies on manual scans and heads-up messages sent by students. Depending on their content, old pages are either archived or removed from the site. With an audience composed of students and instructors, a key feature of Spectrum's dynamic content strategy has been to encourage repeat visits and the formation of a long-time online community. For this reason, dynamic chat and discussion areas are available to all. The update team carefully analyzes log traffic and adjusts site content for maximum use by the current students and alumni. Rapid feedback to standard queries uses auto-responders created using Procmail (check the how-to page at www.gl.umbc.edu/~ian/procmail .html).

Interface

The look-and-feel of the Spectrum Virtual University is a major factor in its success. Interface changes have occurred on an average of every six months since the site was founded. The most recent change moved the site from a newspaper-style format to a 99-channel archi-

Figure 12.4 Event calendar page for the Spectrum Virtual University.

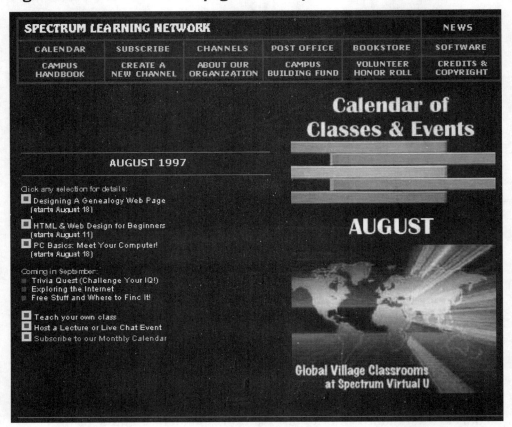

tecture that provides greater efficiency. Interface upgrades have also improved navigation and ensured compatibility with the rapidly changing Web browser market. The overall site interface is standardized through a mix of manually produced templates, pages generated from custom groupware/workflow software, and fill-out forms attached to CGI scripts. Careful interface design helps the Virtual University to cope with high traffic and traffic spikes. Individual graphics are processed using Raspberry Hill Publishing's GifWizard (www.raspberryhill.com/gifwizard.html) to optimize appearance while minimizing file size.

Future Plans

Spectrum expects the percentage of dynamic content on the site to jump from 65 percent to 90 percent within three months. In order to manage this level of throughput, the developers plan to implement a unified groupware/workflow strategy centered around Netscape's (www.netscape.com) SuiteSpot platform. The features on online education (e.g., fixed course material used on a regular basis) lend themselves naturally to push technology, and Spectrum plans to evolve its current channel interface into a true push system. In order to avoid being locked into a proprietary architecture, Spectrum has dismissed Microsoft's CDF format and plans to create push channels using Netscape's Netcaster protocol. Spectrum also plans to introduce real-time audio/video streaming and a hybrid CD-ROM/Internet product in the near future.

Case Study: DigitalThink, Inc.

URL: www.digitalthink.com (see Figure 12.5)

Contact: Steven C. Zahm

Email: info@digitalthink.com

Size of Web site (pages): 5,555

Pages with dynamic content: 90%

Weekly visitors: 600,000 hits; 10,000 unique IPs

Site online: January 1997

Dynamic content online: January 1997

DigitalThink develops and delivers training over the Web. The site includes a course promotion area and delivery system. Students sign up for courses and pay online through a secure transaction system. After signing up, they select a student ID/password and create accounts. Active students work in a dynamic environment created by Java applets linked to a database system. The students' course work study is enhanced with chat rooms, discussion forums, a one-to-one messaging system, as well as animation, sound, and Java applets that are designed to enhance the learning experience.

Figure 12.5 DigitalThink (www.digitalthink.com).

Infrastructure

The DigitalThink site is on a dedicated server remotely hosted by an ISP. A mix of Unix and Windows NT servers is used to power the site. Installed software includes Web servers from Netscape and Microsoft, the Progressive Networks RealMedia server (www.real .com) for audio and video (Chapter 10), and additional utilities enabling secure commerce and cybercash transactions (Chapter 7). Site information is stored in a Sybase database interfaced with Java front ends through a JDBC gateway (Chapter 5).

Team Structure

A large team is necessary to manage the DigitalThink site. Job descriptions include an overall site producer, editor-in-chief, secondary editors, writers, content converters, uploaders, copy editors, site testers, and individuals who specifically remove outdated material. Team interaction is organized through a mixture of email messages, printed orders/reports, and groupware/workflow software. As with many other Web-based companies, time rather than resources presents the greatest challenge for maintenance and updates.

Site Maintenance

The DigitalThink site experiences large changes in traffic on short notice, but commercial performance or load-balancing tools have not been installed. Instead, monitoring proceeds at the system level. To manage the load, the maintenance team has installed enough extra capacity to handle unexpected traffic jumps. The rapid growth of the service has caused considerable reorganization of the server facility. In the first six months of operation, the maintenance team has had to move content to new servers and across operating systems.

Dynamic Content Strategy

DigitalThink developed a dynamic content system to keep its course offerings updated and to effectively compete with other educational services. In managing updates, the team has adopted a model most similar to software and CD-ROM publishing. Updates are developed from original documents, graphics, database information, original multimedia, and content contributed by visitors to the site. The complexity of the course information requires the use of multiple staging servers and editing cycles. Actual course work is generated directly from the Sybase system through middleware using Java and a JDBC gateway. Output pages contain a mixture of HTML, Java/JavaScript, streaming audio/video, chat/bulletin board interfaces, and push technology. Course promotion information is not entered into the system; instead, it is created using static pages with individual media elements generated by CGI scripts. Students interact onsite through a one-to-one messaging system. The update team makes extensive use of personalization strategies enabled by Web Trainer, a proprietary software application developed specifically for the site. The program constructs personalized content using grades, stated preferences, course enrollment, recently viewed course pages, and records of interactions with other students and tutors. Outdated material is recognized and removed by manual scans, search/replace using HTML editors, and custom utilities that recognize expired tags created by site management software. Old information is archived, and the site can roll back to earlier versions if necessary.

Interface

Since the site's launch, the DigitalThink developers have made two significant changes in its appearance. The interface was changed to accommodate new types of content, improve site navigation, and attract new interest from regular users. Interface consistency is maintained through a combination of manually generated page templates, CGI scripts with fill-out forms, and templates generated within the site's groupware/workflow environment. During development, the update team has frequently processed older pages on the site to standardize them to the new interface. Other pages have been converted from static HTML to on-the-fly database generation.

Future Plans

In the near future, DigitalThink intends to expand its current software management tools rather than replace them with commercial software. The developers expect steady growth in courses and students, and they plan to incorporate new dynamic features (e.g., DHTML) into the site as they become available.

Case Study: Smithsonian's Seeds of Change Garden

URL: horizon.nmsu.edu/garden (see Figure 12.6)

Contact: C. C. Chamberlin

Email: ccc@acca.nmsu.edu

Size of Web site (pages): 100

Pages with dynamic content: 100%

Weekly visitors: 15,000 hits; 300 unique IPs

Site online: August 1996

Dynamic content online: August 1996

Smithsonian's Seeds of Change Garden provides an educational service and support for an online community developing and using unique course work based on an exhibit developed by the Smithsonian. Its primary purpose is curriculum development for

Figure 12.6 Smithsonian's Seeds of Change Garden site (horizon.nmsu.edu/garden).

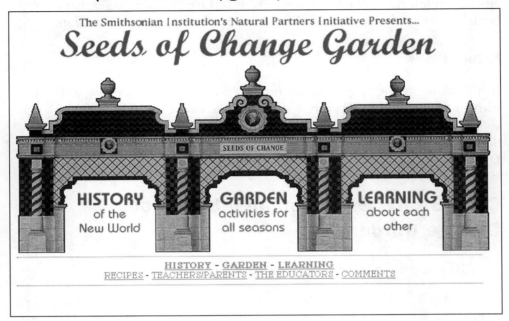

middle schools, and content is developed by teachers working with the Smithsonian to create classroom materials based on the exhibit. The course information allows teachers to develop a hands-on project that emphasizes the rich diversity that can result from cultural exchange. Students, parents, and educators use the site to plan, cultivate, and harvest from a garden, and learn about the similarities and differences among themselves through the experience of growing, cooking, and eating food from different cultures. Dynamic content is implemented on a relatively small scale but allows substantial savings in administration and provides personalization for its specialized audience.

Infrastructure

Seeds of Change is hosted on a dedicated server on a remote ISP, and runs on a Power Macintosh 8500 with 49 megabytes of RAM and a 2-gigabyte hard drive. Connection to the Internet is at T1 speeds. A remote tape backup system is used to archive site material. The system runs Mac OS 7.5.3, WebSTAR 2.0 (www.starnine.com), a RealAudio server (www.real.com), and Maxum's (www.maxum.com) NetCloak software.

Team Structure

Since so much of the site's information is contributed by its audience of teachers and universities, the update team's role is largely editorial. Individual teachers write and maintain editorial control content, while the dedicated update team provides markup, graphics creation, and dynamic programming. The dedicated team consists of editors and a Web administrator. Specialized workflow software is not employed; instead, the team and teachers communicate face to face, through paper-based orders and reports, and through email messages. Like many educational sites, the developers work part time, and cite responding to audience contributions as their biggest challenge.

Site Maintenance

No special programs are currently used to monitor site performance. ServerStat (www.kitchen-sink.com/ss.html) is used to keep track of basic access statistics, but passive access statistics are not used in site maintenance. Instead, actively contributed feedback submitted through registration forms and email is used to tune the content. Part of the reason for this is the Smithsonian name, which attracts a significant number of random visitors to the site and would skew log analysis. The site managers frequently cope with sudden changes in traffic, usually caused by an entire classroom logging on at the same time. To date, this has not caused problems; the maintenance team simply increases the maximum number of allowed users in the Web server's configuration files. Old material is generally removed completely rather than being archived. The site can be rolled back to an earlier version using backup tapes, but special functionality has not been added to this system.

Dynamic Content Strategy

The primary purpose of adding dynamic content to the site is support for the online community of parents, teachers, and students. Virtually all pages contain simple dynamic dates and counter elements, and approximately one-fifth provide personalized information depending on whether the visitor is a parent or teacher. As with many other Mac-based servers, CGI-style programming using NetCloak implements dynamic content. Additional content is added manually, derived primarily from written documents and non-Web documents translated to HTML format. Content is typically added to staging servers (running on the same hardware platform) and is published simply by moving it under the Web server's directory tree. Since the middle-school classrooms that are part of the target audience usually do not have advanced media support, all dynamic operations are done server side and delivered as simple HTML compatible with all Web browsers. Obsolete content is detected by the contributing teachers or update team and is removed using search/replace functions in HTML editors.

Interface

The site has made only one interface change, driven by testing it with focus groups within its audience. Changes resulting from this study included reorganizing the content so it would be in a more intuitive place, and improving general navigation. The combined use of Mac OS and NetCloak has allowed a major reorganization event to be accomplished in about an hour. During its time online, the site has also undergone significant internal reorganization, including changing the overall directory structure and moving the site to a new server. Since the switch was made between Mac systems, the entire process was relatively painless.

Future Plans

At present, the developers do not envision increasing the proportion of dynamic content or substantially changing the infrastructure of the site. However, a companion site is being developed to handle gardening projects associated with arid regions. There are tentative plans for a one-time content addition covering the material in the Smithsonian's own exhibit.

The case studies in this chapter reveal additional features found in many dynamic educational sites. The SUNLINK site demonstrates that groups with modest resources and tools can create an effective system for serving their audience. In this case, close attention to primary content and interface were more important than elaborate interactive schemes or cutting-edge software. A similar theme is found on the Smithsonian Seeds of Change site, where response to direct input from teacher and parents replaces programs for monitoring access statistics. The Seeds of Change site also manages to provide some personalization for its audience through basic dynamic media elements rather than high-end integrated programs. The Spectrum experience demonstrates the need for the maintenance team to anticipate the effects of changes in hardware and software on site performance. Despite the widely perceived ascendance of Windows NT as a Web server platform, an attempt to migrate from Unix caused serious problems and eventually had to be abandoned. The Spectrum experience also demonstrates how careful interface design and close monitoring of site activity may be used to support a large audience with a small number of servers. Taken together, these four examples show how planning and hard work may stretch the often limited resources of educational groups. However, it appears that if online instruction (rather than support for an educational community) is desired, high-end dynamic programming is necessary. Both Spectrum and DigitalThink have created dynamic sites using advanced programming and site maintenance techniques. As is the case for many dynamic sites currently on the Internet, the Spectrum and DigitalThink sites both developed proprietary management systems instead of purchasing a commercial product. Of the two, DigitalThink has taken the ambitious step toward an all-dynamic system based on the Java programming language.

PART FIVE

THE DYNAMIC FUTURE

TRENDS IN DYNAMIC WEB SITES  13

T he state of dynamic technology on the Web is the product of only a few years of design and innovation, yet it is already hard to remember when the Web was a static show of text and pictures. Dynamic technology has rapidly brought all the capabilities of multimedia—including audio, video, and animation—to the Web and has incorporated communication and collaboration systems characteristic of the rest of the Internet. Relational and object-oriented database links have provided the Web's worldwide audience with rapid access to information. Where is dynamic content going in the future? This chapter considers some trends appearing in the industry as a whole, often illustrated in the various case studies presented in earlier chapters.

Trends in Current Dynamic Technology

Despite the short history of dynamic content on the Web, a strong trend can be summed up in a single phrase: *media convergence*. By providing a common visual format for the distribution of images, audio, video, and interactive multimedia, the Web fuses formerly different information models into a seamless whole. This affects the final display of dynamic content as well as the traditional models discussed in the previous case-study chapters. In the future dynamic Web, many business and communication models that are distinct today will come together into a new medium.

Convergence of Periodic and Incremental Updates

In the print world, production costs require publishers to bunch content into single hard-copy editions. In contrast, many dynamic Web publishing sites seem to be drifting from periodic to continuous update models. The hunter-gatherer model for user interaction with the Web encourages users to frequent familiar sites, constantly on the lookout for something new. In such an environment, periodic updates, even if conscientiously performed, may interest users less than a site that always contains something new. Evidence for this shift is found in the sites profiled in Chapter 9, all of which appear to be dropping periodic postings in favor of incremental strategies. The main reason cited by the developers was a competitive edge over broadcast and print media, and this advantage seems likely to drive the Web's dynamic model in the future.

Convergence of Interactive and Broadcast Models

Current Webcast models for real-time audio and video on the Web leave little room for user feedback. With the introduction of new interactive standards, this is likely to change. A primitive example of this is illustrated in the "hot start" unicast option for encoding Internet-aware video using Apple's QuickTime (quicktime .apple.com). As the video progressively downloads, users move forward and backward within the frames they have already received. It is a small jump to extend this strategy to elements within the video itself. For example, it will soon be possible to define clickable areas within moving video images that follow individual characters and camera movements. In the future, Internet-based video servers may have an additional processing layer where these meta-hyperlinks are dynamically imposed on live broadcast streams. This kind of user control will change the very nature of broadcast media.

Convergence of Commerce and Online Communities

Many sales sites are working hard to develop long-term relations with customers and vendors. When these groups solidify into stable communities, the dynamic site becomes a meeting ground for exchange rather than a billboard or order form. In this environment, vendors create increasingly personalized proposals for their clients, who respond with purchases and commentary on products. Forming tight, community-based loops will increase business efficiency and make online commerce nearly indistinguishable from today's chats and threaded discussions.

Integration of Interface into Dynamic Content Strategies

Virtually all the Web sites that provided case studies for this book reported making frequent and extensive changes to their interface, color scheme, navigation, and content organization. These rapid changes—usually orchestrated through manual updates apart from other dynamic software—are likely to become automated in the near future. Document and site management systems may treat the overall interface as another kind of dynamic data with a regular workflow for modification.

Convergence of Physical and Virtual Commerce

To date, most product sales have involved discrete, nonelectronic items such as golf sets and audio CDs. As the quality of Web content improves, selling access to electronic information will become a feature in dynamic commerce sites. The fastest growth is currently occurring in music, where pay-per-download systems are undergoing rapid development. Companies such as LiquidAudio (www.liquidaudio.com) are enabling music delivery for a fee, and other companies are experimenting with for-fee software distribution by a similar scheme. For products capable of being converted to digital format, the distinction between hard copy and electronic files may soon disappear.

Convergence of Sales, Auctions, and Games

Dynamic sites allow rapid updates of product information on a scale of seconds to hours. In the future, personalization systems might allow the customer to define the features of a desired product and have vendors dynamically adjust their products to accommodate the request. Prices might be dynamically adjusted through an auction-like scheme, and sites providing product catalogs would take on many of the attributes of competitive games and auctions (Chapter 11).

New Forms of Dynamic Content

Dynamic Web content also has the potential to move beyond existing media systems to create entirely new ones. As developers and users become familiar with the Internet environment, they continue to explore limits of the medium, exploiting its unique communication and collaborative features. In recent times, several forms of dynamic content have appeared that have no counterpart outside the Internet. Some of these new concepts are discussed next.

Tele-Operation

This unique form of dynamic content was briefly discussed in Chapter 5. Running in reverse from the Webcast model, tele-operation allows users to send their own content streams that dynamically alter the behavior of a robot arm, spy camera, or other physical devices. Beyond the mundane concept of turning on your microwave through its own personal Web site, more realistic possibilities seem likely to be implemented. Web-based systems could substitute for beepers and other systems currently activated by phone, and equipment in dangerous or remote locations could be operated with relative ease. Tele-operation may also have entertainment value; NASA's Jet Propulsion Laboratory (www.jpl.nasa.gov) is already considering building a copy of the rover it sent to Mars and open it to control from the Internet.

Hybrid Media

One form of dynamic media likely to become very common in the next few years is so important that it deserves separate discussion—linking read-only CD-ROM and DVD discs with dynamic data delivered from the Web. Developers are enhancing their Web authoring environments by adding universal "drivers"—translation systems that publish the same formatted information through the Internet, CD-ROMs, or any mixture of the two. This allows developers to archive static information on the disc—thereby reducing download time—and deliver only dynamic media elements through the user's Internet connection. An effective hybrid system requires a high degree of sophistication acting at many levels between disc media, server, and Web browser (Figure 13.1). Business applications might include a "company in a box"—a complete mini-Intranet that may be carried by remote users and updated when necessary over the Internet. Other possibilities include rich game and virtual community environments that pull high-resolution images, audio, and video from the disc and combine them with messages from other users received online. This strategy has significant advantages over streaming media approaches discussed in Chapter 10. Examples of systems currently being developed to realize these concepts are presented next, and additional information is found at sites such as Teleshuttle (www.teleshuttle.com/resource).

Figure 13.1 Diagram showing the complex interactions necessary to support hybrid CD/DVD Internet technology.

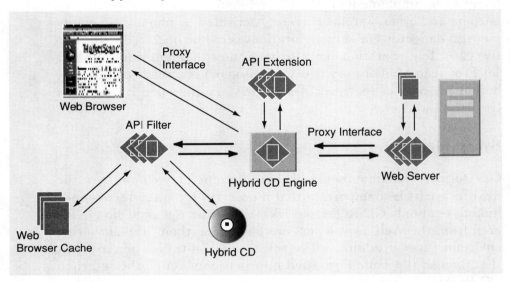

MarketScape's WebCD Pro (www.marketscape.com; $2995; Windows, Macintosh) is being used by major companies including Microsoft (www.microsoft.com), Tektronix (www.tek.com), and Byte Magazine (www.byte.com). The system uses a second-generation Hybrid Engine with client-side intelligence that optimizes browsing speed and content. Designed to provide more than a self-contained, disc-based Web site, it works with the Internet connection to accelerate online browsing and integrate downloaded files with content from CD and local disk caches. This complex behavior is accomplished by running the Hybrid Engine as a local server. It supports embedded navigation elements and dynamic URLs created by Java applets, ActiveX programs, or scripts without editing or recompiling programs. MarketScape customizes WebCD using industry-standard ISAPI (Internet Server API) extensions and filters to support local database queries, shopping-cart interfaces, or ad rotation. The

WebCD Publisher authoring environment imports a Web site directly to CD-ROM, integrates multimedia, and completes the final "build" of an ISO 9660-compliant, platform-independent master image for duplication. No specialized server is required on the Internet. Completed discs are accessed through the WebCD Viewer on computers with an installed Internet connection.

Panasonic's (www.panasonic.co.jp) DVD/Internet system is designed for interactive video. The user's computer requires a DVD-ROM drive and an MPEG-2 board that decodes and plays full-screen, full-motion video within a Web browser window. DVD-ROM-based user identification is possible through the prerecording of a disc-specific identification number on the DVD-ROM disc. The identification number is transmitted from the Web client to the server and checked with the user information management database to create individual information. For example, a group developing a travel service could link a DVD with movies of selected destinations combined with dynamic Web data including airline schedules and ticket purchases.

Macromedia's Director 6 (www.macromedia.com; $950; Macintosh, Windows) is being offered as a painless way to remain in the most popular CD-ROM environment while providing direct links to the Web. Standard Web servers may be used to deliver information to the hybrid system. Using Shockwave commands and new commands in Lingo (Director's proprietary scripting language), it is possible to have individual media elements in CD-ROM programs draw their content from HTML pages, images, streaming audio/animation, or even other Shockwave movies that are online at the same time. This last feature offers the potential for developing Internet-based multiuser games within Director. Macromedia's goal seems to be an alternative interface to the classic Web browser.

New Alloy's LiveCD (www.newalloy.com; $3,400–$5,000; Windows NT/95, Unix) promotes a "write once, publish anywhere" approach to content. LiveCD applications integrate media that reside anywhere—CD-ROM, DVD, hard disk, and the Web. The software's

Persistent Cache Update Management technology manages delivery of content from each source in an efficient fashion. The system consists of a Publisher authoring environment, a central LiveCD push server, and LiveCD client software. Each time users log on to the Internet, the LiveCD requests updates from the server that are pushed downstream via defined channels. On the client site, a special Xtras interface is available for integrating LiveCD with Director 6 applications.

Virtual Worlds

The ultimate goal in the minds of many Web developers is the creation of rich 3D virtual environments that react to visitors in ways reminiscent of the real world. Virtual world development has slackened during 1997, partly due to the poor performance of many VRML-based software companies. As user hardware and bandwidth improves, virtual worlds may again become a promising source of dynamic content. It is possible that some of the self-generating programs from artificial life (discussed in Chapter 5) will form the beginning of the second wave of virtual environments. Ultimately, however, developers need to be careful with virtual worlds and remember that the Web and Internet in themselves are virtual worlds—optimized for delivering information in a fundamentally different way than real-world exchanges. Most Web users cite quick access to information as their reason for being online, and they are distracted and irritated by excessive noninformational multimedia "padding." Will Web users treat dynamic virtual worlds as bandwidth hogs to be avoided, or environments that enhance their quest for useful knowledge? Only the future will tell.

Dynamic sites are among the most exciting and challenging aspects of Internet development. Individuals, companies, and other groups considering a move to the dynamic Web need to be aware of its potential and limitations. Resources such as this book may help in making the correct decisions, but they need to be supplemented with the real-world experience of dynamic sites. Prospective developers should conduct their own case studies and learn what is really necessary to manage and host dynamic content. Developers need to explore the state of the dynamic Web and find contacts to help them select and use dynamic content in a useful and efficient way. They also need to compare the features offered by dynamic sites to their own goals and determine how they might adapt them to their particular brand of promotion, sales, entertainment, or publishing on the Web. The final result will be a medium appreciated by all—a dynamic Web that is flexible and responsive to the needs of its users.

APPENDIX
WHAT'S ON THE WEB SITE?

The Web site for this book at www.wiley.com/compbook/novak is full of resources. You'll find:

> **Software**: A useful set of links to freeware and shareware software that developers may use to add dynamic content to their own Web sites as well as commercial software sites for which demonstration/trial software is available. Both maintenance and update software are listed. The quantity of dynamic software available is growing rapidly, and the Web site contains additional links to software not available at the time of publication. Examples of software and resources follow.

- Web server software
- Link-checker programs
- Site code and HTML compatibility checkers
- Programs for access log analysis
- Storage/archiving programs
- Programs identifying "bottlenecks" in Internet traffic
- Programs for Web traffic balancing across multiple servers
- Web site performance
- Document conversion to Web format
- Dynamic HTML
- Java program archives
- CGI program archives

- Web-enabled databases
- Database/Web "middleware" and Web-based programming languages
- Obsolete content detection
- Mailing list and threaded discussion software
- Personalized chat systems
- Commercial site management software for large sites
- Web-based workflow systems
- Agents and content personalization software
- Push software, Netcaster and CDF

Updates: Announcements of new and useful dynamic site technology. For example, recent advances in freeware/shareware for Web/database connectivity technology such as mSQL/mySQL will be featured as they become available.

Case Studies: Links to public Web sites that were featured in the book's case studies and that provide outstanding examples of dynamic programming, including:

- Content Promotion and Sales
  - MoviePeople (film database)
  - Ostry Internet Solutions (online catalog development)
  - Claims Information Network (insurance claims)
- User-driven Community Sites
  - The Ultimate Band List (music search engine)
  - Womex Online (merchandise exchange)
- Periodic Publishing Media
  - Internet Review (real estate and shopping cyberzine)
  - HotNews.com (media aggregration)
- Events and Webcasting

- Showtimes (movie schedules)
- LA Live (netcasting)
- UltimateTV (television programs and news)
- Online Games and Auctions
  - Auction World (online auctions)
  - TEN (Total Entertainment Network, online games)
  - PrizeFight (online auctions)
- Online Classrooms and Virtual Universities
  - SUNLINK
  - Spectrum Universal's Virtual University
  - DigitalThink
  - Smithsonian's Seeds of Change Garden

What Is Freeware/Shareware?

Freeware is software that is distributed via disk, BBS systems, and the Internet at no charge. The software may be used and distributed freely as long as the use it is put to follows the license agreement included with it.

Shareware (also known as user supported software) is a revolutionary means of distributing software created by individuals or companies too small to make inroads into the more conventional retail distribution networks . The authors of Shareware retain all rights to the software under the copyright laws while still allowing free distribution. This gives the user the chance to freely obtain and try out software to see if it fits his needs. Shareware should not be confused with Public Domain software even though they are often obtained from the same sources.

If you continue to use Shareware after trying it out, you are expected to register your use with the author and pay a registration fee. What you get in return depends on the author, but it may include a printed manual, free updates, telephone support, etc.

Hardware Requirements

Dynamic site software is available for three major platforms: Unix, Windows NT/95, and Macintosh. Since this software usually runs on the same system supporting a Web site, the hardware must support standard Web server operation and the CGI programming interface. Typical Unix configurations include a system with a 1 gigabyte hard drive and at least 32 megabytes of RAM, coupled with an operating system such as SunOS, Solaris, Linux, BSDi, or FreeBSD. If this software is installed on other systems (e.g., Silicon Graphics or VMS or AIX), it may require modifications to the program's source code. Hardware requirements for Windows NT are comparable to Unix. Macintosh systems will need at least 16 megabytes of RAM, a 1 gigabyte hard drive, and System 7.5 or greater. All platforms must support an Internet connection (e.g., leased line) providing 24-hour access to the Web server and its contents. If your site is hosted on a remote ISP or home page service (such as Tripod or GeoCities), you may need to get permission from the service to install the software.

Installing the Software

To install the software, follow these simple steps:

1. Download the software from the Internet.
2. If the software has been compressed with a program such as gzip (Windows/Unix) or compress (Unix), run the appropriate decompression program.
3. Read the instructions to determine if the software needs to reside in a specific installation directory.

4. Start the installation program. On Unix systems, you will usually use the commands "make," "make test," and "make install." Mac and Windows systems usually provide custom installers that prompt the operator at each step of the installation.

Using the Software

Once installed, software use depends on the specific nature of the dynamic program. Maintenance programs usually run immediately with only minor configuration changes. In contrast, programs supporting dynamic updates frequently require extensive preference settings. Typically, configuring the software will require that user, filename, directory, and version information is taken from the Web server and added to preference files. In many cases, dynamic software only provides a development environment rather than a complete program, so it will be necessary to write custom applications specific to your site. Content destined for dynamic presentation will also need to be converted to the appropriate format for use by the programs.

User Assistance and Information

Developers of freeware/shareware programs often provide support for their programs through mailing lists and discussion groups on the Internet. If you plan to actively develop using freeware/shareware products, you will find these free services to be an invaluable resource. Most high-end commercial programs come with formal technical support available by phone, fax, or email. Valuable information for both freeware/shareware and commercial programs is available through Usenet. A simple way to explore this information is to visit DejaNews (**www.dejanews.com**) and search their Usenet archives via the Web.

The software accompanying this book is being provided as is without warranty or support of any kind. Should you require basic installation assistance, or if your media is defective, please call our product support number at (212) 850-6194 weekdays between 9 A.M. and 4 P.M. Eastern Standard Time. Or, we can be reached via e-mail at: **wprtusw@wiley.com**.

To place additional orders or to request information about other Wiley products, please call (800) 879-4539.

GLOSSARY

ActiveX. Proprietary programming environment developed by Microsoft that allows Web browsers to download and execute Windows-compatible programs. Unlike Java, ActiveX does not define a language of its own; programs are compiled and executed in the native code running on the end user's client.

Adbot. Software program designed to communicate with visitors to chat rooms and discussion groups obsessed with discussing its sponsor's products and services.

Agent. Program that creates a model of an individual's tastes and interests, and acts as a proxy in searching for and prioritizing information for that individual. Usually used to classify and prioritize content for custom delivery via push technology.

Agent log. Access statistics written by most Web servers that identify the type of browser being used by visitors to a site.

Alias. Operating-system command that creates a pointer to a file. In most cases, the pointer can be moved, read, and written to as if it were the real file. Useful in simplifying the design of Web site files and directory structure.

Applet. Client-side program written in the Java programming language that downloads and executes on the end user's computer.

Application Programming Interface (API). Standard interface built into a program that allows other programs to communicate with it. Usually added to Web browsers and databases as a speedier alternative to the generic CGI gateway.

Attributes. A basic set of features used to describe an object (such as price, color, size, or age) used in database design and programming. Objects sharing attributes may be ranked according to the value of the attribute (e.g., price ranking).

Autobot. Class of programs that mimic human behavior and communicate with people in the restricted environment of chat rooms and discussion groups. Simple autobots may help to start or maintain online conversation, but rapidly become irritating if they are too insistent (see **Adbot**).

Bulletin Board System (BBS). A dialup system that supports file transfer, email, and conferencing. Originally used as a standalone system, it is now frequently used over the Internet for managing discussions and organizing workgroups.

Caching. Storing local copies of files accessed from the Internet on the user's hard disk. If there have been no changes in the original file, browser and server software will use the cached copy, saving processing and download time. In another form of caching, a Web site's database generates static copies of frequently requested dynamic pages, which speeds up processing.

Cascading Style Sheets (CSS). Extensions to standard HTML allowing the control of multiple Web page styles from a single file.

Channel. Name for an agreed-upon schedule for the delivery of push content to end users. Also, a Web interface design method that organizes information into a few easily understood topics.

Channel Definition Format (CDF). Push standard for Web pages proposed by Microsoft that provides flexibility and control over individual elements but requires some recoding of individual HTML files.

Clickstream. Statistic that tracks the succession of pages visited by a Web site user that analyzes visitor interest and performance of the site's navigation system.

Click-through. Frequency with which a user selects a particular graphic or text hyperlink, usually provided by a sponsor or advertiser. Click-throughs are frequently expressed as a percentage of selections versus loading the page and moving on.

Client. End-user software designed to query a remote server for specific information and display it. A standard language is used to define client-server interaction. Web browsers are a common and highly successful example of client software (see **Server**).

Client pull. Mechanism underlying some "push" schemes in which code on a downloaded Web page automatically requests content from the Web server after a given amount of time.

Client-side program. A special program that is downloaded from a server and executed using the end user's computer hardware. Examples of client-side programs include Sun Microsystems' Java and Netscape's JavaScript.

Collaborative filtering. Specialized method for personalizing a Web site using advanced software to combine user profiles into a consensus, which is then used to rank content. Allows individual site users to compare their tastes and interests to those of the virtual community as a whole.

Collaborative software. Type of software that allows several individuals to share a common working document or participate in a running discussion; usually installed to organize efforts of a workgroup.

Common Gateway Interface (CGI). Generic communication standard supported by all Web servers for accessing external programs. Examples of CGI programs include gateways to databases and scripts that process and return HTML commands to the server. CGI-based programs are the most common methods used to add dynamic media elements to Web pages.

Content. Name used in this book for all forms of information that might appear on the Web (e.g., text, graphics, audio, video, and multimedia).

Cookie. Special file stored by Web browsers on the user's local computer. Web servers may use cookie information to uniquely identify their visitors.

Copy editor. The individual within the update team responsible for examining dynamic site content for spelling, grammar, and punctuation.

Demographics. Statistics that create a profile of an individual according to external measures (e.g., age, gender, geographic location, and nationality).

Document root. Location of the default home page accessed by a Web server.

Dynamic system. Environment in which there is a continuing flow of new information from content providers to the site audience. Most dynamic systems also provide for the removal or storage of old content. Dynamic Web sites add and delete HTML, graphics, audio, video, multimedia, and links to non-HTML programming to give visitors a unique experience each time they log on.

Dynamic HTML (DHTML). Two competing strategies for increasing the interactivity of Web pages proposed by Netscape and Microsoft. Both DHTML standards provide a specialized client-side extension to HTML allowing simple animation and response to user input—without repeatedly accessing the Web server.

Extranet. Specialized virtual community created by linking closely interacting business groups—typically buyers, sellers, and facilitators—through the Web. Extranets use Internet and Web technology to enable communication and collaboration, but they may or may not use the public Internet to connect to each other. Many Extranets convert Intranets into a larger mini-Web.

Groupware. Software designed to coordinate and enhance communication between teams working on common jobs. Most groupware provides enhanced email, access control to documents, discussion groups, and a calendar system to synchronize work on the project (see **Workflow**).

Imagemap program. A CGI script or client-side <MAP> HTML directive that translates user mouse clicks on a graphic into XY coordinates for further processing.

Information Server Application Programming Interface (ISAPI). System created by Microsoft for tight integration between separate programs in the Windows environment. It is commonly used to link Microsoft's Internet Information Server (IIS) to databases and other programs.

Intranet. Enterprise-wide networked communication that uses Internet and Web technology to replace proprietary software.

Interactive system. Computer-generated user interface that responds actively to user input. Common examples of interactivity include onscreen controls that make noises when they are selected with a mouse, animation cued to specific software operations, and user-adjustable background colors and format. Interactive systems may or may not be dynamic, depending on whether they provide access to static or changing content.

Java. Client-side programming language developed by Sun Microsystems with many advanced features. The language is ideal for cross-platform, Internet-based software development. Java programs are usually downloaded and executed by Web browsers, though some traditional software has utilized Java as its programming language as well.

Java DataBase Connectivity (JDBC). Standard protocol for exchanging information between relational databases and Java applets. Implementing JDBC allows Java-based programs to access server-side dynamic content.

JavaScript. Subset of the Java programming language developed by Netscape, and executed when a Web page downloads. Compared to Java, JavaScript is easier to write, but less powerful.

Layers tag. Proprietary HTML extension developed by Netscape and used in its proposal for Dynamic HTML (DHTML). This tag allows a single browser window to contain visible and hidden text/graphics arranged on top of each other.

Mail robot. Software that receives and processes email messages, frames an appropriate reply, and sends it back to the requester.

Commonly used to answer frequently asked questions that don't require human intervention.

Mailing list. Specialized software that sends messages to all or part of a maintained list of email addresses. Often used in one-to-many mode to send messages to an interest or working group.

Maintenance. The general process necessary for hardware and software running on a dynamic site, and a strategy for response to traffic and other changes affecting Web server performance.

Maintenance team. Subgroup of the overall development team or workgroup charged with keeping the hardware and software of a dynamic Web site up and running. The team also monitors and responds to events affecting Web site performance, such as increased visitor traffic.

Management system. Commercial or locally developed software that organizes the maintenance and update teams and their work. Management tools may include graphic design interfaces, document control, discussion/collaboration tools, and templates for generating dynamic Web pages.

Media convergence. Process in which advanced computers and network technology convert print, film, phone, television, and other communication systems into a seamless whole.

Media element. Individual module placed into a Web page that contains information, usually corresponding to a specific block of text, graphics, audio, or video. On dynamic sites, a media element may remain in place while the content within it changes.

Motion Picture Expert Group (MPEG). Video compression standard common in the video and multimedia worlds, and used in some Internet video products. MPEG gives reasonable compression rates but is not as efficient at extremely low data rates (e.g., modem speeds) as other compression technologies.

Multicast. Method for distribution streaming audio over the Internet in which the main signal is downloaded to a set of key secondary distribution points, which in turn download the material to the end user. By distributing the primary signal across multiple servers, it is practical to Webcast to audiences numbering in the thousands— instead of the dozens to hundreds characteristic of unicast mode (see **Unicast**).

Multipurpose Internet Mail Extension (MIME). Standard used to map files downloaded through email and over the Web to the appropriate media type. The end-user's computer uses MIME typing to figure out which editing/listening/viewing software to launch when the file is received.

Netcaster. Push standard for Web pages proposed by Netscape that uses a combination of JavaScript and Marimba's Castanet technology. Does not require modifying pages included in the push channel, but it is generally less flexible than Microsoft's CDF (see **Channel Definition Format**).

Netscape Application Programming Interface (NSAPI). System created by Netscape for tight integration between separate programs running on Unix and Windows NT platforms. It is commonly used to link Netscape server products to databases and other external programs.

Network Access Point (NAP). Internet network-switching station where major Internet providers exchange user traffic between their backbones.

Object oriented. Programming and database style that records information by mixing attributes with the code used to process them. For example, an object-oriented database for cars might link fields for color and model year with algorithms calculating market value.

One-to-many. Information distribution paradigm in which one message is sent from a single provider to a large number of end users. Direct mail, broadcast, and Internet mailing lists may all use this mode.

One-to-one. Information distribution paradigm in which two users exchange messages on an equal basis. Telephone calls and Internet chat provide examples of one-to-one information distribution.

Open DataBase Connectivity (ODBC). Communication standard for exchanging information between relational databases and external programs.

Paging. Memory management system found on Unix servers in which information contained in RAM may be temporarily swapped to a partition on the hard disk acting as virtual memory. Servers that go into a paging/virtual memory mode slow down substantially.

Peering network. Private connections implemented between Internet providers for mutual traffic sharing, usually set up to bypass the congestion of the public NAPs (see **Network Access Point**).

Personalization. Dynamic programming technique that takes information collected about Web site visitors and uses it to select and return content relevant to their interests. Personalization systems use contact information, geographic information, demographics, and psychographics to construct a model of the user (see **Demographics** and **Psychographics**).

Practical Extraction and Reporting Language (PERL). C-style interpreted language popular for quick programming of applications and utilities linked to Web pages.

Presentation. Term for the particular interface used to present Web-based content to the end user; it can include browser type, form, style, color, and type of media used.

Profile. Coded description of an individual based on demographics and psychographics. May be used to construct a computer model of the individual's interests and tastes and to personalize information.

Prosumer. Term coined by futuristic author Alvin Toffler, it describes an individual who both produces and consumes information. Characteristic of an environment such as the Internet where production costs for content are low.

Psychographics. Method for constructing individual profiles that relies on answers to questions abut lifestyle patterns (e.g., motivation, music tastes, opinions about social issues) instead of demographic information (e.g., gender, geographic location). Since psychographic information may be used to develop a model of an individual's tastes without knowing the person's name or other sensitive information, it is ideally suited to the anonymous world of the Internet.

Push. Generic term referring to a large number of schemes for automatically delivering information from a producer to an end user over the Internet.

Replication. Strategy for synchronizing information between central members of a workgroup and remote "road warriors" making intermittent connections to the network. When remote users connect, the replication system determines differences between local and remote files, and downloads only those components necessary to bring both systems up to date.

Seat. Term for the number of users allowed to use a particular piece of software at the same time, usually applied to proprietary client/server packages run on corporate networks.

Secure Sockets Layer (SSL). Protocol for secure exchange of sensitive information through the Internet, used by most commerce servers on the Internet.

Server. Central software run by content providers that operates continually and automatically responds to requests sent from client programs over the network. A standard language is used to define client-server interaction. Web and video servers are common examples of this kind of software (see **Client**).

Server root. Location of the Web server program in the directory tree of the Web server's hard disk.

Server-side program. Type of program that is triggered by a request from a client but uses the server computer's hardware to execute. Examples of server-side programs include databases and CGI programs.

Shopping cart. Electronic commerce metaphor for purchasing goods and services. Customers check out a virtual shopping cart, place products into it while they browse the site, and check out/pay for their accumulated items when leaving the Web site.

Spam. Slang for unwanted, unsolicited mass email messages sent through the Internet.

Spider. Specialized software program that automatically accesses Web sites, indexes text content, and loads the information into a search engine database.

Structured Query Language (SQL). Standard protocol for communication with relational databases, running on top of proprietary commands used to access the particular vendor's software.

Staging. Strategy that divides the process of creating content for the Web or other media into a series of steps, each involving development, testing, and approval before moving on to the next stage. Custom software is used to set up staging systems for dynamic Web sites.

Static. Web-based content that is not altered after being added to a site. Since the content is not linked to any external program, there is no way it may respond to a user visiting the Web site.

Template. "Placeholder" HTML page coded so that it may be used as a starting point for constructing dynamic Web pages. In practice, templates have dynamic content inserted into them through manual editing or execution of external programs.

Threaded discussion. Communication system specific to electronic networks in which correspondents add comments to a growing document. Users may post after the most recent comment, or within or at the end of discussion threads representing subconversations.

Unicast. Mode for audio/video streaming over the Internet in which the end user has VCR-type control over which part he or she listens to. Unicast is flexible and puts the power in the user's hands, but places greater demands on hardware and software than multicast mode (see **Multicast**).

Updates. Addition or removal of content from a Web page, or from within media elements (e.g., blocks of text or images) on the page. Updated Web pages (no matter what mechanism is used to effect the update) turn static sites into dynamic ones.

Update team. Subgroup of the overall team charged with creating a dynamic Web site that is specifically responsible for content added to and removed from the Web site.

Virtual Reality Markup Language (VRML). Page-coding language designed to expand the 2D world of Web pages into interactive 3D environments. Despite widespread support, application of VRML has been slowed due to compatibility problems and the extremely reduced speed of most VRML environments.

Webcast. Delivery of a constant stream of audio, video, or multimedia through the Internet.

Whiteboard. Collaborative tool found in some game programs and groupware/workflow software that allows networked users to write/draw figures and images that everyone within the group may view.

Workflow. A strategy for managing large projects by breaking them up into jobs distributed among members of a development team. When implemented in software, its meaning is identical to groupware (see **Groupware**).

INDEX

Bulldog Software, 172

Caching, 95, 159
Cadis Software's
  Krakatoa, 208–9
Cascading style sheet
  (CSS), 30, 134–35, 220
Castanet. *See* Marimba
Catalog Navigator.
  See Firefly
CDF. *See* Channel
  Definition Format
Centra's Symposium, 306
Central Ad Software, 113
CGI. *See* Common
  Gateway Interface
Chaco Communications'
  Pueblo, 233. *See also*
  virtual worlds
Channel Definition
  Format (CDF), 142,
  196–97. *See also* push
  technology
Chat, 166–67
Chili!Soft's Chili!ASP, 149
Cisco Systems'
  Distributed Director, 101
Claims Information
  Network Site (CINS).
  See PJW Associates
Clear Communications
  Corp., 61–62
ClickOver Software's
  ClickWise, 113
Clickstream, 105
Client pull, 197. *See also*
  push technology
Coast Web Administrator,
  77
Cold Fusion. *See* Allaire
Collabora. *See* Netscape

Comedy Central, 36
CommercePoint. *See* IBM
Common Gateway
  Interface (CGI), 15
  bottlenecks, 90
  and dynamic links to
  external programs, 135
  NT scripts, 152
  Public Domain CGI
  Script Archive (*see*
  Selena Sol)
  Resource Index, The,
  136–37, 147, 232
  and Web/database
  gateways, 138
Commonwealth Network,
  130
Communicator. *See*
  Netscape and Intermind
Connected (remote back-
  up service), 81
Content
  aggregation, 131
  audio, 129–30
  computer-generated,
  131–32
  electronic documents,
  127–28
  environmental informa-
  tion, 131
  features, 22–24
  images, 128–29
  links on remote sites,
  130–31
  obsolete, 157–59
  printed documents,
  126–27
  sources and formats,
  126–32
  static, 23
  video, 130

Cookie. *See* Netscape
Counters. *See* media
  elements
CSS. *See* cascading style
  sheet
CUChat. *See* NetDive
CurrentIssue. *See* Inlet
  Software
CyberCash, 210. *See also*
  Micropayments
CyberChart, 154
Cymbiont's Meridian Map
  Server, 154
C|Net, 176, 257

Data mining, 184
Database
  accessing a database
  server via the WWW,
  139
  flat-file, 147
  object-oriented, 149–50
  page generation, 17
  relational, 148–49
  Web hybrid, 139
DBM, 71
DeBabelizer, 129
DejaNews. *See* Usenet
DHTML. *See* Dynamic
  Hypertext Markup
  Language
DigiCash. *See*
  Micropayments
Digital Versatile Disc
  (DVD), 82, 335. *See also*
  hybrid media
DigitalFacades' Xpound!,
  231
DigitalThink, Inc., 306,
  317–21
Director. *See* Macromedia

and dynamic links to external programs, 135
link validation, 74

IBM
CommercePoint, 210
Net.Commerce System, 206, 209
Surf-Aid, 111, 184
iCat's Electronic Commerce Suite, 206
ICentral Incorporated's ShopSite, 207
ichat, 232, 279. *See also* Chat
ICQ. *See* Mirabilis
ICVerify's MacAuthorize and PCAuthorize, 210
i-depth, 147
IDS Software, 142
IETF Working Group for Distributed Web Authoring and Versioning, 248
Illustra. *See* Informix
Image Communications' WebThreads, 183. *See also* personalization
Imagemap, 74–75, 121
InContext
Site Command, 248
WebAnalyzer, 78
Infoaccess' HTML Transit, 128
Infodata Systems' Virtual File Cabinet (VFC), 179
Informix's Illustra, 68, 137, 150, 172
InfoSeek, 76, 183
Ingot Software's Disk Imager 81–82. *See also* storage

Inktomi
Network Of Workstations (NOW), 102
Virtual Network Cache, 102
Inlet Software's CurrentIssue, 173–74, 252
Insight. *See* Accrue Software
Instant Messenger. *See* America Online
Interaction Manager. *See* Afficast
Interjet. *See* Whistle Communications
Intermind's Communicator, 195. *See also* push technology
Internet connection:
alternative options, 62–63
bandwidth, guaranteed, 59–60
leased-line, 58
redundant, 58–59
security and, 60
speed, 57
tech support and, 60–62
traffic spikes and, 60
Internet Information Server (IIS). *See* Microsoft
Internet Link Exchange, 130
Internet Service Provider (ISP), 53–54, 93–95
Intertec Publishing's Internet Review, 249–53
InterVU, 281. *See also* Webcasting
Interwoven

Teammaker, 177
Teamsite, 31
Intranet, 10, 95–96
Inverse Network Technology's Benchmark Report Works, 95
I/PRO
I/COUNT, 113
Netline, 112–13
and Prizefight, 299
Ipswitch's WhatsUp, 96
Iptscrae. *See* Palace, the
ISAPI. *See* Microsoft
IsoView. *See* Skunk New Media

Java, 139, 143, 145, 334
JavaScript, 143–44, 145, 152, 290
Jet Propulsion Laboratory. *See* NASA
Joint Photographic Experts Group (JPEG), 128

Kaleidospace (Kspace), 79, 133–34, 208
KeepItUp, 218
Krakatoa. *See* Cadis Software
Kruse, Matt
Mkstats, 106
Server-Side Includes Tutorial, 157

LA Live. *See* Virtual Netcasting Corporation
Lariat. *See* FreeRange Media
Lightweight Directory Access Protocol (LDAP), 169

WHAT'S ON THE WEB SITE?

Visit the companion Web site at www.wiley.com/compbook/novak. You'll find:

Software: A useful set of links to freeware and shareware software that developers may use to add dynamic content to their own web sites as well as commercial software sites for which demonstration/trial software is available. You'll also find additional links to software not available at the time of publication.

Updates: Announcements of new and useful dynamic site technology. For example, recent advances in freeware/shareware for Web/database connectivity technology such as mSQL/mySQL will be featured as they become available.

Case Studies: Links to public Web sites that were featured in the book's case studies and that provide outstanding examples of dynamic programming, including Content Promotion and Sales; User-driven Community Sites; Periodic Publishing Media; Events and Webcasting, Online Games and Auctions, and Online Classrooms and Virtual Universities.